Foundations of
Intellectual Assessment

RELATED TITLE OF INTEREST

Psychological Testing: History, Principles, and Applications,
Second Edition
Robert J. Gregory
ISBN: 0-205-15816-1

For more information or to purchase a book, please call
1-800-278-3525.

Foundations of Intellectual Assessment

The WAIS-III and Other Tests in Clinical Practice

Robert J. Gregory

Wheaton College
Wheaton, Illinois

Allyn and Bacon

Boston • London • Toronto • Sydney • Tokyo • Singapore

Series editorial assistant: *Susan Hutchinson*
Manufacturing buyer: *Suzanne Lareau*

Copyright © 1999 by Allyn & Bacon
A Viacom Company
Needham Heights, MA 02494

Internet: www.abacon.com

Library of Congress Cataloging-in-Publication Data

Gregory, Robert J.
    Foundations of intellectual assessment: the WAIS-III and other tests in clinical practice / Robert J. Gregory.
      p.   cm.
    Includes bibliographical references and index.
    ISBN 0-205-19833-3
    1. Intelligence tests.   2. Wechsler Adult Intelligence Scale.
  I. Title.
    [DNLM: 1. Wechsler Scales—in adulthood.   2. Brain Diseases—diagnosis.   3. Cognition Disorders—diagnosis.   4. Neuropsychology.
BF 432.5.W2 G823f 1999]
BF431.G784 1999
153.9′32—dc21
DNLM/DLC
for Library of Congress   98-21398
                                       CIP

Printed in the United States of America
10 9 8 7 6 5 4 3 2   02 01 00 99

CONTENTS

PREFACE

As a clinical psychologist who has taught individual intelligence testing for over 25 years, I have been struck continually by the absence of useful resources for introducing essential concepts of assessment. Although a few good books have been published, these existing materials tend to be encyclopedic in length and narrow in focus. What I have found lacking is a work that embodies a wide frame of reference combined with enough details to convey the challenge of assessment. The purpose of this text is to fill that void.

The book was designed particularly for graduate students in clinical, counseling, and school psychology taking their first course in intellectual assessment. In addition, the text should prove helpful for established clinicians who want a brief sourcebook on the essentials of intellectual assessment in adulthood. As the title indicates, the goal is to provide practitioners (both neophyte and more seasoned) with the foundations of intellectual assessment.

The heart of the book pertains to the administration, scoring, and interpretation of the WAIS-III (with some attention to its recent predecessor, the WAIS-R). Coverage of this test is extensive, found in Chapter 4 (The WAIS-III: Introduction and the Meaning of IQ), Chapter 5 (The WAIS-III: Clinical Issues and Alternative Tests), and Chapter 7 (Report Writing and Professional Standards), which together constitute nearly half of the volume. Yet the proper use of any intelligence test extends beyond the capacity to pose questions, record answers, and compute scores. The mandate of intellectual assessment is to *understand* test results in context. This means that the examiner must discern what the client brings to the testing table: relevant history, current mental status, and possible cognitive impairment. All of these factors influence the interpretation of intellectual test results. For this reason, I summarize essential concepts of history taking, mental status evaluation, and cognitive screening alongside the ample coverage of intelligence testing with the WAIS-III.

Although this is not a book on neuropsychological assessment, I do advocate that intellectual assessment should be informed by neuropsychological concepts. Let me illustrate the advantages of this perspective. My experience has been that clinicians who approach assessment from this perspective see things overlooked by others. For example, the practitioner with a rudimentary knowledge of organic syndromes will recognize that word-finding difficulty in a 70-year-old gentleman might signal the onset of Alzheimer's disease or other dementia. Ideally, the practitioner also could select and administer appropriate screening tests to determine whether the word-finding difficulty was truly suspicious or merely a consequence of normal aging.

In general, clinicians sensitive to a neuropsychological perspective are more inclined to look for hidden or subtle influences that might help explain current functioning. Consider the case of a college student whose grades begin to decline for no apparent reason. A counselor could interpret the faltering academic record as indicating any of several possibilities. Perhaps the student's part-time job takes too much time away from studying, or possibly the aspiring scholar is experiencing the onset of a depression, or maybe the explanation is simply that the student has chosen the wrong course of study. But suppose that the counselor learns that his client fell off her bicycle the previous summer, striking her head on the pavement. The case conceptualization now takes a different turn, and a brief screen for cognitive impairment becomes imperative. However, this will happen only if the counselor sees the possible connection between a very mild head injury and subsequent impairment of the ability to concentrate. Such are the advantages of allowing neuropsychological concepts to inform the practice of intellectual assessment.

It also has been my experience that brief, simple, and practical tools often provide the most useful results. Gradually, I have evolved a philosophy of test usage that might be called brief intellectual assessment informed by neuropsychological concepts. This book approaches assessment with that philosophy in mind. There are three interlocking components to this perspective: (1) basic knowledge of conditions that might lead to cognitive impairment, (2) competence with an assortment of screening tests, and (3) facility with the Wechsler Adult Intelligence Scale—III (WAIS-III).

The first component is basic knowledge of the nature, signs, and symptoms of prominent syndromes of cognitive impairment. I am referring here to a variety of developmental and acquired conditions that manifest impairment of cognitive functions. These include, but are not limited to: dementia, especially from Alzheimer's disease or stroke; mental retardation and other conditions of diminished intelligence; learning disability; and traumatic brain injury. I mention these conditions because they represent the kinds of cognitive impairment most frequently encountered by the generalist practitioner.

The second component is facility with an assortment of efficient screening tests for cognitive impairment in adults. Practitioners do not have the luxury of referring every client with possible cognitive impairment to a clinical neuropsychologist for assessment with a 6-hour test battery at a cost that may approach a thousand dollars. In many cases a short battery of screening tests will satisfy the clinician that further testing is unnecessary—or on occasion confirm that referral to specialists is warranted. Several good screening tests are prominently featured throughout this book, and where possible I provide norms and interpretive guidelines. The selection of screening tests is necessarily selective and intended mainly to illustrate the role of these instruments in assessment. Dozens of other useful tests could be cited, but space does not permit discussion of these.

The heart of the book is found in its third focus, which is the Wechsler Adult Intelligence Scale—III (WAIS-III). The WAIS-III is *the* cornerstone of adult intellectual assessment. Any discussion of adult assessment would be woefully incomplete without extensive coverage of this instrument. The essentials of WAIS-III administration, scoring, and interpretation are found in Chapter 4, whereas special topics and concerns are pursued in Chapter 5. Chapter 7 also features the WAIS-III.

Two disclaimers need to be mentioned. First, even though this work refers to basic concepts in neuropsychology, this is first, foremost, and exclusively a sourcebook on the essentials of *intellectual* assessment. The practice of clinical neuropsychological assessment requires extensive specialized training and a broader base of knowledge than is supplied here (Lezak, 1995). Nonetheless, the practice of intellectual assessment is substantially enriched when informed by the basic precepts of neuropsychology—which is precisely what this book seeks to accomplish. The second disclaimer is that the assessment of children is not covered here. This book focuses exclusively on the assessment of intellectual and cognitive functions in adulthood. I discuss only adult testing because, in my experience, the assessment of children requires a qualitatively different approach that incorporates a more cautious set of interpretive hypotheses.

Readers familiar with my earlier book, *Adult Intellectual Assessment* (Gregory, 1987), will recognize that the current text has evolved from it. Yet, in spite of slight overlap and superficial similarities, the present work is really a new book with a broader emphasis. Some of the same instruments are discussed, but so much has happened in assessment during the last 10 years that the material included here is substantially new.

Outline of the Text

The book consists of seven chapters, as follows:

Chapter 1: Introduction to Intellectual Assessment
Chapter 2: The Mental Status Examination
Chapter 3: Introduction to Brain–Behavior Relationships
Chapter 4: The WAIS-III: Introduction and the Meaning of IQ
Chapter 5: The WAIS-III: Clinical Issues and Alternative Tests
Chapter 6: Screening Tests for Cognitive Impairment
Chapter 7: Report Writing and Professional Standards

Chapter 1 discusses the relevance of intellectual assessment and establishes the rationale for using basic neuropsychological concepts when thinking about assessment. Also included is a discussion of how to obtain relevant background information about the client. The chapter contains a structured questionnaire for this purpose.

Included in Chapter 2 are a detailed presentation of the categories of a mental status examination with sample questions; discussion of how to conduct a clinical mental status exam; and detailed presentation of the administration, scoring, and interpretation of prominent instruments, including the Test of Temporal Orientations, the Mini-Mental Status Exam, and the Short Portable Mental Status Questionnaire. The chapter also features a short section on the nature and diagnosis of dementia, particularly Alzheimer's disease.

Chapter 3 discusses brain structure and functional systems, including memory, language functions, motor control, the visual system, and so forth. The chapter also highlights the signs and symptoms encountered when these brain systems are impaired, for example, aphasic symptoms when the language system is damaged. This chapter introduces foundational knowledge for a later chapter on screening tests for cognitive impairment.

The WAIS-III is prominently featured in Chapter 4 (with occasional reference to the WAIS-R). This is the first of two chapters devoted to this test. The chapter introduces the reader to issues that arise in the administration, scoring, and interpretation of this important measure. Also included is a discussion of the traditional model of general intelligence as measured by mainstream instruments.

Chapter 5 provides a survey of clinical issues in WAIS-III interpretation. One focus is the use of the test in the assessment of impaired functioning such as mental retardation, neurological problems, and learning disorders. Other topics pertain to special circumstances such as short forms and serial retesting. The potential for misuse of test results, especially in the assessment of minority individuals, is featured here. The chapter closes with a review of five alternative measures of intellectual functioning.

Chapter 6 features the presentation of brief tests useful in screening for cognitive impairment. The chapter details the administration, scoring, and interpretation of several representative instruments. Readers are warned that the coverage is not intended to be exhaustive—dozens of good screening tests could be cited. The selected instruments exemplify the role of screening tests in the assessment of possible cognitive impairment.

The primary focus of Chapter 7 is report writing. It is difficult to discuss this topic, however, without referring to issues of informed consent, provision of feedback to clients, sensitivity in assessment of minorities, and a host of other ethical and practical concerns. For these reasons, the text includes a discussion of these elements of clinical practice. The chapter closes with four reports drawn from the author's practice.

Criteria for Test Selection

With the exception of the WAIS-III, this book advocates tests and procedures that are short, simple, and practical. Some of the approaches are in the public domain and require no purchase on the part of potential users. I provide interpretive guidelines for these more generic tools. A few short tests are reproduced with the kind permission of publishers. For these I have provided appropriate norms and interpretive guidelines. In all cases, specific addresses are provided so that qualified users can purchase these instruments, usually at nominal cost. Collectively, all of the tests and procedures discussed in this book can be carried in one large briefcase.

Ease of administration is an important characteristic of practical assessment. The most difficult and time-consuming test discussed in this book is the WAIS-III, which may require an hour and a half to administer. Most of the other tests take 10 minutes or less to administer and interpret; several can be given in 5 minutes or less. Only one of the ancillary tests (Short Category Test, Booklet Form) requires more than 15 minutes for administration.

For the most part, then, I have selected tests and procedures that are easy to learn and interpret. Where possible I have provided guidelines and summaries to make the process of interpretation as simple as possible. Abundant charts, figures, tables, and sample reports are provided to help the practitioner understand the meaning of individual test results.

The limitations and caveats surrounding the instruments also are discussed. Too often, psychologists adopt a defensive posture in which test results are deified and the shortcomings of their instruments are overlooked. This is unfortunate because it is unnecessary. Our methods need not be perfect in order for our assessments to be useful. We do not diminish our influence by admitting that our interpretations include a band of error or that certain tests might be misleading for specific clients. The more usual effect of such truth in advertising is an increase in respect from those whom we hope to serve.

In addition to extensive coverage of the WAIS-III, the following tests and procedures are discussed in the book:

Assessment of Mental Status	Mental Status Examination
	Test of Temporal Orientations
	Short Portable Mental Status Questionnaire
	Mini-Mental State Exam
Attention/Concentration	Subtracting serial 7s
	Paced Auditory Serial Addition Task
	Trail Making Test
Sensory/Perceptual	Finger Localization Test
Psychomotor Speed	Symbol Digit Modalities Test
Memory	Rey Auditory Verbal Learning Test
	Serial Digit Learning Test
Language Tests	Clinical Examination for Aphasia
	Word Fluency Test
	Peabody Picture Vocabulary Test—Revised
Drawing/Constructional Tests	Bender Gestalt
	Greek Cross Test

Higher Cognitive Functions	Clinical Assessment of Executive Functions
	Short Category Test, Booklet Form
Intelligence and Related	WAIS-III
Capacities	Kaufman Brief Intelligence Test
	Shipley Institute of Living Scale
	Scales of Independent Behavior–Revised
	Stanford-Binet: Fourth Edition
	Raven's Progressive Matrices

Use of the Text

This book was designed for graduate courses in intellectual assessment, but it is my intention for it to have broader appeal as well. Thus, the first audience is graduate students in psychology and related fields taking their initial assessment course. In addition, generalist practitioners who need a useful summary of the foundations of intellectual assessment will find value in this volume.

Knowledge of the tests and procedures presented here will provide a solid foundation for the practice of intellectual assessment in mental health centers, counseling centers, schools, hospitals, and other settings. Of course, not all skills can be learned from a textbook. The practice of intellectual assessment also presupposes an extensive amount of supervised experience in test administration and report writing. In order to develop a minimum competency in the assessment process, aspiring practitioners usually need months or years of supervised experience, such as provided by practicum and internship placements.

Note on Case Histories and Reports

As a means of illustrating the principles of intellectual assessment, I have included several case histories, brief vignettes, and written reports. This is the special focus of the final chapter, which contains four lengthy reports featuring the WAIS-III. All of the individuals highlighted in these case histories and reports are real. The scores presented are from actual protocols—with only slight changes. Specifically, owing to the recency of the WAIS-III, several prior assessments with the WAIS-R have been "upgraded" to the WAIS-III with comparable results. Of course, unessential details such as age, occupation, or referral source have been altered to preserve the privacy of these persons. For ease of discussion I refer to each case by first name and last initial (such as Robert G.); however, these have no reference to real names.

Acknowledgments

Thanks are due to several reviewers who identified many subtle errors (and a few glaring ones, too!). The following individuals provided helpful reviews:

Michael D. Franzen, Allegheny University of the Health Sciences
Robert E. Deysach, University of South Carolina
C. Munro Cullum, University of Texas Southwestern Medical Center at Dallas
Maura Mitrushina, University of California, Los Angeles
Eric B. Larson, Rehabilitation Institute of Chicago

I owe a debt of gratitude to my editor, Carla Daves, who was tireless in locating effective reviewers. Her assistant, Sue Hutchinson, provided invaluable logistical support at several key points. Thanks are due to my wife and two children, who continue to tolerate my preoccupation with writing. Finally, I want to acknowledge my academic family at Wheaton College—students, colleagues, staff, and administrators—who provided a supportive, encouraging atmosphere for this prolonged project.

1 Introduction to Intellectual Assessment

Psychologists have found it useful to view behavior as the product of three functional systems: cognitive, emotional, and executive (Lezak, 1995). Cognition has to do with the information-processing abilities of the brain: How well does the individual process incoming information, organize the information, and communicate a response? Emotion has to do with the feeling and motivational aspects of behavior: Which feelings arise in the context of behavior and which motivational systems (e.g., anger, fear, sex) are invoked? Executive functions consist of those capacities that promote successful goal-directed behavior: How well does the individual plan, modify, and carry out selected goals?

The assessment of the cognitive domain is the primary focus of this book—although invariably this will invoke executive capacities to some extent because of the psychometric difficulty of partitioning these two functional systems. Psychologists have achieved the greatest success in measuring and assessing the cognitive realm, for which numerous tests and other structured approaches are available. In this chapter we discuss the aims of cognitive assessment, also known as intellectual assessment, and provide a philosophical orientation to its practice.

Properly conceived, intellectual assessment embraces a broad focus that extends beyond the testing of intelligence into related domains such as mental status, memory, language capacity, visual-motor skills, and screening for cognitive impairment. A first course in assessment—the topic of this book—should consist of more than learning how to administer, score, and interpret a few standardized instruments. The competent practitioner needs to appreciate ancillary tests and procedures, understand the essentials of cognitive function and dysfunction, and recognize the limitations of testing and assessment.

Flowing from these premises, the dual purposes of this text are to introduce graduate students and clinical practitioners to intellectual assessment (broadly conceived) and to instruct qualified persons in the application, scoring, and interpretation of selected instruments. These goals are pursued within a philosophy of assessment that is informed by basic neuropsychological concepts that are brief, simple, and practical in application.

The Rationale for Cognitive Assessment

We begin with a question: What is the relevance of cognitive assessment? For many practitioners the answer is "more than you might think." Three case vignettes illustrate this point. Similar cases abound in mental health professions such as psychology, psychiatry, counseling, and social work.

Case 1 involves a 62-year-old woman referred by her concerned children. She lives alone in a retirement home and has been independent and high-functioning all of her life. But recently the children have noticed that mom seems forgetful and continually misplaces important items (e.g., glasses, checkbook). They took her to see an internist, who talked with her and completed a routine physical examination. He also referred her to a neurologist, who ordered a computerized tomography (CT scan), which was interpreted as being unremarkable. Ultimately, the physician found nothing wrong and concluded that the concerns of the children were misplaced. They were initially reassured but then discovered that their mother left a kitchen burner turned on "high" overnight. At this point they decided to seek a second opinion.

Case 2 concerns a 21-year-old college student brought by his parents to a consulting psychologist after a disastrous semester in which his grades plummeted. Although he earned As and Bs during the first 2 years of college, his most recent academic record consists of a few Cs and several incompletes. The student appears irritable and slightly depressed. He is confused as to why his coursework has slipped so badly. He alludes to a rollerblading accident 3 months ago in which he fell to the ground, struck his head on the pavement, and lost consciousness briefly. He says, "I just haven't felt right since then." But his parents dispute this explanation, noting that their son was not hospitalized, that his CT scan was normal, that his diagnosis was mild concussion, and that the emergency room physician gave him a clean bill of health.

Case 3 involves a 37-year-old high school English teacher who reports that he began experiencing difficulty reading about 4 months ago. He would attempt to read a sentence, but it would "read like a Lewis Carroll poem." Consultation with an ophthalmologist revealed no visual impairment, but the patient was told, "You've probably had a stroke." In an office visit a physician found no evidence of a stroke and suspected that the reading problem was stress-related. The teacher has now appeared in the consultant's office, seeking an explanation for his mysterious symptoms.

Regarding Case 1, a competent practitioner from any field should recognize the suspicious signs of early dementia in the brief history recounted here. Issues of cognitive screening then become paramount. The clinician would want to know the following: What are the distinctive signs and symptoms of dementia? Which alternative diagnoses should be ruled out? What kinds of structured tools and objective tests would be helpful in the process of differential diagnosis? When is referral to a medical or neuropsychological specialist warranted?

Case 2 raises a strong suspicion that the college student has experienced a mild head injury. Even the best medical and neurological evaluations cannot detect the effects of diffuse injury in which brain function is subtly compromised while leaving no evidence of overt lesions. A short battery of screening tests is essential in the evaluation of these cases. The practitioner needs to be familiar with the following issues: What symptoms are typical of postconcussion syndrome? What is the natural history of mild head injury? Which screening tests might be helpful in determining the effects of mild head injury? When is referral for specialized testing justifiable?

In Case 3 the astute practitioner would find reason to go beyond the initial conclusions of the physicians. Although a difficulty with *concentration* while reading might have a purely psychological explanation, that is not the teacher's complaint. His symptom is in regards to the cognitive processing of what he sees. The manner in which he describes his difficulty has a distinctly neurological flavor. The clinician would want answers to several questions: Which symptoms raise a suspicion of neurological involvement? What kinds of patient complaints are likely to be stress-related? Which tests are helpful for general-purpose screening of neuropsychological impairment? When is referral to a specialist appropriate?

These three cases illustrate only a few of the many circumstances in which a psychologist or other clinical practitioner might encounter the need for intellectual assessment in which a knowledge of basic neuropsychological concepts would also prove helpful. One purpose of this book is to provide the foundations for knowing when a client's presentation is "suspicious" from the standpoint of possible cognitive impairment. Another purpose is to introduce useful tools for intellectual assessment and screening for impairment in these cases. In chapters 4 and 5 we will focus on the Wechsler Adult Intelligence Scale—III as the cornerstone of intellectual assessment. Chapter 6 discusses briefer instruments for detecting possible cognitive impairment, and, finally, Chapter 7 outlines report-writing guidelines and professional standards in assessment.

First, we provide a more comprehensive survey of the many justifications for evaluation with structured tools. The specific rationale for cognitive assessment tends to fall within one of these four categories: diagnosis, screening, treatment planning, or evaluation.

Diagnosis

Intellectual assessment is an important component in the diagnosis of many developmental and acquired conditions that feature impairment of cognitive abilities. It is rare that a practitioner from any single discipline makes the definitive diagnosis for conditions such as Alzheimer's disease, progressive neurological disease, mild head injury, or mental retardation. What is more common is that several health care practitioners each provide additional certainty that a specific diagnosis is appropriate. In regard to the three cases just outlined, brief assessment for cognitive impairment was crucial in focusing attention upon the proper diagnosis:

- Case 1 appeared to be an instance of early onset dementia, possibly Alzheimer's disease. A brief mental status examination revealed that the patient maintained strong conversational skills and was alert and engaging, but displayed repeated memory lapses in conjunction with serious loss of orientation to time and place. The likely diagnosis of Alzheimer's disease was further supported when additional medical evaluation was uneventful and the patient continued to decline in her cognitive capacities over the next 6 months.
- Case 2 showed all the signs of a very mild head injury, the consequences of which can linger for many months. The young college student revealed impairment of information-processing capacity on several tests, including the Symbol Digit Modalities Test, a simple and brief instrument discussed later in the book. Although the student needed to withdraw from college, his cognitive capacities slowly improved and he was able to enroll the next semester and continue his academic pursuits.
- Case 3 is a sad instance of the psychologist being the first health care professional to confirm serious neurological impairment. The patient scored Verbal IQ of 119, Performance IQ of 77, and Full Scale IQ of 97 on the WAIS-R. The 42-point discrepancy between Verbal and Performance IQ was strikingly indicative of serious neurological impairment, which was corroborated by several other brief tests (e.g., serious errors and distortions on the Bender Gestalt, a design-copying test). A neurologist eventually confirmed that the patient was in the initial stages of multiple sclerosis, a degenerative disease characterized by loss of myelin sheath in the nervous system that leads to progressive sensory, motor, and cognitive disability. He died 2 years later.

Screening

Another application of brief cognitive assessment is to screen for impairment of cognitive functions. A common scenario for this application is when a physician refers a patient to a mental health practitioner, thinking that certain puzzling symptoms might be "psychological" in origin. For example, one patient reported visual-perceptual distortions to his physician. Specifically the patient said that the right side of road signs would occasionally appear distorted. Routine medical and visual examinations were unremarkable. The physician concluded that the symptoms were hysterical in origin and referred the patient to a psychologist. When the consultant administered a simple drawing test discussed later in this text—copying a Greek cross—the patient showed dramatic and incontrovertible evidence of cognitive impairment. A later, more extensive test battery indicated a significant neurological problem warranting referral to a neurologist.

Screening for impairment with cognitive assessment tools is appropriate in a wide variety of situations. For example, many mental health practitioners work with elderly clients who may complain of memory loss. This complaint could be a normal part of aging, a symptom of depression, or the initial presentation of a progressive dementia. How is the clinician to decide whether specialized assessment is needed? A short battery of screening tests might prove helpful in deciding whether a client should be referred for an expensive, time-consuming, and anxiety-inducing workup for dementia. Additional applications of cognitive assessment in screening include the identification of adults with possible learning disorders, the initial evaluation of persons with potential mild head injury, and the flagging of children with suspected reading difficulties. In summary, the purpose of screening is to identify persons in need of further diagnostic evaluation. The tools of cognitive assessment are essential for this screening function.

Treatment Planning

For some clients the reality of their cognitive impairment is undisputed and the question then becomes what to do about it. The tools of cognitive assessment can provide important clues to treatment planning. After all, test results furnish the practitioner with a description of the client's mental capacities. Implications for treatment often flow naturally from this description.

A case in point is a head-injured client who performed abysmally on one portion of the Wechsler Memory Scale—Revised (WMS-R), a general-purpose test of memory functions (Wechsler, 1987) that has been revised recently (WMS-III; Tulsky, Zhu, & Ledbetter, 1997). This client functioned well on most parts of the test but had striking difficulty with a 30-minute delayed recall of orally presented narrative passages. This test-based demonstration of a marked deficit for verbal memory was highly relevant to treatment planning. In particular, the therapist recommended to the spouse and the client's employer that they write out requests rather than delivering them orally. The therapist also concluded that the client needed notebook training to remediate the memory defect (Schmitter-Edgecombe et al., 1995).

The clinician must furnish the link between assessment results and treatment planning, but the formulation is rarely so simple as "for deficit X on test Y provide treatment Z." Treatment planning needs to be individualized, based upon assessment results and the unique situation of the client. This is where the clinician's ingenuity, training, and experience come into play. For one client an assessment finding of attentional impairment might suggest the need for new study habits. For another client the same kind and degree of impairment might indicate the desirability of changing jobs. Treatment planning is as much art as science. Unfortunately, the topic of cognitive remediation is beyond the scope of this book.

Evaluation

The results of cognitive assessment also provide ongoing evaluation of client status. Serial evaluation of cognitive abilities can be used to measure therapy-based improvement, confirm spontaneous recovery, or document the effects of progressive illness. A few examples will serve to clarify the contributions of cognitive assessment in evaluation.

One application of serial assessment is to determine whether a prescribed drug therapy is having an intended effect. For example, it is not unusual for young adults with attentional problems to receive a trial prescription of Ritalin or other psychoactive drug (Spencer et al., 1996). The client's self-report of the drug effects is certainly important. But an objective method for determining whether the drug has improved attentional capacities is preferable. A useful approach is serial testing of attentional capacities—before, during, and after the drug prescription. A few of the tests discussed in Chapter 6 (Screening Tests for Cognitive Impairment) might prove helpful for this purpose.

Another application of serial assessment is to confirm the pattern of recovery after injury or illness. For example, an elderly patient with profound depression initially may be disoriented and unable to complete simple items on a mental status exam. Serial application of a brief measurement tool such as the Mini-Mental State Exam can help gauge improvement as the patient emerges from the depths of a psychotic depression. Direct measures of depression such as the Geriatric Depression Scale also would help with this form of evaluation (Yesavage, Brink, & Rose, 1983).

Serial evaluation can serve a wide variety of purposes in assessment. Briefly, repeated testing may be used for these additional purposes:

- Identify dementia early in its course
- Measure the effects of surgical procedures
- Document improvement after a concussion
- Check for the possible recurrence of a brain tumor

Of course, in all applications of serial testing the examiner must apply appropriate correction factors for expected practice effects, so that the consequences of mere practice are not confused with real improvement.

Client Background and History

Common to any application of cognitive assessment is the need to obtain relevant background and history on the client. Regardless of the referral issue, the unique background of the examinee will bear upon the interpretation of any assessment. For example, a finding that a client reveals attentional difficulties will mean one thing if this is a new symptom but might prove unremarkable if the client was diagnosed with attention deficit disorder prior to the accident that prompted the assessment.

The current functioning of the individual should not be evaluated in isolation from his or her life history. Of particular relevance is the educational history, which provides important clues as to the level of test functioning that might be expected from the examinee. Consider the case of a head-injured adult with a current IQ of 93. Does this score indicate a decline in functioning caused by the head injury? Many factors need to be considered in relation to this question, but a vital piece of data is the prior academic achievement of the examinee. If she finished college with an accounting degree, we are likely to surmise that her current functioning is probably depressed (and perhaps substantially so) from pre-accident functioning. But if she dropped out of school in the tenth grade to become a child care worker, most likely our interpretation will differ.

In their manual on screening for brain impairment, Berg, Franzen, and Wedding (1994) identify the neuropsychological history as the single most important element of the evaluation:

> A careful history is the most powerful weapon in the arsenal of every clinician, whether generalist or specialist. Brain–behavior relations are extremely complex and involve many different moderator variables, such as age, level of premorbid functioning, and amount of education. Without knowledge of values for these moderator variables, it is virtually impossible to interpret even specialized, sophisticated test results. (p. 51)

In summary, a thorough history is not just helpful—it is crucial to the proper interpretation of assessment results.

The essentials of history taking as a precursor to intellectual assessment will differ from one practitioner to another, but clinicians commonly delve into the following topics with the client or a knowledgeable informant:

- Current complaints
- Family history
- Prenatal history
- Developmental milestones
- Educational background
- Work history
- Medical history
- Psychiatric history
- Current situation

Some sources would include observation and interview impressions as part of the client history. The appearance of the client, language abnormalities, and behavioral oddities are certainly relevant to an intellectual assessment. However, these evaluative components are more commonly included under the category of mental status. This will be split off as a separate topic and discussed along with relevant concepts in Chapter 2 (The Mental Status Examination).

History taking should be guided by hypotheses and not conducted in a lifeless, perfunctory manner. The purpose of history taking is to obtain information that will aid in understanding the current functioning of the client, not simply to amass huge amounts of data. Thus, a compulsive examination of every topic for every client is unwarranted. In working with a high-functioning college professor who is experiencing memory problems, for example, it would be sufficient to determine that he received a doctorate degree—a chronology of intermediate degrees and colleges attended is probably irrelevant. On the other hand, details of his psychiatric history might be highly relevant. In particular, an exploration of whether he has experienced episodes of depression could be valuable in understanding current test results, as memory complaints are common in major depression.

It is usually appropriate for the clinician to ask the client or a trusted informant (e.g., spouse) to fill out a structured background information questionnaire in advance of the initial assessment appointment. Areas of confusion or uncertainty can be clarified quickly during the first contact. Wolfson (1985) has assembled a highly detailed questionnaire that probes almost every conceivable aspect of the client's background and history. Her questionnaire is excellent but its length (thirty-eight pages) may prove prohibitive for many referrals. Appended to the end of this chapter is a short but reasonably comprehensive protocol for the background history.

BACKGROUND HISTORY SURVEY

General Information

Name: _____ Age: _____ Sex: ☐ male ☐ female

Marital Status: ☐ single ☐ divorced ☐ separated ☐ married Handedness: ☐ left ☐ right

Race/Ethnicity: _____ How many kids?:_____ Their ages: _____ _____ _____ _____

What is your primary language? ☐ English ☐ Other: _____

Family Information

For your *biological* family:

	Age	Years of Education	Occupation	Academic Problems?	Medical Problems?	Psychological Problems?
mother	_____	_____	_____	☐ No ☐ Yes	☐ No ☐ Yes	☐ No ☐ Yes
father	_____	_____	_____	☐ No ☐ Yes	☐ No ☐ Yes	☐ No ☐ Yes
sibs	_____	_____	_____	☐ No ☐ Yes	☐ No ☐ Yes	☐ No ☐ Yes
	_____	_____	_____	☐ No ☐ Yes	☐ No ☐ Yes	☐ No ☐ Yes
	_____	_____	_____	☐ No ☐ Yes	☐ No ☐ Yes	☐ No ☐ Yes
	_____	_____	_____	☐ No ☐ Yes	☐ No ☐ Yes	☐ No ☐ Yes

If "Yes" for any of the above, please explain:

_____

_____

(continued)

Background Survey, *continued*

Reason for Assessment

Reason for Referral:_____

Is your case likely to involve a lawsuit, now or later? ☐ No ☐ Yes   If Yes, explain:

_____

_____

Circumstances of Birth

During pregnancy, did your mother:

Use alcohol? ☐ No ☐ Yes   Use prescription drugs? ☐ No ☐ Yes   Smoke? ☐ No ☐ Yes

Use street drugs? ☐ No ☐ Yes   Were there problems during pregnancy? ☐ No ☐ Yes

If Yes to any of the above, please explain: _____

_____

Weight at birth: ____ Was the birth premature?: ☐ No ☐ Yes   If Yes, weeks premature ___

Early Development

Mark all that applied to you as a child:

☐ late walking	☐ late talking	☐ delayed reading	☐ hyperactive
☐ attention problems	☐ sleep problems	☐ bed wetting	☐ depression
☐ nervous	☐ seizures	☐ truant from school	☐ conflict with teachers
☐ held back in school	☐ many fights	☐ police contact	☐ disobedient
☐ defied authority	☐ poor coordination	☐ many ear infections	☐ attention problem
☐ low self-esteem	☐ aggressive	☐ shy	☐ frustrated easily
☐ impulsive	☐ tantrums	☐ daydream often	☐ fidgety

For boxes checked, please explain: _____

_____

Medical History

Mark all that apply now or in the past:

☐ head injury	☐ unconscious	☐ coma	☐ seizures
☐ high blood pressure	☐ stroke	☐ balance problem	☐ loss of smell
☐ loss of taste	☐ alcohol problem	☐ drug problem	☐ hospitalized
☐ high fever	☐ vision problem	☐ hearing problem	☐ paralysis
☐ loss of touch sense	☐ heart attack	☐ heart disease	☐ angina
☐ HIV or AIDS	☐ lead poisoning	☐ double vision	☐ hallucinations
☐ slurred language	☐ numbness or tingling	☐ extreme fatigue	☐ memory problems
☐ tremor	☐ headaches	☐ dizziness	☐ learning disability
☐ hearing aid	☐ clumsiness	☐ sleep problems	☐ electric shock therapy
☐ neurological problem	☐ exposure to toxic chemicals	☐ drug treatment program	☐ other serious illness

For boxes checked, please explain: _____

_____

Please list the current medications (prescription and over the counter) that you take. Indicate the dosage and number of times per day, if possible:

_____   _____

_____   _____

_____   _____

_____   _____

(continued)

Background Survey, *continued*

History of Counseling and Testing

Have you ever received counseling or other treatment for an emotional or psychological difficulty? ☐ No ☐ Yes   If Yes, please specify the approximate year, the nature, and the duration of the treatment(s):

_____

_____

_____

_____

Have you ever been administered psychological tests before? ☐ No ☐ Yes   If Yes, please indicate the approximate year and the kinds of tests administered:

_____

_____

_____

Academic and Work History

How many years of education have you received? _____
[Note: high school = 12, bachelor's degree = 16, master's degree = 18]

What is your highest degree or diploma earned? _____

If employed, what is the title of your current job?   _____

Please describe the nature of your work: _____

_____

_____

How long have you held your current job?   _____

How many jobs have you had in the last 5 years?   _____

Before-and-After Comparisons

Most persons consult with a psychologist because of a problem, accident, injury, or illness. Please rate how your current functioning compares with your functioning prior to the problem, accident, injury, or illness that is the reason for this evaluation.

	Severe decline	Moderate decline	Slight decline	No change	Improvement
Compared to before, how is your functioning in the following areas:	☐	☐	☐	☐	☐
level of energy	☐	☐	☐	☐	☐
irritability	☐	☐	☐	☐	☐
efficiency of thinking	☐	☐	☐	☐	☐
ability to concentrate	☐	☐	☐	☐	☐
ability to drive	☐	☐	☐	☐	☐
efficiency at your job	☐	☐	☐	☐	☐
frustration tolerance	☐	☐	☐	☐	☐
following conversation	☐	☐	☐	☐	☐
finding your way around	☐	☐	☐	☐	☐
understanding what you read	☐	☐	☐	☐	☐
expressing yourself verbally	☐	☐	☐	☐	☐
recent memory	☐	☐	☐	☐	☐
remote or long-term memory	☐	☐	☐	☐	☐
coordination	☐	☐	☐	☐	☐
vision	☐	☐	☐	☐	☐
hearing	☐	☐	☐	☐	☐
learning ability	☐	☐	☐	☐	☐
sense of touch	☐	☐	☐	☐	☐
sense of smell	☐	☐	☐	☐	☐
sleeping	☐	☐	☐	☐	☐
impulse control	☐	☐	☐	☐	☐
getting along with spouse/partner	☐	☐	☐	☐	☐
participation in social activities	☐	☐	☐	☐	☐

2 The Mental Status Examination

The mental status examination (MSE) is a short, organized interview that usually precedes all other forms of psychological assessment. Many clinicians include a structured, objective questionnaire as part of the MSE, but this should not be confused with the full MSE, even when the terminology "mental status" is found in the title (e.g., Mini-Mental State Exam, Short Portable Mental Status Questionnaire). Regardless of its title, a brief questionnaire is ancillary only—not a substitute for the full MSE, which spans a wide range of psychological functions.

This chapter aspires to three intertwined goals: (1) introduce the essential elements of the MSE, (2) review prominent questionnaires that are often part of the examination, and (3) review the nature and assessment of dementia. The reason for including the third goal is that mental status questionnaires perform an important role in the detection and diagnosis of dementia. In fact, some well-known tools such as the Mini-Mental Status Exam were developed *primarily* as screening tools for the identification of suspected dementia. In order to make effective use of structured mental status questionnaires, the clinician must also understand essential signs and characteristics of Alzheimer's disease, cerebrovascular disorders (stroke), and other conditions. Hence, a primer of dementia concepts is included in this chapter.

Nature and Purpose of the MSE

The specific purpose of the MSE is to provide an accurate description of the patient's current functioning in the realms of memory, thought, language, feeling, and judgment. In addition, the evaluation furnishes a description of the appearance, attitudes, and motor behaviors of the patient. The MSE is the psychological equivalent of the physical exam given by a general practitioner. Just as the physician reviews all the major organ systems looking for evidence of disease, the psychologist reviews the major categories of personal and intellectual functioning, looking for signs and symptoms of neuropathology or psychopathology.

The general purpose of the MSE is to aid the clinician in the diagnosis, assessment, and treatment of clients. A complete and thorough MSE is an essential precursor to clinical work with individuals who may (or may not) reveal evidence of cognitive impairment. Of particular interest is whether clients exhibit significant personal or intellectual impairment relevant to subsequent diagnosis, testing, or treatment.

In some cases the few minutes that it takes to conduct a mental status examination can save hours of misdirected effort. The MSE might reveal that a patient is disoriented, unaware of the month or year, and experiencing a general slowing of thought processes and bodily movement. Under these circumstances, administering a battery of psychological tests would be pointlessly misleading, not to mention thoughtlessly cruel. The highest priority would be to determine the cause of these acute symptoms and to refer the patient for appropriate treatment. Assessment should be postponed—or at least the test battery should be shortened and the results reported with appropriate cautions.

In other cases the client will breeze through an MSE with little or no difficulty. An unremarkable outcome provides confidence that appropriate standardized tests will reveal the client's usual functioning. Knowing whether test results are typical—as opposed to temporarily compromised—is very important in the practice of assessment. Typical results predict future functioning more accurately than anomalous findings. The patient who is delirious from a reversible brain infection will fail any and every question on a mental status examination. This same patient might show great potential for recovery when tested later.

Another use of the MSE is to determine which kinds of additional tests to administer. The client might do generally well on the MSE but reveal some difficulty on those parts of the structured interview having to do with short-term memory. This is a clear mandate for administering specialized tests of memory functions to determine the scope and degree of memory difficulties.

Textbooks in clinical psychology and related fields list topical areas that the examiner should investigate during the MSE (e.g., Trzepacz & Baker, 1993). Although the components differ slightly, these areas are usually included:

- Appearance, attitude, and behavior
- Speech and language functioning
- Thought process and content
- Emotional functioning
- Insight and judgment
- Cognitive functioning

We review these components of the MSE before moving on to presentations of several widely used questionnaires.

Appearance, Attitude, and Behavior

The MSE begins the moment the examiner meets the client. Based upon the client's physical appearance and demeanor, a sensitive and well-trained clinician begins forming impressions about intellectual and emotional functioning even before the

(Note to bot: the MSE is in observation section of Interview)

client speaks. Clothing, cleanliness, and other aspects of appearance are highly relevant to psychodiagnostic sleuthing.

The importance of evaluating the client's appearance is illustrated by the case of a distinguished retired professor in his 70s who was referred for assessment by his daughter. She was concerned by his gradual withdrawal from prior hobbies and social activities. This gentleman-scholar was effusive and gracious when shaking hands with the psychologist. He was well groomed and wore a handsome three-piece suit. But one anomaly of his appearance virtually screamed at the consultant: The Professor's vest bore the remains of at least three different food stains.

Of course, food stains per se do not furnish any particular diagnostic indication. But their presence on the clothing of an otherwise socially skilled gentleman is a dramatic omen that something is awry. Does it signal that the professor is depressed and no longer cares about his appearance? Does it indicate the onset of dementia and a consequent loss of social judgment? We would need more information to fathom the meaning of this oddity. The important point here is that almost any aspect of the client's appearance can be pertinent to the MSE.

Grooming and hygiene are also relevant components of the mental status evaluation. The examiner must regulate expectations based upon the context of the evaluation. For example, when seeing an inpatient at a hospital, it is probably unremarkable if the client's hair is uncombed and she is dressed in pajamas. The same grooming and dress in an outpatient would raise questions about cognitive or emotional functioning. Hygiene is especially relevant to the MSE. The unkempt patient with strong body odor may be experiencing a psychiatric disturbance or an organic mental disorder.

The clinician also should make note of any salient and unusual physical characteristics present in the client. This would include indications of self-harm such as scars on the forearms and evidence of drug abuse such as needle marks. Tattoos are also noteworthy because of their association with social deviance and personal psychopathology. (There are exceptions, of course, as many young adults now adorn their bodies with small, stylish tattoos.) Physical handicaps such as amputated limbs should be noted. Demographic data including age, sex, and ethnic background need to be recorded.

Facial expression is invaluable in monitoring the mental status of clients. A person who has an inappropriate, tortured facial expression and who engages in stereotypic, repetitive hand movements has said more by his presentation than may be revealed by subsequent verbalizations. Especially when combined with unusual mannerisms, a bizarre facial expression may signal a psychotic process and indicate the need for psychiatric referral rather than intellectual assessment.

Much has been made of eye contact in the psychological and psychiatric literature, and the general thrust of the findings is that the absence of eye contact signifies suspiciousness, shyness, or other pathology. This is probably a correct inference, assuming that cultural differences are not at play. In some cultures (e.g., Islamic, Native American) it is considered rude to make direct eye contact; some Native Americans, for example, have been socialized to avoid eye contact as a means of indicating respect. The opposite extreme of excessive eye contact is also considered significant. Hostile, aggressive individuals may engage in unblinking, excessive eye contact as a means of intimidating others.

Attitude toward the examiner is another variable of interest in the MSE. A cooperative client will probably reveal all relevant details of mental and emotional functioning. At the other extreme, the guarded and suspicious patient will resist intrusions into mental life, with the result that the clinician may not gain an accurate picture of the patient's functioning.

Activity level and motor abnormalities also offer clues to the examinee's functioning. Gross motor behaviors such as rapid pacing may indicate excessive anxiety or the onset of a manic episode. At the other extreme, a patient who is motorically slowed may be illustrating one of the classic symptoms of severe depression. These behaviors are relevant to assessment because they may affect the validity of intellectual tests.

Speech and Language Functioning

Regarding the language functioning of the client, the examiner should make note of the rate of speech, tone quality, volume, fluency, and prosody. A pressured push-of-speech is often observed in manic episodes, whereas slow, halting speech may indicate depression or neurological impairment. Dysfluent speech that is halting also suggests neurological impairment. Prosody refers to the emotional tone or affective components of speech that are conveyed by the fluctuations or musicality of speech. The absence of prosody, often described as flat affect, may indicate the presence of schizophrenia. Test results should be interpreted cautiously in these cases.

Difficulty in finding words, verbal confusion, and misuse of words by the examinee also are diagnostically significant. Difficulty in naming well-known objects such as a pencil, watch, cup, coat, or chair may be a symptom of an aphasia caused by underlying cognitive impairment. This would indicate that referral for a comprehensive aphasia assessment would be desirable. Likewise, the patient who engages in empty speech or speech that never directly answers the question may reveal an acquired aphasia.

In addition to observing language skills, the examiner may pose tasks to the patient, such as requesting him or her to repeat certain phrases like "no ifs, ands, or buts" or to interpret well-known proverbs. Asking the patient to read a short passage out loud or to write a simple sentence also might prove diagnostically instructive. For example, when given the assignment to write a simple sentence of her choosing, one accomplished 62-year-old woman produced, "I would t come for my appoint." She was later diagnosed with Alzheimer's disease.

Thought Process and Content

In the course of the interview most patients will demonstrate logic, clarity of thought, and appropriateness of associations. Seriously disturbed patients, however, may reveal gross illogicality ("I am growing my grandfather's hair"), or ramble on vaguely about an ill-defined problem, or display looseness of association ("Nice mobile you got there—it's like the bloodmobile I gave blood at"). The examiner also looks for clinical signs such as blocking of thought (sudden cessation in the train of thought) or ideas of reference (the morbid but erroneous belief that others are talking about the patient). All such symptoms indicate that the referral issue may involve psychiatric disability as well as intellectual dysfunction.

Blatantly delusional thinking usually will be well known in advance of the assessment interview, although a direct question or probe occasionally is needed to reveal an underlying psychosis. To do this, the examiner must be sensitive to the leads given by the patient. A seemingly innocuous statement such as "I've been made to think too much lately" might lead to disclosure of an elaborate delusional system about being controlled by TV towers, for example. The delusion will be revealed only if the examiner asks the patient to clarify what he means by such a queer statement.

Emotional Functioning

In the examination of emotional functioning the practitioner infers the predominant mood and observes the affective range in the patient. Mood refers to the more stable and internal feeling state (e.g., calm, angry, cheerful, dysphoric, anxious) and must be inferred from the patient's verbalizations. In contrast, affect is the objective, external manifestation of the patient's internal emotional state. Whereas mood is more stable, affect typically shows range and variability.

> Affect is judged in terms of its type, intensity, range, variability, and degree of correspondence to the content of the conversation. Normal individuals demonstrate a variety of emotions, of variable intensity, that usually match and change in accordance with the thoughts and feelings being verbally expressed. (Trzepacz & Baker, 1993, p. 39)

Flatness of affect or inappropriateness of affect may indicate a psychiatric disability. The client who rarely modulates his affect or who smiles while discussing the death of his mother might be exhibiting schizophrenia or other serious psychiatric condition.

Of particular interest to the examiner is the presence of depressed mood, which may result in less than optimal functioning on standardized tests. Depressed mood is usually easy to identify because of the melancholic, gloomy demeanor, accompanied by lowered self-esteem, lack of self-confidence, harsh personal criticism, and somatic symptoms such as sleep disturbance, appetite disturbance, headache, or gastrointestinal complaints. But some clients present with a "smiling depression" and do not acknowledge their anguish. In these cases an assessment for depression is important insofar as unacknowledged depression can be mistaken for cognitive deficit.

Insight and Judgment

Insight and judgment refer to the self-understanding, expectations, and plans of the client. Usually, insight and judgment are revealed by the way the client responds to his or her difficulties in the initial interview. Occasionally, specific hypothetical questions are posed to the client, for example, "What would you do if you saw a fire in a theater?" An alcoholic who answers "Yell fire" may have suffered some degree of cognitive impairment from his abusive drinking. Such an answer would certainly suggest the need for additional assessment and testing.

Insight is measured by the extent to which the client is aware of having problems, and the degree to which their impact is acknowledged. In general, it is important to note whether the client appreciates the purpose of the assessment and whether she has realistic plans for the future. Although we can only touch upon the topic here, an important component of insight/judgment is the nature of the patient's defense mechanisms (Vaillant, 1977). Patients who use immature defense mechanisms such as outright denial ("There's nothing wrong with me and they're going to let me out of the hospital tonight") obviously show less insight than those who employ mature defense mechanisms such as humor ("Well, this would certainly be a crummy night to kill myself").

Cognitive Functioning

This section of the MSE often begins with the examiner asking the client to answer some questions that may seem simple, perhaps foolish. The examiner begins by asking the classic orientation questions, namely: What is your name? Where are we? What time is it? Normal persons will be aware of their name, their location, and the approximate time. A patient who answers all three inquiries correctly is said to be "oriented × 3." The evaluation might then proceed to a more detailed inquiry about day of the week and date (month, day, and year).

The patient's basic fund of information might then be assessed by asking who is president now and who was president before him. In addition, the examiner might ask the client to answer questions about well-known persons, such as "Who is governor of this state?" or "Who was Robert Kennedy?"

Simple computational ability might be assessed by having the examinee subtract 7s from 100 or 3s from 20. Alternatively, simple story problems such as "Adam had seven marbles but gave away three—how many were left?" might be used. Short-term memory can be tested by asking the client to repeat a series of digits such as "7-4-3-6-1" with the expectation that a person with normal intelligence should have a digit span of at least five numbers. Another useful test is to tell the client to repeat the names of three objects that the examiner presents verbally (e.g., "Apple, cup, shoe"). Most clients easily can repeat this list after only one presentation, whereas the need for repeated administrations is an indication of impaired short-term memory. The useful aspect of this task is that it can be introduced later as a surprise test of incidental long-term memory. If retested within a half hour, most persons will remember at least two of the three objects. Occasionally, an individual with impaired memory functions will be unable to recall any of the three items. Another method of testing recent memory is to inquire what the client had for breakfast or what he or she did on the previous day. Of course, some collateral source of information is needed to determine the accuracy of the answers.

Abstracting ability is usually tested by asking the examinee to interpret common proverbs such as the meaning of "Still waters run deep" or "Don't cry over spilled milk." The tendency to personalize proverbs ("I never swim where the water is deep" or "I had a cat that spilled milk") or to interpret them concretely ("It is deep where the water is still" or "Spilled milk is sticky") may indicate a psychiatric disorder such as schizophrenia or a diffuse cognitive impairment.

In review, a comprehensive MSE includes the structured, clinical evaluation of a wide gamut of psychological capacities, including language, thought, insight, emotions, and cognitive functions widely conceived. One challenge faced by the examiner is how to describe the findings, especially those that are out of the ordinary. Table 2.1 presents a series of topics and terms useful in conceptualizing the diverse areas of functioning typically evaluated in the MSE.

Several tests are available to aid the clinician in the assessment of mental status. Three prominent instruments are surveyed later in this chapter. Because these tools are especially valuable in the evaluation of dementia, relevant concepts of that disorder are presented before we return to the topic of the MSE.

The Nature and Diagnosis of Dementia

The MSE is particularly important in the assessment of dementia. For this reason, a brief review of the nature and diagnosis of prominent forms of dementia is included here. The term *dementia* refers to a variety of conditions characterized by multiple cognitive deficits that include memory impairment. Dementia was previously classified as an organic mental disorder, but this terminology is no longer used, due to the misleading implication that other mental disorders do not have biological contributions. Yet the older terminology does correctly convey that dementia is a brain disorder. Degenerative brain diseases are especially likely to cause dementia. The dementias are usually categorized according to presumed cause and include the conditions outlined in Table 2.2. All of the dementias share the following common symptoms (American Psychiatric Association, 1994):

1. Memory impairment
   a. impairment of the ability to learn new information, and/or
   b. impairment of the ability to recall previously learned information
2. One or more of the following cognitive disturbances
   a. aphasia—disturbance in language comprehension or expression
   b. apraxia—disorder in the execution of learned, skilled movements
   c. agnosia—loss of ability to recognize or identify objects despite intact senses
   d. impairment of executive functions—disorder in planning, organizing, sequencing, or abstracting

TABLE 2.1   Mental Status Examination Topics and Terms

Topic	Applicable Terms or Concepts
Demographics	Age, sex, race, ethnicity, native language
Apparent Age	Appears younger/older than age
Dress	Neatly dressed, attire appropriate/inappropriate
Cleanliness/Grooming	Neatly groomed, body odor, unkempt, unshaven, hair dirty/uncombed
Appearance	Fresh, relaxed, tense, tired
Eye Contact	Avoided, excessive, unnerving, appropriate
Level of Consciousness	Alert, drowsy, lethargic, stuporous, comatose
Unusual Features	Tattoos, scars, physical disabilities
Attitude toward MSE	Cooperative, uncooperative, suspicious, hostile, guarded
Motor Features	Paralysis, paresis (weakness), psychomotor retardation, masked facies, restlessness, agitation, tremor, tardive dyskinesia, stereotypic behavior, mannerisms
Mood	Calm (friendly, pleasant), angry (belligerent, sullen), euphoric (elated, jovial), apathetic (dull, flat), dysphoric (despondent, remorseful), apprehensive (anxious, tense)
Affect	Appropriate/inappropriate, congruent/incongruent, reactive/nonreactive, blunted, exaggerated, constricted, fixed, labile
Speech and Language	Fluent/nonfluent, pressured/slowed, prosodic/flat, loud/soft, excessive/restricted, stuttering, word salad, word-finding difficulty, poor articulation (dysarthric)
Thought Process	Circumstantiality, loose associations, flight of ideas, tangentiality, word salad, clang associations, neologisms, thought blocking, echolalia
Thought Content and Percepts	Delusion, hallucination, obsession, phobia, paranoia, suicidal/homocidal thoughts, suspiciousness, insightful/ not insightful
Cognitive Processes	Constructional apraxia, distractibility, acalculia, concrete thinking, confabulation, impairment of immediate memory, impairment of delayed memory, retrograde/anterograde amnesia, perseveration, word-finding difficulty, loss of orientation, altered consciousness (alert, drowsy, lethargy, stupor, coma)
Insight and Judgment	Insight, denial, humor, intellectualization, indifference, projection, repression, suppression, other defense mechanisms

Source: Based on T. P. Trzepacz & R. W. Baker. *The Psychiatric Mental Status Examination* (New York: Oxford University Press, 1993).

TABLE 2.2   Major Types of Dementia Based on Presumed Etiology

Dementia of the Alzheimer's type

Vascular dementia (e.g., multi-infarct dementia, hemorrhage)

Dementia due to head trauma

Dementia due to medical conditions (e.g., HIV, tumor, Parkinson's disease)

Substance-induced persisting dementia (e.g., drug or alcohol abuse, toxins)

3. The impairments listed above must be serious and interfere with social or occupational functioning.

4. The impairments listed above must represent a decline from prior functioning.

Note that memory impairment is a cardinal symptom of dementia and is often the most prominent early symptom. Yet memory impairment alone is not a sufficient basis for the diagnosis—the patient must meet other criteria as listed.

In addition to these common features, each subtype of dementia has unique features as well. Both the common and the unique elements of the dementias are reviewed in this chapter and the next. Of course, a thorough mental status evaluation is pivotal in making a diagnosis of dementia. The reader will recall that the subcategories of a typical mental status evaluation include memory, language functions, sensory and motor functions, and higher-level processes of planning, organizing, and abstracting—precisely the elements listed here for a diagnosis of dementia.

Many cases of dementia develop slowly, such that friends and relatives are unable to pinpoint exactly when the patient started to go downhill. Even some cases of vascular dementia—characterized by the gradual accumulation of small strokes—can follow this pattern. Dementia is typically irreversible, although some forms can be controlled with therapeutic interventions. Andreasen and Black (1995) estimate that up to 15 percent of cases are potentially reversible but that only 3 percent fully resolve. A search for treatable causes of dementia (e.g., brain infection, hypothyroidism, exposure to certain toxins) is mandatory. If a patient with suspected dementia has not had a thorough medical evaluation, immediate referral is warranted.

Delirium refers to a group of cognitive disorders that may be confused with dementia. In contrast with dementia, which typically features insidious onset, a hallmark of delirium is rapid onset. The patient becomes disoriented and confused and reveals widespread cognitive impairment over a period of hours or a few days. Delirium almost always signifies a serious medical, surgical, or neurological illness. It is usually easy to recognize because the patient displays a reduced level of consciousness (including stupor) and exhibits a reduced ability to focus, sustain, or shift attention. In addition, delirium typically develops over a short period of time (hours or days) and fluctuates throughout the day. Properly diagnosed and medically treated, delirium may be reversible. Obviously, medical referral is obligatory. This disorder is found mainly among persons who are medically ill, and it is associated with high mortality—an estimated 40 to 50 percent of delirious patients will die within 1 year (Andreasen & Black, 1995).

Dementia of the Alzheimer's Type

Dementia of the Alzheimer's type is commonly referred to simply as Alzheimer's disease. This is a dementia of insidious onset and gradually progressive course in which other specific causes have been excluded by the history, medical examination, and laboratory tests. As the disease progresses, CT or MRI scans reveal brain atrophy with resultant enlargement of the ventricles and fissures. Histopathological changes at the cellular level also are evident at autopsy (Whitehouse, 1993). These changes include increases in senile plaques (degenerating neurons tangled around a core of amyloid) and in neurofibrillary tangles (helical filaments tangled within neurons). These plaques and tangles are found in normal aging, but in Alzheimer's disease their presence is accelerated and excessive; that is, the differences between Alzheimer's disease and normal aging may be primarily quantitative, not qualitative. The plaques and tangles are dispersed throughout the brain with heavier concentrations in the hippocampus (a brain structure important in consolidation of new memories) and the cerebral cortex. This helps explain why memory loss is the primary presenting complaint in Alzheimer's disease.

Alzheimer's disease is named after Alois Alzheimer, the German physician who identified it in 1907. The disease is known to cause degeneration of the basal nucleus and the hippocampus, leading initially to deficits in short-term memory. Later, logical and social capacities are lost, followed by abstracting ability. Finally, behavior and personality are more obviously affected. In the final stages the person is totally incapable of self-care.

It is estimated that about 5 percent of the population over the age of 65 suffers from Alzheimer's disease (Andreasen & Black, 1995). The risk increases precipitously with age—the disorder affects 20 to 30 percent of those over the age of 85. There is also a familial pattern, and first-degree relatives (parents or siblings) are at greater risk for developing the disease earlier in life than are members of the general population (Heston & White, 1991).

Risk factors for Alzheimer's disease include age, female gender (but this may be confounded with age), a history of head injury (at any age), Down's syndrome, low social class, and having a first-degree relative with Alzheimer's disease. When evaluating a referral with suspected Alzheimer's disease, the practitioner should pay special attention to the symptoms listed in Table 2.3. Some of these behaviors also apply to other forms of dementia, but the presence of several of these distinc-

TABLE 2.3   **Symptoms and Examples Suggestive of Alzheimer's Disease**

1. Memory impairment that interferes with work or social functioning: forgets assignments and appointments, fails to remember recent transactions

2. Difficulty with commonplace activities: can't balance the checkbook, prepares the same meal repeatedly

3. Loss of orientation to time or place: often wrong as to date or time, becomes lost even when visiting familiar sites

4. Insidious onset: initial disability is minimal, others recognize problem only in retrospect

5. Noteworthy problems with language: word-finding difficulties, substitution of inappropriate words

6. Difficulty with abstract thinking: does not understand the rules of card games, no longer can fill out a simple form

7. Impairment of social judgment: dress is no longer appropriate, endangers self or others

8. Misplacing important items: keys and eyeglasses, etc., simply disappear, or show up in inappropriate places

9. Changes in personality: rapid mood changes, onset of suspiciousness or confusion

10. Loss of initiative: marked preference for the familiar, needs prompting to become involved

Source: Based on Alzheimer's Association (1998), Andreasen and Black (1995), and other sources.

tive symptoms is suggestive of Alzheimer's disease. In addition to this symptom pattern, the examiner should consider the age and family history of the client. The suspicion of Alzheimer's disease is heightened for older clients and for those with a family history of the disorder, particularly if first-degree relatives (parents and siblings) exhibited early onset.

Practitioners are reminded that the diagnosis of Alzheimer's disease is difficult, as certain medical conditions and some forms of severe depression can mimic the symptoms. Currently the diagnosis is made by a careful process of elimination and verified at autopsy by means of characteristic brain pathology. Diagnosis is serious detective work that involves the exclusion of all other possibilities. In every case of suspected Alzheimer's disease, referral for medical workup is mandatory.

Vascular Dementia

The primary type of vascular dementia is multi-infarct dementia, which involves a series of small strokes over a period of months or years. The mechanism of stroke is that small arteries in the brain become occluded by the buildup of fatty, atherosclerotic deposits. Often, a stroke occurs when a small piece of atherosclerotic plaque breaks loose within a larger artery and travels to the brain, where it closes off a smaller, partially obstructed artery. Once an artery is completely blocked off, all brain tissue supplied by that artery dies from lack of oxygen. Thus, the effect of each small stroke depends on the size and location of the brain tissue previously supplied by the blocked artery. The symptom picture may include confusion, visual disturbance, slurring of speech, weakness on one side of the body, or difficulty in writing.

Multi-infarct dementia is the second most common type of dementia (after Alzheimer's disease) but accounts for only about 10 percent of all cases. Approximately 300,000 to 400,000 individuals, mainly elderly, are affected each year (Starkstein & Robinson, 1992). The disorder is usually easy to distinguish from other dementias because of the patchy, stepwise decline in cognitive and sensory-motor abilities caused by the succession of small strokes. Significant cerebrovascular disease usually is evident from history, physical examination, or laboratory tests. High blood pressure is common. Plateau periods in which functioning is reasonably constant are followed by episodes of sudden decline reflecting the onset of a cerebrovascular accident. Some improvement is typical after each event, but each succeeding stroke leaves a residual effect. The long-term accumulation of deficits can leave the patient with significant disability. Unlike Alzheimer's disease, for which treatments are largely palliative, the course of multi-infarct dementia can be slowed with proper medical treatment.

A more serious form of vascular dementia is caused by the hemorraghic rupture of an artery within the brain. The rupture of an artery causes damage by direct physical contact of the blood spurting into brain tissue, resultant physical displacement of brain tissue, and loss of circulatory supply downstream from the point of rupture. Hemorrhage causes widespread brain damage and is often fatal. Both multi-infarct dementia and hemorrhage are easily diagnosed by medical personnel who have access to modern brain-imaging techniques. Patients with suspected vascular dementia usually have seen a physician, but if they have not this is mandatory.

Other Dementias and Pseudodementia

Almost any condition that affects the brain can lead to dementia, which means that the number of subtypes is vast. A prominent cause of dementia is head injury, which is discussed at the end of the next chapter. We have not considered a lengthy list of neurological diseases such as invasive tumor, Parkinson's disease, multiple sclerosis, and Huntington's disease, nor have we looked at medical conditions such as dementia from human immunodeficiency virus or the Wernicke-Korsakoff syndrome from severe alcohol abuse. These conditions constitute a very small proportion of the dementias in comparison to Alzheimer's disease, vascular dementia, and head trauma. Space does not permit a full discussion; the interested reader is referred to Albert and Moss (1988), La Rue (1992), and Storandt and VandenBos (1994) for details.

Finally, we consider the concept of *pseudodementia*, even though it is not an official diagnosis. The term is used inconsistently, but most sources indicate that pseudodementia refers to a potentially reversible dementia that sometimes accompanies depression. The patient appears to have dementia as evidenced by memory problems and cognitive lapses. Characteristically, the patient often complains bitterly about lost cognitive skills. However, the disorder is an artifact of the depression and will dissipate if the primary disorder is successfully treated.

The concept of pseudodementia stands as a warning to clinicians that they should look for reversible, treatable causes whenever they encounter what appears to be a case of dementia. This is particularly true of impaired elderly patients, for whom the default diagnosis of Alzheimer's disease is so easily offered. What appears to be Alzheimer's disease might actually be an atypical manifestation of depression. Particularly in elderly patients, major depression can be accompanied by cognitive impairment. Individuals who experience a severe depression often complain of memory impairment, difficulty in thinking, and a reduction in intellectual abilities. In some cases these complaints are not verified by objective testing, whereas in other cases there will be substantial deficits in objective test performance. Table 2.4 lists the clinical features that distinguish dementia from pseudodementia.

Tools for the Assessment of Mental Status

It should be evident from the wide-ranging nature of the topical areas covered by a full examination that the MSE would be difficult to quantify in any objective, standardized format. For example, it is difficult to devise questions or tasks for the examinee that capture the extent to which he or she reveals good insight and judgment. These are clinical assessments, inherently subjective, and substantial clinical sensitivity on the part of the examiner is needed.

Another impediment to a global measure of mental status is the disparate nature of the topical areas. It is unlikely that a client's speech quality and his knowledge of the date have anything in common, at least from a psychometric point of view. Combining these and other unrelated symptoms into one global measure probably would not yield a useful instrument.

In spite of these cautions about devising a global measure of mental status, the *cognitive* aspects of the MSE are natural targets for the development of short screening tests. Cognition, memory, and orientation are all intellectual functions that can be easily tested in a structured interview format. Several brief measures of mental status have been developed around this core of intellectual functions. While none

TABLE 2.4   Clinical Features Distinguishing Dementia and Pseudodementia

	Dementia	Pseudodementia
Onset	Insidious*	Abrupt
Duration	Longer	Shorter
Complaints	Fewer and vague	More and detailed
Social Skills	Later loss	Earlier loss
Mood	Shallow and labile	Pervasive mood change
Attention	Preserved	Faulty
Test Responses	Successes emphasized	Dwells on failures
Effort at Tests	More effort	Less effort
Test Answers	Near misses	"Don't know" answers

*Except multi-infarct dementia, which may show stepwise, progressive disability.

Source: Based on C. E. Wells, (1979), "Pseudodementia," *American Journal of Psychiatry, 136,* 895–900. Also based on S. J. Nixon, Secondary Dementias: Reversible Dementias and Pseudodementia, in R. L. Adams, O. A. Parsons, J. L. Culbertson, and S. J. Nixon (Eds.), *Neuropsychology for Clinical Practice: Etiology, Assessment, and Treatment of Common Neurological Disorders* (Washington, DC: American Psychological Association, 1996).

of them is particularly good at assessing the nonintellective aspects of the MSE— such as appearance, mood, thought content, and speech processes—they are nonetheless quite useful as screening devices for intellectual impairment.

We focus here on three useful tests of mental status, each of which has found a niche of its own. The Test of Temporal Orientations (Benton et al., 1994), which measures orientation to day, date, and time and requires only a minute or two to administer, is a general-purpose tool that can be used as part of any intellectual evaluation. The Short Portable Mental Status Questionnaire (SPMSQ) is slightly longer—a ten-item test that is particularly useful with elderly clients suspected of cognitive decline. The Mini-Mental State Exam (MMSE) is a 5- to 10-minute test that yields an index of global intellectual functioning. The MMSE is particularly useful in screening for dementia.

Test of Temporal Orientations

The MSE always includes assessment of a patient's temporal orientation, that is, awareness of time, day, and date. Most adults provide reasonably accurate answers when asked "What time is it?" or "What day is it?" or "What is the date today?" Minor errors such as being off by a half hour for time or missing the date by a day or two may occasionally occur in normal persons; missing the day of the week is a rare error. Gross errors such as missing the time by 3 hours or giving the wrong year for the current date are therefore of particular diagnostic significance and may signal an abnormal condition such as dementia, schizophrenia, or mental retardation. Of course, this is a one-directional sign only: Major errors in temporal orientation signify that an abnormal condition might exist, but not all abnormal conditions will lead to deficiencies in temporal orientation.

The temporal orientation portion of a MSE usually is administered in an informal, unstandardized manner. The examiner typically asks the client for the current time, day, and date and then applies a liberal and subjective interpretation as to the accuracy of the answers. Unfortunately, most examiners are too forgiving in their judgment of "normal" versus "impaired" functioning on this task, with the result that many clinically impaired individuals escape immediate detection (Benton, Van Allen, & Fogel, 1964). For example, Knights and Folstein (1977) found that 37 percent of cognitively impaired general medical ward patients went unidentified by the attending physicians. DePaolo and Folstein (1978) studied thirty-three patients with cognitive impairment on a neurologic inpatient service and found that 30 percent were not recognized as impaired by the attending neurologists.

The Test of Temporal Orientations (TTO) was developed by Benton, Van Allen, and Fogel (1964) to provide an objective method for administering, scoring, and interpreting temporal orientation. A summary of the test with extensive normative data is found in Benton and others (1994). The TTO is administered by asking the examinee to give the current month, day, and year, the day of the week, and the present time (Table 2.5). Of course, calendars and wrist watches must be placed out of view before the test is given. In all, then, five pieces of information are obtained from the examinee.

Scoring is in terms of error points. A perfect performance results in a score of zero. One error point is earned for each day of the week removed from the current day (maximum of 3), and 1 error point is earned for each day of the month removed from the correct day (maximum of 15). An incorrect month results in 5 error points for each month removed from the correct month, while an incorrect year results in 10 error points. As detailed in Table 2.5, certain exceptions for scoring error points are made if the month or year have just changed. Finally, 1 error point is earned for each 30 minutes removed from the correct time (maximum of 5).

The value of objective scoring for the TTO is that normal persons usually make perfect or near perfect scores. The likelihood of a "false positive" outcome in which a normal individual is classified as impaired is correspondingly quite low. In fact, 93 percent of three combined samples of normal subjects (N = 434) earned between 0 and 2 error points. Benton et al. (1994) advise that scores of 3 can be considered borderline, while scores of 4–7 are moderately defective, and scores of 8 or higher (obtained by 0.6 percent of normals) are severely defective.

In the experience of most clinicians, normal individuals almost never misidentify the year. It is also unusual for a normal person to misidentify the month, although it seems within the realm of possibility that this might happen at the very beginning of a new month. A more common error (resulting in scores of 1 or 2 points) is for a normal client to miss the day of the month by one or more days.

[handwritten: 0 = perfect score. the higher the score, the more impairment]

TABLE 2.5   Test of Temporal Orientations

Administration

What is today's date? (The patient is required to give month, day, and year.)

What day of the week is it?

What time is it now? (Examiner makes sure that the patient cannot look at a watch or clock.)

Scoring

Day of week: 1 error point for each day removed from the correct day to a maximum of 3 points.

Day of month: 1 error point for each day removed from the correct day to a maximum of 15 points.

Month: 5 error points for each month removed from the correct month with the qualification that, if the stated date is within 15 days of the correct day, no error points are scored for the incorrect month (for example, May 29 for June 2 = 4 error points).

Year: 10 error points for each year removed from the correct year to a maximum of 60 points with the qualification that, if the stated date is within 15 days of the correct date, no error points are scored for the incorrect year (for example, December 26, 1982 for January 2, 1983 = 7 error points).

Time of day: 1 error point for each 30 minutes removed from the correct time to a maximum of 5 points.

The total number of error points constitutes the patient's obtained score.

Source: From *Contributions to Neuropsychological Assessment: A Clinical Manual* (2d ed.), by Arthur L. Benton, A. B. Sivan, K. Hamsher, et al. Copyright © 1983, 1994 by Oxford University Press, Inc. Used by permission of Oxford University Press, Inc.

Missing the time of the day by more than 30 minutes also happens occasionally, although it is rare for a normal person to miss it by 60 minutes or more.

A particular virtue of the TTO is that it can help identify patients with impaired orientation who appear temporally oriented in a routine clinical examination. Benton et al. (1964) found the test to disclose temporal disorientation in twenty-seven patients with brain disease, only thirteen of whom were judged to have such impairment during interview. Of course, many brain-impaired persons will score in the normal range on the TTO. Nonetheless, a sufficient percentage of brain-impaired individuals do poorly that the test is highly cost-effective. The value of a suspicious finding—even if rarely found—is substantial in view of the small amount of time invested in the procedure.

Research by Joslyn and Hutzell (1979) indicates that alcoholic patients are very unlikely to score in the moderately or severely impaired range (4 and above points), whereas only five of sixty-seven patients diagnosed with schizophrenia had such deviant scores. These results speak well for the discriminant validity of the test—it is mainly patients with dementia who obtain high scores. Of course, the fact that some persons with schizophrenia score in the impaired range validly may reflect their current temporal disorientation.

Short Portable Mental Status Questionnaire

The Short Portable Mental Status Questionnaire (SPMSQ; Pfeiffer, 1975) is a tool for identifying cognitive deficits associated with brain impairment. It differs from the other instruments discussed in this section in that it is specifically intended for use with older subjects, those age 50 and above.

Elderly patients with brain impairment often experience disorientation to time, place, or person, loss of recent memory, and difficulty with simple cognitive tasks. Clinicians who work with the elderly frequently are called upon to assess the presence or degree of such impairment. This assessment can be crucial in determining if the patient is still capable of self-care or should be placed under the supervision of nursing home staff or responsible family members. In many cases the SPMSQ can help the clinician in this diagnostic task by providing an accurate and brief assessment of cognitive competence in such basic areas as recent memory, simple computation, and orientation to time, place, and person.

The test consists of ten questions that are scored right or wrong. The questions involve knowledge of the date, day of the week, telephone number (or street address), place of birth, mother's maiden name, and name of the current and previous U.S. president. The age and birthdate of the patient also are requested. Finally, serial subtraction of 3 from 20 is tested. Scores can range from a severely impaired 0 to a perfect 10.

Two noteworthy features of the SPMSQ are, first, that the scoring system was normed to compensate for differences in educational background and race, and, second, that the score yields four levels of mental function (intact, mild, moderate, and severe impairment). These levels of function can be used to aid the clinician in determining an older person's capacity for self-care (Pfeiffer, 1975). The first category is considered normal, while the second might be termed "frail elderly," implying that some assistance is required, but the subject is still capable of independence. The third and fourth categories are consistent with dementia. Of course, other sources of evaluation would be essential to the evaluation.

Pfeiffer (1975) has provided normative data on 602 Caucasian persons and 323 African American individuals from which the level of function can be derived. For a Caucasian client with 7 through 12 years of education the cutoffs for the four levels of function are as follows: 8–10, intact; 6–7, mildly impaired; 3–5, moderately impaired; 0–2, severely impaired. If the client is African American, the cutoffs are 1 point lower; that is, 7–10 is intact, and so on. If the individual has had only a grade school education, the cutoffs are also adjusted downward 1 point. Conversely, if the client has had post-high school education, the cutoff values are raised by 1 point.

Considering the brevity of the scale, the reliability of the SPMSQ is good. A 4-week test-retest study produced reliability coefficients of .82 and .83 for two groups

(N = 29 and 30) of older subjects (Pfeiffer, 1975). Test-retest reliability was .85 in a sample of nursing home patients (Lesher & Whelihan, 1986).

Questionnaire validity has been investigated by comparing agreement between test classification and global clinical diagnosis derived from interview and collateral sources of information. In the original study by Pfeiffer (1975) a SPMSQ rating of moderate or severe impairment was confirmed by a clinical diagnosis of dementia in thirty-six of thirty-nine cases (sensitivity of 92 percent). Conversely, a SPMSQ rating of intact or mild impairment was confirmed by the absence of a clinical diagnosis of dementia in seventy-seven of ninety-four cases (specificity of 82 percent). These are very respectable hit rates for a short screening instrument.

Wolber and others (1984) studied the diagnostic precision of the SPMSQ in a mixed sample of ninety-five consecutive admissions to an inpatient geriatric unit. Fifty-six percent of the sample had a primary diagnosis of organic disorder (1 percent mild, 18 percent moderate, and 37 percent severe), while the remaining 44 percent had a primary diagnosis of some type of psychiatric disorder. While it is true that persons with psychiatric disorder also might show deficits in mental status, we should expect that, on average, the degree of their deficits would be less than that observed in persons with dementia. It is reassuring, then, that the group with a primary diagnosis of psychiatric disorder scored far higher (M = 6.6, SD = 3.0) than the group with organic disorder (M = 2.5, SD = 3.1). In this same study the SPMSQ revealed good concurrent validity with other neuropsychological measures. There was a strong and consistent correlation with other measures of cognitive impairment such as the Bender Gestalt ($r = .60$), Digit Span ($r = .66$), and a measure of basic living skills ($r = .57$).

Wolber and colleagues (1984) do issue one caution in the use of the SPMSQ. In their research the instrument was accurate at the two extremes of level of functioning but misleading at the two intermediate levels. Of their patients scoring in the severely impaired level, 88 percent were independently diagnosed as being organically impaired. At the other extreme, the intact level, 78 percent were diagnosed as nonimpaired. However, for those classified as mildly and moderately impaired by the SPMSQ, 64 percent and 70 percent, respectively, were diagnosed as not organically impaired. Thus, at the middle levels of impairment the test tends to *overdiagnose* the presence of organic conditions. So long as examiners are aware of this tendency, it is nonetheless clear that the SPMSQ is a very useful screening test for mental status in the elderly.

Smyer, Hofland, and Jonas (1979) came to a similar conclusion in a validity study of the SPMSQ. They collected information on twenty-six variables related to independent functioning in 103 institutionalized subjects and 78 community dwellers. The variables involved such practical matters as continence, ability to use the telephone, and ability to cook for oneself. All subjects were also administered the SPMSQ. The mean age for the entire sample was 75 years. Smyer, Hofland, and Jonas (1979) reasoned that if the SPMSQ was a valid mental status instrument with the elderly, then a discriminant function analysis should predict the four SPMSQ categories (intact, mild, moderate, and severe impairment) from the twenty-six independent variables involving activities of daily living and the like. Initial results were somewhat discouraging: Only 69 percent of the sample could be correctly classified using the original four-group system outlined by Pfeiffer (1975). The accuracy of classification for the mildly impaired group was a disappointing 22 percent. Most of those subjects with SPMSQ scores in the mildly impaired range were, according to independent external criteria, functioning normally. To refine the SPMSQ classification system, subjects were then divided into three groups: no or minimal impairment (6–10 points), moderate impairment (3–5 points), and severe impairment (0–2 points). This system combined the first two categories from Pfeiffer (1975) in an attempt to reduce errors of classification for the mildly impaired group. The modified scheme for determining intellectual function showed a respectable 79 percent accuracy, a significant improvement over the original four-group method.

An extensive study by Scherr and others (1988) also provides reason for caution when interpreting intermediate scores on the SPMSQ. This study evaluated nearly 1,000 community-dwelling elderly persons ages 65 and over. For the youngest group (65–69 years of age) the average score was 7.8, whereas for the oldest group (85–89 years of age) the average score dropped to 6.1, indicating that the interpretation of SPMSQ scores must be moderated by age as well as by education and race.

In sum, examiners need to grant diagnostic leniency to subjects who make three to four errors, particularly if they are less educated, older, African American, or other minority. In terms of nontest criteria, these persons may appear normal and function independently, in spite of their apparent deficits in mental status. Practitioners need to be reminded that the SPMSQ is a *screening* test only. A poor score raises a concern about dementia, but additional evaluation is needed to confirm (or disconfirm) that suspicion.

Mini-Mental State Exam

The Mini-Mental State Exam (MMSE; Folstein, Folstein, & McHugh, 1975) is a 5- to 10-minute screening test that provides an objective global index of cognitive functioning (Figure 2.1). The index ranges from an extremely impaired score of 0 to a perfect score of 30. The examinee must answer brief questions from the clinician and perform simple tasks on command. The authors list five areas of cognitive functioning that are assessed. In addition, their copy-design task can be regarded as a sixth and separate subtest. *Orientation* is measured by asking the usual questions about time, day, date, and location. Note that this section of the MMSE overlaps entirely with the TTO. Hence, by administering the TTO, the examiner has also completed most of the first section of the MMSE. *Registration* is actually a short-term memory task for which the examinee must recall three things named by the examiner. *Attention and Calculation* is measured by having the subject begin with 100 and count backwards by 7 (serial 7s). If the patient cannot or will not perform this task, the alternative task is to spell the word "world" backward. In *Recall* the subject must recall the same three objects named previously. *Language* functions are assessed by having the subject name simple objects, repeat a sentence, and follow a three-stage command. A *Constructional* task also is included in the language section. The examinee must copy overlapping pentagons, a task borrowed from the Bender Gestalt. Each discrete subtask completed correctly (such as naming the year) earns 1 point toward a maximum possible score of 30.

		Score	Points

Orientation

1. What is the

		Score	Points
	Year?	_____	1
	Season?	_____	1
	Month?	_____	1
	Date of Month?	_____	1
	Day of Week?	_____	1

2. Where are we?

	State	_____	2
	County	_____	1
	City	_____	1
	Hospital/Building/Home	_____	1

Registration

3. Name three words (shirt, brown, honesty), taking 1 second to say each. Then ask the patient all three after you have said them. Give 1 point for each correct answer. Repeat the words until the patient learns all three.   _____   3

Attention and Calculation

4. Spell WORLD backwards (DLROW)   _____   5

Recall

5. Ask for three words learned in item 3. One point for each correct response.   _____   3

Language

6. Point to a pencil and a watch. Have the patient name them as you point.   _____   2
7. Have the patient repeat "No ifs, ands, or buts."   _____   1
8. Have the patient follow a three-stage command: "Take the paper in your right hand. Fold the paper in half. Put the paper on the floor."   _____   3
9. Have the patient read and obey the following: "Close your eyes." (Write in large letters).   _____   1
10. Have the patient write a sentence of his or her own choice. (The sentence should contain a subject and an object and make sense. Ignore spelling errors.)   _____   1
11. Enlarge the design printed below to 1–5 cm per side and have the patient copy it. (Give 1 point if all sides and angles are preserved and if the intersecting sides form a quadrangle.)   _____   1

Total: [_____]   30

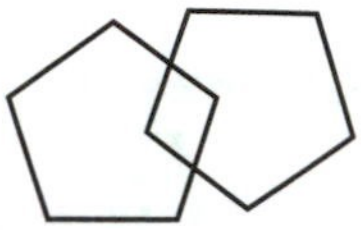

FIGURE 2.1   The Mini-Mental State Exam

Source: Reprinted with permission from M. F. Folstein, S. E. Folstein, and P. R. McHugh (1975), "Mini-Mental State: A Practical Method for Grading the Cognitive State of Patients for the Clinician," *Journal of Psychiatric Research, 12*, 189–198. With permission from Elsevier Science.

*ask • why so many cog. tests in MSE
& when to use what

Several dozen studies of the MMSE have investigated the traditional psychometric properties of reliability and concurrent validity with generally positive findings. Regarding reliability, the inaugural study by Folstein, Folstein, and McHugh (1975) reported excellent 24-hour test-retest reliability for twenty-two patients with varied depressive symptoms ($r = .89$). When two testers were used over a 24-hour test-retest period for nineteen patients with major depression, the reliability dropped somewhat ($r = .82$) but was still respectable for such a short scale. Test-retest reliability over a 28-day period for twenty-three clinically stable patients with diagnoses of dementia, depression, and schizophrenia was exceptional ($r = .99$). More recent studies generally confirm strong reliability coefficients for diverse patient samples. For example, Uhlmann, Larson, and Buchner (1987) reported a 12-month test-retest reliability of .86 in a sample of patients with dementia. Somewhat lower coefficients on the order of .70 were reported by Grace and others (1995) in a sample of seventy-seven geriatric stroke patients and by de Leon and others (1993) in a sample of twenty-two inpatients diagnosed with schizophrenia.

One determinant that probably reduces the reliability of the MMSE somewhat is the original design of the instrument, which allows for discretionary variations in administration and scoring of some items. The following components of administration and scoring can vary at the choice of the examiner:

1. In the Registration section the examiner names three unrelated objects. No guidance is given as to which objects to name, so the stimuli might be "apple, cup, shoe" or "kumquat, tureen, abacus." Some clinicians modify the procedure further by using a mix of concrete and abstract terms such as "shirt, brown, honesty" which probably changes the difficulty level (Tombaugh et al., 1996). Of course, using triads of unequal difficulty level for test and retest will diminish the reliability of the instrument.

2. In the Attention and Calculation section the examiner has the choice of using serial 7s or asking the examinee to spell "world" backward. Switching from one option to the other also will reduce reliability, because these two choices are not of equal difficulty (Feher et al., 1992).

3. The scoring in the spell "world" backward item also is unclear (Gallo & Anthony, 1994). For example, how many points should be awarded for "dlorw"? Viewed rigidly and literally, both "o" and "r" are not in proper reversed order (two errors), so it appears that the score is 3 out of the maximum 5. But by this logic, a score of 4 is impossible—how could only a single letter be out of order? In response to this dilemma, some clinicians recommend a "chess move" strategy to determine the score. In this approach the examiner determines the number of "single jumps" needed with one or more letters to produce the correct sequence. With "dlorw" only one letter needs to be moved one place ("jump" the "o" over the "r") to produce the correct reversed sequence. With this more liberal scoring approach the appropriate score is 4 out of 5. Of course, using different scoring strategies for test and retest will further reduce the reliability of the instrument.

Further modifications of the original MMSE also are encountered in some applications. For example, Tombaugh et al. (1996) modified the "Where are we?" portion of the Orientation section, worth a total of 5 points, by scoring *state* as 2 points and replacing *floor of building* with *type of building*. Scoring is thus as follows: *state* (2 points), *county* (1 point), *city* (1 point), *hospital/building/home* (1). These alterations were necessary so that the MMSE could be used with community-dwelling elderly for whom *floor of building* would be irrelevant.

Finally, we look briefly at a substantial revision of the MMSE known as the Modified MMSE or 3MS (Teng & Chui, 1987). The 3MS is a worthy and valuable instrument, but the changes from the MMSE are so substantial that it really constitutes a new test. For this reason, the coverage is restricted here to the MMSE, with its long and rich history of normative and validation research.

The variant forms of the MMSE present a quandary to practitioners, namely, which version should they adopt? When administering the Registration items, should examiners use "apple, cup, shoe" or some other choice? What about serial 7s versus spelling "world" backward for the Attention items? For Orientation, should the examiner ask for *floor of building* or *type of building*?

I recommend the version reprinted in Figure 2.2 for several reasons. First, this form specifies the three words used in the Registration section (shirt, brown, honesty), which provides standardization not present in the original MMSE. Second, the use of the "world" backward item instead of serial 7s in the Attention section is consistent with common practice. Serial 7s is substantially more difficult and therefore frustrating to many normal elderly persons. Third, the Orientation section employs *type of building* instead of *floor of building*, which renders the test more useful in community settings. The final reason—and probably the most important one—is that excellent norms and cutoff scores exist for this version (Tombaugh et al., 1996).

The validity of the MMSE has been investigated from two perspectives, one theoretical and the other practical. From a theoretical perspective, it is important that scores on the test correlate positively and substantially with other tests known to be sensitive to cognitive impairment. For example, in the original study by Folstein, Folstein, and McHugh (1975) the MMSE revealed robust correlations with Wechsler Adult Intelligence Scale (WAIS) IQ scores, thereby demonstrating a form of concurrent validity. Specifically, in a heterogeneous group of twenty-six psychiatric patients, the MMSE correlated highly with Verbal IQ ($r = .78$) and with Performance IQ ($r = .66$). In a study of twenty patients with diverse forms of brain damage the MMSE also correlated substantially (as high as .74) with scores on the Luria-Nebraska Neuropsychological Battery (Horton & Alana, 1990). Finally, a factor analysis of MMSE scores for 892 nursing home residents revealed a solution with four meaningful and theory-confirming factors: Executing Psychomotor Commands, Memory, Concentration, and Language (Abraham et al., 1994).

From a practical standpoint, the validity of the MMSE rests upon its capacity to discriminate patients with dementia from normal patients and from other examinees with less severe forms of cognitive impairment such as depression. Data from the original study are quite encouraging in this regard (Folstein, Folstein, and McHugh, 1975). In one substudy, twenty-nine patients with dementia averaged 9.7 points (range 0 to 22), while thirty depressed patients averaged 25.1 points (range 8 to 30). A sample of sixty-three normal individuals averaged 27.6 (range 24 to 30) out of the possible 30 points. Notice that scores for patients with clear-cut dementia (0 to 22) showed no overlap with scores for normal persons (24 to 30). These results provided a basis for a cutting score of 23/24; that is, scores of 23 and below indicate organicity, whereas scores of 24 and above suggest normal cognitive functions.

Anthony and others (1982) evaluated the validity of the 23/24 MMSE cut score in detecting dementia and delirium in ninety-seven patients from a general medical ward. Their sample was quite diverse in demographic characteristics, but females, African Americans, and persons over age 40 were overrepresented. The validity criterion was an independently derived psychiatric diagnosis of delirium/dementia present versus absent. These diagnoses were methodically derived by two psychiatrists highly knowledgeable about organic brain syndromes. Considering that such clinical diagnoses nonetheless must have some degree of unreliability, it is impressive that the MMSE cut score of 23/24 correctly identified 87 percent of the patients diagnosed as impaired (dementia or delirium) and 82 percent of the patients diagnosed as not impaired.

More recent studies have acknowledged that the ideal cut score depends on the kind of diagnostic precision that the examiner wishes to maximize or, alternatively, the kind of imprecision that the examiner desires to minimize. Furthermore, the best cut score also may depend on the age and the education of the examinee. In some contexts a lower cut score of 20/21 is desirable, whereas in other situations a more stringent cut score of 25/26 might be preferable. The psychometric concepts of sensitivity, specificity, positive predictive power, and negative predictive power enter into the discussion here, so we take a brief detour to look at these tools.

All of these concepts are based on the presupposition that the researcher has a criterion of truth against which the test-based classifications will be compared. Thus, in a typical investigation of the sensitivity and specificity of a test the researcher ultimately knows whether each examinee is normal or impaired. The designation of normal or impaired is usually based on extensive medical tests such as brain-imaging techniques in combination with detailed neurological examinations. The diagnosis of dementia, normality, or other outcome is considered truth—at least for purposes of test validation.

The sensitivity of a test is the percentage of *impaired* subjects who fall at or below the cutoff score. In this context, then, the sensitivity of the MMSE is the percentage of patients with dementia who score at or below a designated value. In particular, if the cut score is 23/24, then the sensitivity is the percentage of patients with dementia who obtained a score of 23 or less. Put simply, sensitivity is the percentage of correct classification of impaired subjects as impaired.

The specificity of a test is the percentage of *normal* subjects who fall at or above the cutoff score. As before, if the cut score is 23/24, then the specificity of the MMSE is the percentage of normal patients who obtain a score of 24 or more. Put simply, specificity is the percentage of correct classification of normal subjects as normal.

Obviously, it is desirable for a test to have both high sensitivity and high specificity, and the closer to 100 percent, the better. But these two indices do not convey all the important information about test-based classification. What is missing is some sense of how well the test does at identifying cognitively impaired patients from a group that contains both cognitively intact persons and impaired patients. This information is provided by the positive predictive power (PPP) of a test, which is given by this formula:

$$PPP = (\text{true positives})/(\text{true positives} + \text{false positives})$$

In this context a "true positive" is a dementia patient correctly classified with dementia, whereas a "false positive" is a normal patient falsely classified with dementia. Thus, PPP indicates the percentage of patients that are truly impaired out of those that the test score classified as impaired.

Similarly, it is also useful to know how well the test does at identifying cognitively intact (normal) patients from a group that contains both cognitively intact and impaired patients. This information is provided by the negative predictive power (NPP) of a test, which is given by this formula:

$$NPP = (\text{true negatives})/(\text{true negatives} + \text{false negatives})$$

A "true negative" is a normal patient correctly classified as normal, whereas a "false negative" is a dementia patient falsely classified as normal. Thus, NPP indicates the percentage of patients that are truly normal out of those that the test score classified as normal.

Just as with sensitivity and specificity, the ideal test is one with high levels of both PPP and NPP, and the closer to 100 percent, the better. But ideal tests do not occur in the real world, and the reality of assessment is that the examiner must choose a balance between sensitivity and specificity. A cut score that increases sensitivity will *by necessity* reduce specificity. These concepts are inversely related not just on an empirical basis but on a logical basis as well—if one improves, the other *must* decline. The same is true for PPP and NPP: As one increases, the other *must* decrease.

The point of this diversion into psychometrics is that practitioners should use a cut score that produces a livable balance between sensitivity and specificity and between PPP and NPP. Tombaugh et al. (1996) have expressed this point as follows:

> The selection of a cutting point depends on the relative benefits of detecting a dementia case, compared to the disadvantages of labeling a normal person as impaired. The former hinges on how treatable the dementia is; that is, does early detection imply a better prognosis? The latter considers the possible distress that may be caused by a fuller clinical assessment, as well as the financial cost involved. (p. 57)

There are no cut-and-dried answers to these questions. What is important is for practitioners to be aware of the issues and to avoid the unwise reliance upon a single cut score for every examinee regardless of age, education, or setting.

With these prefatory points in mind, then, we peruse tables useful in the interpretation of MMSE scores for elderly individuals with different levels of education. In Table 2.6, norms for 406 normal community-dwelling elderly are presented. These individuals were judged to be cognitively intact by physicians and clinical psychologists on the basis of history, clinical and neurological examination, and an extensive battery of neuropsychological tests (not including the MMSE). In this sample a fairly sizable portion of these intact, community-dwelling elderly obtained scores in the low 20s. This was particularly true for those persons with 8

TABLE 2.6   MMSE Percentile Ranks for 406 Cognitively Intact Elderly by Age and Years of Education

MMSE Score	Age 65–79		Age 80–89	
	0–8 years (N = 58)	9+ years (N = 168)	0–8 years (N = 65)	9+ years (N = 115)
30	98	86	100	93
29	88	62	97	77
28	76	41	89	57
27	62	29	83	37
26	48	21	66	30
25	36	14	58	18
24	26	9	49	11
23	19	6	35	6
22	16	5	23	4
21	10	4	14	3
20	5	4	8	1
19	5	3	5	<1
18	4	1	<5	
17	4	<1		
16	3			
<16	<3			

Source: From T. Tombaugh, I. McDowell, B. Kristjansson, and A. Hubley, "Mini-Mental State Examination (MMSE) and the Modified MMSE (3MS): A Psychometric Comparison and Normative Data." *Psychological Assessment, 8,* 48–59. Copyright © 1996 by the American Psychological Association. Reprinted with permission.

or fewer years of education. For example, scores of 22 or below were obtained by 16 percent of the 65- to 69-year-old persons and by 23 percent of the 80- to 89-year-old individuals with 8 or fewer years of education.

In Table 2.7, data pertinent to sensitivity, specificity, PPP, and NPP are presented. These results are based upon the combined data for the 406 normal subjects discussed above and 119 community-dwelling patients judged to have Alzheimer's disease after extensive evaluation. In this sample a cut score of 22/23 provides a good balance of sensitivity and specificity, although PPP is marginal at 55 to 59 percent.

Practitioners need to be mindful that the MMSE is a screening test only, not a sufficient basis for accurate assessment. A low score raises a suspicion that the examinee exhibits significant cognitive impairment. However, further diagnostic evaluation is essential to confirm or disconfirm the initial suspicion.

limitations   Several limitations of the instrument must be considered when administering or interpreting the MMSE. First, it should be obvious that patients with motor handicaps, impaired vision, or hearing problems may do poorly on the test for reasons unrelated to dementia. Patients with aphasia likewise are not the best candidates for the MMSE, because their language disability may prevent them from understanding the verbal and reading tasks on the test.

Education is a substantial moderating factor in understanding MMSE results. Because the test involves reading and writing, those with educational deficits may do poorly on it. In fact, Anthony et al. (1982) reported a discouraging 39 percent false positive rate when a cutting point of 23/24 was used on a general medical ward. It is noteworthy that all of the false positives had fewer than 9 years of education. The false positive rate for their sample dropped to 19 percent when a more lenient cutting point (20/21) was used for patients with 8 years or less of education. However, this modified cutting point causes the false negative rate to shoot up for this subsample.

Mental Status Examination: Case Illustration

This chapter concludes with an abbreviated MSE so that the reader can see how concepts discussed in this chapter are incorporated into a written report. This case also illustrates the importance of conducting a mental status evaluation before launching into formal testing. In this case the assessment provided sufficient evidence to make a medical referral. Total time for the evaluation was 20 minutes, instead of the hour or two that a test battery might have taken. Although the TTO was formally administered, most of the information was obtained through a brief interview.

A few facts about the context of the referral are necessary to understand the format of the report. The client was a 71-year-old widow who was living in a progressive housing complex for the elderly. Residents of this facility ranged from completely independent apartment dwellers at one extreme, to completely institutionalized and bedridden persons with advanced Alzheimer's disease at the other. The

TABLE 2.7   Sensitivity, Specificity, Positive Predictive Power, and Negative Predictive Power for the MMSE

MMSE Criterion Score	Education							
	0–8 years				9+ years			
	SEN	SPE	PPP	NPP	SEN	SPE	PPP	NPP
Age 65–79								
27	100	24	29	100	96	59	23	98
26	100	38	33	100	93	71	30	98
25	100	52	39	100	91	79	36	99
24	100	64	46	100	82	86	46	97
23	100	74	55	100	68	91	55	96
22	89	81	59	96	59	94	60	95
21	83	84	63	94	52	95	62	93
20	67	90	67	90	46	96	59	93
19	33	95	67	82	36	96	59	92
18	28	95	63	81	27	98	62	91
17	24	96	60	79	25	99	86	91
Age 80–89								
27	100	10	41	100	100	43	37	100
26	100	17	43	100	100	63	48	100
25	98	34	48	96	97	70	52	99
24	93	42	49	90	95	82	63	98
23	88	51	52	87	82	89	71	94
22	70	65	55	78	69	94	79	90
21	63	77	63	77	44	96	77	83
20	50	86	69	74	39	97	83	82
19	48	92	79	74	36	98	93	82
18	45	95	86	74	28	98	100	80
17	35	96	82	71	26	100	100	80

Note: All results are given in percentages. MMSE = Mini–Mental Status Examination, SEN = Sensitivity, SPE = Specificity, PPP = Positive Predictive Power, NPP = Negative Predictive Power. These concepts are discussed in the text.

Source: Reprinted with permission from T. Tombaugh, I. McDowell, B. Kristjansson, and A. Hubley. "Mini–Mental State Examination (MMSE) and the Modified MMSE (3MS): A Psychometric Comparison and Normative Data." *Psychological Assessment, 8,* 48–59. Copyright © 1996 by the American Psychological Association. Reprinted with permission.

majority of the residents were somewhere in between, occupying private apartments but receiving support and supervision from nearby staff when necessary. Alice E. was living alone and received very little supervision, but certain peculiarities in her behavior had caused her son to request an intellectual evaluation. In particular, the son noticed on two occasions that Ms. E. had forgotten to turn her range off, leaving the burner on "high" for hours at a time. Also, she had gone for a walk one afternoon and needed assistance in finding her way back to her apartment.

 Brief Report: Mental Status Exam of Alice E.

This 71-year-old widow was evaluated at the request of her son, who expressed concern that she was dangerously forgetful (leaving the range on "high" for hours at a time) and occasionally disoriented (needing help to find her way home). The client was well dressed and well kempt, in a good mood, and conversed eagerly about superficial matters. She maintained good eye contact and sat in a stiff, upright position on a couch while conversing with the examiner. She appeared to be highly alert and was generally cooperative although slightly evasive at times.

Her rate, tone, and volume of speech were appropriate; however, the content was occasionally a little bizarre. For example, at one point she talked about pushing the blood out of her fingers so that it could go up her arms. Some word-finding difficulty was evident, as when Ms. E. referred to the janitor as "the cleaner guy." Thought content was otherwise appropriate, and no delusions were evident. No loose associations were noticed.

Cognitive and memory functioning revealed several noteworthy failures. Initially, she refused to do serial 3s from 20, claiming that it was too easy. However, it became clear that this was part of a generalized strategy for covering up her many impairments by making a joke out of questions and requests. For example, she was totally uncertain as to her age and turned this question back upon the examiner ("Well, how old do you think I am?"). Her social judgment appeared to be impaired as well. She judged the examiner's age to be 71, then 64. In fact, the examiner is a youthful looking 42. Ms. E. has memory disturbance as well. At one point she insisted that she needed to return to her private home (she has not lived there for 2 years) to prepare dinner.

Temporal orientation is grossly impaired: She correctly reported the time of day and day of the week but missed the date by 2 years and 2 months. On the Test of Temporal Orientations, her error score was 32 points (0–2 points is normal), which indicates severe impairment.

Considering the apparent degree of impairment in her cognitive functions, Ms. E.'s emotional functioning appears to be surprisingly good. She is able to maintain her jovial mood by means of massive denial, which is adaptive in the short run. Her insight is judged to be minimal—she appears unaware that her functioning is impaired.

All of these symptoms point to cognitive and memory impairment; that is, a significant degree of dementia is indicated. Because certain aspects of dementia may be treatable, it is imperative that Ms. E. receive a comprehensive medical examination, preferably by a practitioner who specializes in the elderly. Based upon the results of that referral, additional intellectual testing may be appropriate to determine the nature and extent of intellectual impairment. In the meantime, Ms. E. should receive close supervision in order to prevent accidental self-harm.

Final Comment

The existence of dementia signifies an impairment of brain function. Although the generalist practitioner should not attempt to serve as a neurologist or neuropsychologist, a modicum of knowledge about syndromes of brain impairment nonetheless proves useful in the practice of intellectual assessment. For this reason the reader will be introduced to brain–behavior relationships in the next chapter.

CHAPTER

3

Introduction to Brain–Behavior Relationships

This chapter presents a primer of brain–behavior relationships. The excursion into clinical neuropsychology has a simple purpose, namely, to prepare the reader for later chapters that review screening tests for cognitive impairment. We begin by considering the diversity of brain functions encountered within different neural systems. The sheer variety of neural systems and cognitive capacities should convince the reader that no single screening test for impairment will perform accurately in all cases. The practitioner needs access to a variety of screening tests—although only a few instruments might be needed for an individual client. The choice of a screening battery depends upon the referral issues and the nature of the suspected cognitive impairment. That is why it is advisable—even for the generalist practitioner—to learn about the neural foundations of cognition and behavior.

The presentation of neural–behavioral relationships in this chapter is both concise and selective. We review mainly those behavioral components of brain functions that can be quickly and easily assessed with simple screening tests. The topical coverage is judicious, which means that the subtleties surrounding the voluminous literature in clinical neuropsychological assessment are by necessity omitted. Readers who desire comprehensive coverage of these issues can begin with Adams and others (1996), Lezak (1995), Kolb and Whishaw (1990), and Tranel (1992). The focus here is on foundations. The intention is to provide the generalist practitioner with sufficient background to understand the role of screening tests in intellectual assessment.

In addition to reviewing basic concepts of brain function, the chapter also features periodic reference to neuropsychological syndromes. The essential features of common disorders are summarized briefly so that practitioners might have an idea of what to expect when they encounter persons with these disabilities. The chapter closes with a succinct review of the diverse neurobehavioral consequences of head injury. Including mild forms, which may leave no lasting sequelae, millions of Americans sustain a head injury each year.

Structure of the Human Brain

The complexity of the human brain defies ordinary language. Words such as "awesome" or "extraordinary" come to mind, but they are totally inadequate in this context. No wonder, then, that otherwise somber neuroscientists resort to hyperbole when discussing the brain. Eccles (1973) describes the brain as "…without qualification the most highly organized and most complexly organized matter in the universe." Considering our limited knowledge of the universe, the truth of this assertion is questionable, but no matter. The point is that scientists who study the intricacies of this wonderful organ come away with a near-religious sense that the human brain is the most inscrutable of all the mysteries in nature.

The central functional element of the brain is the neuron. Estimates of the number of neurons vary from a low of 10 billion or 10^{10} to a high of 1 trillion or 10^{12} (Strange, 1992). For purposes of discussion, we will accept an intermediate position that the brain consists of 100 billion or 10^{11} neurons.

Typically, a neuron consists of dendrites, cell body, axon, and boutons (end feet) that are tiny transmission organs at the end of the cell. The flow of information is from dendrites to cell body to axon to boutons. Within each bouton are tiny packets of neurotransmitters. These are chemical messengers that can be released across the synapse to stimulate other neurons.

The point of interaction between neurons is the *synapse*, an almost infinitesimally small gap that separates the boutons of one neuron from the dendrites or cell bodies of other neurons. An individual neuron may have hundreds, thousands, possibly tens of thousands of synapses with other neurons. Each neuron continuously monitors incoming messages from hundreds or thousands of its colleagues, both near and far. Some of the incoming messages are excitatory, urging the neuron to "fire" a message to the neurons in its transmission network. Other incoming messages are inhibitory, in effect saying "don't fire." When the balance of excitatory to inhibitory messages exceeds a certain threshold, the neuron "fires."

The functional complexity of the brain is further illustrated by the fact that more than 100 different types of neurotransmitters have been identified. These neurotransmitters activate some sites on other neurons but not other sites; that is, they are selective in their activation. To complicate matters further, information can be coded in the *frequency* of neuronal firing. The release of neurotransmitters across a synapse can occur up to a thousand times a second in each neuron.

Another important element of the brain is the *glial cell*. These cells far outnumber the neurons. Traditionally, glial cells have been thought to perform mundane support roles such as conveying nutrition and providing structural support to the neurons. But, with the recent discovery that the brain of Albert Einstein contained an unusually large number of glial cells in those parts of the cortex presumed critical for mathematical skills, it is clear that neuroscience no longer can trivialize the role of these enigmatic elements of brain function.

In the mature human brain, neurons do not divide, multiply, or reproduce in any way. Each human adult possesses all the neurons that he or she will ever have.

As neurons die, they are not replaced. Rather, surrounding tissues such as glial cells (which do reproduce) may fill the void, or the brain may slowly atrophy and its internal cavities enlarge as additional fluid fills the volume within the skull.

To summarize: The human brain contains about 100 billion neurons, each of which can release neurotransmitters up to a thousand times a second to perhaps a thousand other neurons in its transmission network. This means that in a *single second* the human brain is theoretically capable of sending up to $10^{11} \times 10^3 \times 10^3$, which is 10^{17} or 100 *quadrillion* neural transmissions. Furthermore, as noted above, the neurotransmitters come in substantial variety and individualized capacity to activate some receptor sites but not others, and the neurons are surrounded and supported by hundreds of billions of glial cells that may play a role in brain function as well.

Against this backdrop of astounding complexity, it should be clear that assertions about brain function almost always are oversimplified and subject to exceptions and qualifications. It is important for the reader to keep these points in mind when studying the various conclusions about brain function that are encountered in the remainder of this chapter. Although a few broad generalizations have been established—and are outlined below—the relationship between brain and behavior is still substantially a mystery.

The nervous system is traditionally subdivided into the central nervous system, composed of the brain and spinal cord, and the peripheral nervous system, which includes the network of nerves emanating from the spinal cord. Psychometricians are interested mainly in behaviors associated with brain function, so the brain will be the exclusive focus of this chapter.

Skull, Meninges, and Cerebrospinal Fluid

The brain weighs roughly 3 pounds and is one of the most protected organs in the human body. The most obvious form of protection is the skull, an intermeshed set of tough bones that almost completely encases the brain. In addition, the brain is surrounded by the *meninges*, a triple set of membranes encasing the brain and spinal cord. On rare occasions a tumor of the meninges, called a *meningioma*, will develop, pressing into the brain. The exact effects of such a tumor will depend upon which parts of the brain are displaced. Such tumors usually are separated from the brain and are typically globular in appearance. Prognosis is much better than for a *glioma*, a tumor of the glial cells that gradually infiltrates the brain.

The middlemost layer of the meninges is spongy and filled with another form of protection, the *cerebrospinal fluid* (CSF). CSF is a clear liquid that is produced continuously by specialized structures within the *ventricles*, hollow chambers located in the center of the brain (Figure 3.1). About three-fourths of a liter of CSF is produced each day. It flows slowly from the ventricles down through channels and aqueducts until it reaches the meninges on the outer surface of the brain. Eventually it is absorbed by a large vein at the top of the brain. The CSF provides a continuous liquid cushion, such that the brain is literally floating in a perfectly shaped container.

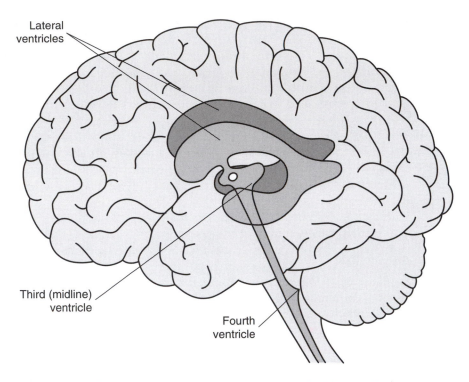

Lateral
ventricles

Third (midline)
ventricle

Fourth
ventricle

FIGURE 3.1   Outline of the Ventricular System of the Human Brain

Not only does this liquid buffer the brain against sharp blows to the head, it also reduces the effective weight of this delicate organ to about three ounces. Without these forms of protection, the brain quickly would bruise from any rapid movement of the head.

If the normal flow of CSF is constricted, the internal pressure from the continued manufacture of CSF will cause hydrocephalus or, literally, "water on the head." This is most commonly a congenital condition observed in children. The continuous pressure can lead to enlargement of the ventricles, compression of the brain against the skull, and, in time, enlargement of the head. Very rarely, as a result of head injury, brain infection, or unknown cause, an adult will develop an acquired condition known as *normal pressure hydrocephalus* (*NPH*). The symptoms of NPH include mild dementia, gait disturbance, and urinary incontinence. Children with hydrocephalus may show dramatic improvement when a shunt is inserted into the ventricles to drain off the excess buildup of CSF. Adult patients with NPH sometimes respond well to this treatment, too.

The location and size of the ventricles offer important clues about the integrity of the brain. With the use of modern brain-imaging tools such as the computerized tomography or CT scan, cross-sectional X-ray pictures of the brain can be obtained. These pictures provide valuable information about the nature and source of brain impairment. For example, if the ventricles are enlarged, a degenerative brain pathology (such as caused by severe alcoholism) might be present. Another common example is a tumor pressing in from one side causing the ventricles to be displaced from the center line.

Magnetic resonance imaging (MRI) is a more recent technology that is also useful in detecting structural brain impairment. This technique uses radio waves to excite hydrogen atoms in the body. A huge magnet surrounding the body monitors these excitations, allowing a computer to produce a composite picture. The structural detail revealed by MRI is substantially better than in CT scans. The procedure is also thought to be safer than a CT scan because it uses harmless radio waves rather than X rays.

Blood Supply to the Brain

Two pairs of arteries carry blood to the cerebral hemispheres and brainstem. The internal carotids and the vertebral arteries join together at the base of the brain in a circular network of vessels called the circle of Willis. This circular network provides a shunting mechanism by which a continual blood supply to the brain is ensured even when one of the input arteries is compromised.

On each side of the brain, three arteries branch off from the circle of Willis to provide blood to the cerebral hemispheres. The anterior cerebral artery supplies the frontal lobe and midline structures. The middle cerebral artery supplies blood to most of the lateral surface of the hemisphere and certain internal structures as well. The posterior cerebral artery supplies blood to the occipital lobe and additional internal structures (Figure 3.2).

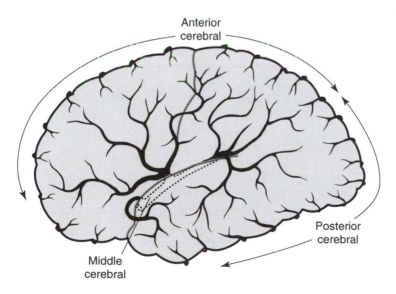

Anterior
cerebral

Posterior
cerebral

Middle
cerebral

FIGURE 3.2 Outline of the Blood Supply to the Human Brain

Occasionally, an artery will become completely obstructed by fatty atherosclerotic plaque, resulting in death to the brain tissues supplied by that vessel. This kind of physiological event is called an *infarct*. More rarely, an artery will burst open from a malformation or weakness (called an *aneurysm*), leaking blood into the brain and causing direct and indirect damage to nerve cells. Whether from infarct (more common) or arterial rupture (rare), the consequence would be referred to as a *cerebrovascular accident (CVA)* or "stroke." The effects of stroke depend on the location and extent of the resulting brain damage. A significant degree of impairment would be diagnosed as vascular dementia, a condition discussed in the previous chapter. The most common form of vascular impairment is multi-infarct dementia, caused by the accumulated effects of several small strokes over a period of months or years.

Structural Organization of the Brain

Hindbrain

From the standpoint of developmental neurobiology, the brain consists of three systems superimposed on top of each other (hindbrain, midbrain, forebrain). At the innermost core sitting immediately above the spinal column is the hindbrain, which mediates the basic survival mechanisms of alertness, breathing, and heartbeat. These functions are capable of going on "automatic pilot" and can operate in the absence of conscious control. Included in the hindbrain are the medulla oblongata, the pons, the reticular formation, and the cerebellum.

The lowest structure on the hindbrain is the medulla, which mediates several vital bodily functions: breathing, swallowing, vomiting, blood pressure, and (partially) heart rate (Restak, 1984). For obvious reasons, lesions in this critical structure can cause immediate death. Even a very small hindbrain stroke can lead to drastic symptoms, including opposite-sided paralysis, partial loss of pain and temperature sense, clumsiness, dizziness, and atrophy of the tongue. This area also contains nerve centers necessary for some aspects of talking and singing, although higher brain sites are intimately involved in these capacities as well.

The reticular formation is a small bundle of fibers that begins in the spinal cord and extends through the medulla and upward, interconnecting with all the major neural tracts going to and from the brain. Although it begins in the hindbrain, the reticular formation actually extends upward into forebrain structures such as the thalamus (see below). The reticular formation helps mediate complex postural reflexes and muscle tone. Portions of this structure known as the reticular activating system (RAS) also govern wakefulness, arousal, and alerting mechanisms. Lesions in this neural system may lead to the profound unresponsiveness of coma. Lesser disruptions of the RAS, such as caused by nonpenetrating head trauma, often result in a period of unconsciousness. The RAS also is responsible for the orienting response to new or surprising stimuli.

The highest structures in the hindbrain are the pons and the cerebellum, or "little brain." Together these structures help coordinate posture, muscle tone, and hand and eye movements. The cerebellum is one of several brain sites involved in the control of movement. In particular, the cerebellum receives sensory feedback from every part of the body and coordinates the details of bodily movements so that they are smooth, controlled, and well organized. The cerebellum is one component of an elaborate motor output system that involves anatomically diverse brain sites, especially the basal ganglia and prefrontal cortex (discussed below). Damage to the cerebellum results in jerky movements and *intention tremor*, a fine motor shakiness mainly affecting the hands that appears only when a deliberate movement is made. Patients with cerebellar damage also walk in a clumsy, stumbling gait and have problems with balance and sense of bodily position. The characteristic wide-based gait found in many chronic alcoholics is a manifestation of this damage. Another symptom of cerebellar damage is *nystagmus*, a condition in which the eyes appear to jitter back and forth even when the patient attempts to hold a steady gaze.

Midbrain

The midbrain is a small area just above the hindbrain. A major portion of the RAS passes through the midbrain. In addition, the midbrain contains two sets of bilaterally symmetrical nuclei known as the superior colliculi and the inferior colliculi. The superior colliculi mediate head and eye movements needed to localize and track visual stimuli. The inferior colliculi provide the same function for auditory stimuli.

Many of the twelve cranial nerves also emanate from the midbrain. The cranial nerves are major neural tracts responsible for a variety of sensory and motor functions. Some are exclusively sensory, relaying information from the external world to the brain; some are exclusively motor, executing commands from the brain; about a third of the cranial nerves possess both sensory and motor functions.

By convention there are twelve pairs of cranial nerves. They are arranged in mirror-like symmetry on the left and right of the underside of the brain. A listing of the nerves and a very condensed presentation of their functions is as follows:

- Olfactory nerve (I): Mediates the sense of smell in each nostril.
- Optic nerve (II): Relays information from the retina of each eye rearward to the striate cortex of the occipital lobes.
- Oculomotor nerve (III), trochlear nerve (IV), abducens nerve (VI): These nerves control the musculature for eye movements.
- Trigeminal nerve (V): Controls sensation to the forehead and cheeks, and motor functions of the jaw muscles.
- Facial nerve (VII): Supplies the anterior two-thirds of the tongue for taste, and controls the muscles involved in facial expression.
- Acoustic nerve (VIII): A sensory nerve involved in hearing and balance.
- Glossopharyngeal nerve (IX): Controls muscles of the pharyngeal cavity and the sensory function of the gag reflex.
- Vagus nerve (X): Mediates motor functions related to swallowing; also has autonomic functions related to heart rate.

- Accessory nerve (XI): A motor nerve controlling muscles of the neck and shoulders.
- Hypoglossal nerve (XII): Provides motor control of the tongue and related muscles.

The assessment of the integrity of the cranial nerves is an important element of any comprehensive neurological evaluation. Typical procedures involve presenting odiferous substances (soap, coffee, wintergreen) separately to each nostril and asking the patient to identify each smell (olfactory nerve, I); checking for pupillary constriction to light (oculomotor nerve, III); examining the ability of the patient to track a stimulus visually (trochlear nerve, IV); assessing the sensitivity of the cheeks to touch such as a pin prick (trigeminal nerve, V); asking the patient to imitate facial movements such as frowning or raising the eyebrows (facial nerve, VII); evaluating sensitivity to vibrations from a tuning fork held near each ear (acoustic nerve, VIII); checking for contraction of the pharyngeal muscle when the back of the throat is touched with a tongue depressor (glossopharyngeal nerve, IX); asking the patient to swallow and perform simple verbalizations such as "ahhhh" (vagus nerve, X); evaluating the capacity to turn the head and shrug the shoulders (accessory nerve, XI); and asking the patient to stick out the tongue, move it rapidly from side to side, up and down, and the like (hypoglossal nerve, XII).

The maneuvers listed here are illustrative only. A comprehensive evaluation of the cranial nerves would involve many other tests and procedures, including some that require expensive equipment. The assessment of the cranial nerves properly belongs within the province of neurology. Nonetheless, some of the neurological techniques highlighted here have been borrowed by neuropsychologists and incorporated into comprehensive test batteries. For example, neuropsychological test batteries often use sensory tests similar to those listed (e.g., touching each cheek lightly with a cotton ball) and motor evaluations as well (e.g., asking the patient to imitate tongue movements). These procedures require significant training in clinical neuropsychology and are not discussed here.

Forebrain

The forebrain is the largest of the main divisions of the brain. It consists of the outermost portions of the brain including the cerebral cortex, and underlying structures such as the thalamus, hypothalamus, basal ganglia, limbic lobe, and corpus callosum. In the main, neuropsychological tests and procedures pertain to function and dysfunction within the forebrain structures, so most of the discussion will address these elements of the brain.

At the base of the forebrain is the *thalamus*, the major relay station for incoming and outgoing neural transmissions. Virtually all incoming or outgoing transmissions are gated through the thalamus, so this cluster of nuclei is crucial for the survival of the organism. Only for the sense of smell, involving the olfactory bulbs, do the incoming stimuli circumvent the central relay station of the thalamus and go directly to the brain site responsible for their processing.

Because it serves as the way station for most sensory pathways to the cerebral cortex, damage to the thalamus may lead to any of several diverse forms of sensory dysfunction. The accurate registration of sensory stimulation may be impaired. One intriguing symptom known as *tactile object agnosia* consists of the inability to identify what is felt. For example, the examinee may be unable to identify an eraser or a key by touch alone, even though sensation is grossly intact.

The thalamus is also the termination site for RAS. As such, damage to the thalamus may result in various impairments of attention and arousal. For example, one prominent sign of thalamic impairment is reduced attention to stimuli impinging on the side of the body opposite the lesion, a symptom known as *unilateral inattention*.

Certain nuclei within the thalamus are also essential for the proper functioning of memory. Discrete lesions may lead to the profound inability to acquire new memories found in chronic alcoholics suffering from Korsakoff's syndrome. This would be one manifestation of *anterograde amnesia*, the impairment of memory from one point in time forward. In fact, the most common cause of anterograde amnesia is prolonged alcohol abuse. Patients with this disorder appear oriented and alert, but they cannot remember what happened even a few hours before. The cause of alcohol-induced amnesia is thought to be thiamine deficiency, and some patients improve if they stop drinking and receive treatment. But a large proportion of these patients, perhaps half, continue to show devastating amnesia even with abstinence and the best treatment (Andreasen & Black, 1995). Patients with thalamic lesions may also experience *retrograde amnesia*—difficulty in recalling information prior to injury or disease. This amnesia often reveals a temporal gradient in which the recall of information that occurred just before the thalamic damage is most difficult whereas older memories are more accurately retrieved.

Damage to the thalamus may result in alterations in emotional responsivity and capacity. Patients may show apathy, loss of spontaneity, and affective flattening (Lezak, 1995). Finally, patients with thalamic lesions may display a variety of perceptual-organizational problems such as difficulty with face recognition and design reproduction.

Located below and in front of the thalamus is the *hypothalamus*, a multipurpose structure that helps govern visceral and somatic functions such as temperature, metabolism, and endocrine balance. The hypothalamus monitors body temperature, concentration of fluids, and amount of hormones, using homeostatic or self-correcting mechanisms to keep these variables at a proper balance. Behaviors important for species survival such as feeding, fighting, and sexual activity also are governed by this vital brain structure.

Basal ganglia is an inexact term that refers to structures found near the inner core of the brain, including the putamen and caudate. The basal ganglia have complex interconnections with the cortex. They appear to be prominently involved in the facilitation and inhibition of sequences of movements, particularly larger movements of the arms and legs. The basal ganglia also are involved in postural adjustments. Damage to the facilitating structures can result in a passive and immobilized individual. Damage to the inhibitory structures can result in a hyperactive person who is incapable of holding still. Patients with damage to the basal ganglia often reveal great difficulty in starting motor acts, or stopping them, or both.

Parkinson's disease is the most common syndrome caused by damage to the basal ganglia (Wooten, 1990). The disorder is found in about 0.5 percent of those over the age of 50 and has a mean age of onset of about 60 years of age (Strange, 1992). The classic signs are tremor, rigidity, and disturbances of movement. The disease is characterized by an immobile, mask-like facial expression, muscular tremor, and a difficulty initiating movements. The cause is a lack of the inhibitory neurotransmitter dopamine and correlated damage to neurons in the basal ganglia. Interestingly, patients show difficulty holding their hands still and reveal a nearly continuous fine tremor of the hands. Yet, once they initiate a movement, the tremor may disappear. The role of the basal ganglia in postural mechanisms is evident in Parkinson's patients: All of the arm muscles are contracted, resulting in a stooped postural rigidity. Such patients also possess an abnormal gait consisting of small shuffling steps and the absence of the normal associated movements such as swinging of the arms. A final diagnostic point is a weakness of voice: The listener has to strain to hear a person with Parkinson's disease.

Patients with Parkinson's disease usually reveal a constellation of intellectual deficits—which indicates that the basal ganglia also mediate important cognitive functions. In particular, patients display problems in the following areas: retrieving information from memory, using spatial information for motor function, and shifting mental set (Strange, 1992; White et al., 1992).

Another neurological syndrome characterized by damage to the basal ganglia is *Huntington's disease*, a rare degenerative disorder distinguished by jerky, random, involuntary movements; progressive intellectual deficits; and personality change. The disorder does not manifest until middle adulthood and is always fatal. Huntington's disease is caused by an autosomal dominant gene, which means that one-half of the children of index cases will be affected. Presymptomatic and even prenatal identification of gene carriers is now possible, which raises delicate and difficult ethical questions.

Psychologists rarely are involved in the initial diagnosis of patients who display neurological disorders such as Parkinson's or Huntington's disease. Nonetheless, it is not unheard of for a psychologist to be the first health care professional to consult with a patient manifesting a recent onset of eye movement difficulty or, perhaps, a mild intention tremor. For this reason, it is appropriate that psychologists possess a general knowledge of inner brain structures such as the cranial nerves and basal ganglia. In the absence of such knowledge, minor neurological symptoms warranting medical referral might be downplayed and dismissed as the benign consequences of anxiety.

The forebrain also includes several structures collectively called the *limbic lobe.* The limbic lobe is sometimes referred to as the limbic system, in reference to early speculations by Papez (1937), who believed that the structures of the limbic lobe constituted a continuous neural circuit responsible for the elaboration of emotion and the control of visceral activity. Although the idea of a simple Papez circuit is now thought to be incomplete, it is generally recognized that the structures of the limbic lobe play a major role in the regulation of emotion (Kupfermann, 1991).

The components of the limbic lobe include the hippocampus, septum, and cingulate gyrus. The hippocampus is actually a dual structure with symmetrical locations within the left and right temporal lobes (plural *hippocampi*). These structures play a special role in memory. They are part of a complex memory circuit that consolidates new experiences into long-term memories. While damage to one hippocampus causes mild deficits in memory, individuals in whom both hippocampi have been damaged or surgically removed experience a catastrophic inability to remember anything new for more than a few seconds. Memories prior to the bilateral hippocampal damage remain intact, but there is no capacity to convert new short-term memories into long-term memories. Such persons are prisoners of the moment. They cannot remember whether they have previously met their current visitor. They will read the same book over and over, enjoying it anew each time. They have difficulty locating the recreation room or remembering the name of their doctor. The memory deficits are so profound that institutional care is almost always required.

In terms of total volume, the forebrain is vastly more significant than the first and second layers (hindbrain and midbrain) that it sits astride. The relationship between brain and behavior is also much better mapped for this outer portion of the brain. Consequently, screening tests for cognitive impairment often are aimed at the functions subserved by structures within the forebrain. The intention of such tests is not to localize sites of damage—CT and MRI are far superior at this task—but to effectively screen for cognitive impairment. We will consider a variety of representative instruments in Chapter 6. Here we review concepts and terminology relevant to this task.

Cerebral Cortex

The outer layer of the forebrain is the *cerebral cortex*. This layer is quite thin, about six cells deep, and is a very recent evolutionary addition. It is the functional capacity of this part of the brain that most dramatically separates humans from the lower animals. The tissue here is folded over into elaborate convolutions. The prominent bulges that stick out are called *gyri* (singular *gyrus*), whereas the clefts, grooves, and fissures are called *sulci* (singular *sulcus*). This arrangement allows the brain to have much more cortical tissue than if the surface were smooth.

A small portion of this tissue is *committed cortex*. It is committed in the sense that it is dedicated to the processing of the senses (vision, hearing, touch) and to the fulfillment of motor output. Damage to particular sections of committed cortex has predictable effects upon vision, hearing, touch, or motor control, as discussed later in this chapter. The remainder of the cortex is *uncommitted*, or *association*, *cortex* that allows for the processing of information by means of comparing, contrasting, inferring, and the like. It is the relatively large proportion of this latter type of cortical tissue that distinguishes *homo sapiens* from other animals. The *Brandenburg Concerti* and the hydrogen bomb are direct results of these evolutionary advances in brain development.

We will look at four aspects of brain function within the cerebral hemispheres: left-right lateralization of cerebral function, specialization of the four major lobes within each hemisphere, language functions within the left hemisphere, and the operation of the visual system. The presentation is selective. The goal is to help the reader understand the screening tests discussed in the next chapter.

Lateralization of Cerebral Function

Hemispheric Symmetry

In some respects, the two hemispheres of the human brain are symmetrical in structure and function, whereas in other domains, asymmetry or lateralization of function prevails. The commonalities between the cerebral hemispheres are especially prominent for the primary sensory and motor centers of the brain. In regard to the processing of touch, vision, and hearing and also the control of motor output, the two halves of the brain operate identically.

With only a few exceptions and qualifications, the brain operates according to the principle of opposite-sided, or *contralateral*, control. What this means is that most of the neural pathways for sensory and motor activation are opposite-sided: The left cerebral hemisphere mediates the sensations and movements of the right side of the body, and vice versa. For example, sensations in the right hand are initially processed in the somatosensory area of the left hemisphere; motor activation of the left hand is guided, in large measure, by the motor cortex of the right hemisphere; auditory input to the right ear is processed substantially by the left auditory cortex; damage to the left motor cortex causes paralysis on the right side of the body.

The only true exception to the principle of contralateral activation is the sense of smell, which is exclusively same-sided, or *ipsilateral*. The sensations received in each nostril travel directly upward to the olfactory bulb on the same side of the brain. Vision appears to be an exception to the principle, but it is not. The neural pathways for vision are complex insofar as stimuli impinging on each retina are sent to *both* halves of the brain—which appears to violate the principle of contralateral activation. However, it is still true that the left half of each *visual field* is projected to the visual centers in the right hemisphere, and vice versa. The visual system is a complex example of contralateral control, not really an exception. We will revisit this point in a later section.

The principle of contralateral activation is relative, not absolute. For example, the vast majority of the neural pathways for motor control cross over to the opposite side of the body (contralateral), but a small minority (perhaps 20 percent) project to the same side of the body (ipsilateral). This is fortunate insofar as it provides a mechanism for regaining partial control over one side of the body even if the opposite-sided motor cortex has been substantially damaged. The same-sided motor connections provide a limited basis for regaining bodily movement. The auditory systems also feature a significant component of ipsilateral connection. As a result of this mixed projection pattern, destruction of the primary auditory cortex on one side of the brain rarely causes total deafness in the opposite-sided ear.

Hemispheric Asymmetry

Although the primary sensory and motor functions of the human brain are largely symmetrical across the cerebral hemispheres, it is relative *asymmetry* that characterizes many higher cognitive functions and qualitative aspects of behavior. The most obvious examples are language capacities (largely left hemisphere) and spatial skills (largely right hemisphere), but several other functional capacities reveal left-right specialization as well (Springer & Deutsch, 1989).

It is intriguing that structural differences underwrite the specializations of each cerebral hemisphere. Consider language, which is predominantly a left hemisphere phenomenon. For most right-handers the top of the temporal lobe (planum temporale) is larger in the left hemisphere, and the left hemisphere contains more gray matter, even though it is slightly smaller and lighter than the right hemisphere (Geschwind & Galaburda, 1987). A structural basis for the right hemisphere superiority in spatial skills is also evident. The lateral sulcus is much longer in the right hemisphere, with the result that the parietal-temporal cortex is slightly enlarged on this side.

It has been known for decades that the left and right hemispheres differ in their underlying cognitive processes. An early synthesis of findings was provided by Sperry (1968), who localized the capacity for language and calculation in the left hemisphere and identified the right hemisphere as important for spatial construction, simple language comprehension, and nonverbal ideation. In general, it is now believed that the left hemisphere controls language and uses linear thought, while the right hemisphere governs spatial arrangements and uses configural thought. A consensual validation for these left-right hemispheric specializations is provided by research traditions as diverse as electrical stimulation of the brain, tachistoscopic studies of split-brain patients, and psychometric studies of patients with lateralized lesions.

Another way of distinguishing the relative specializations of the two sides of the brain is in terms of analysis versus synthesis. Metaphorically expressed, the left hemisphere uses analysis and extracts the individual elements that make up the whole experience. In contrast, the right hemisphere uses synthesis and puts isolated elements together to perceive things as a gestalt or whole.

Lateralization of function holds true for virtually all right-handers, and the majority of left-handers as well. However, perhaps a third of all left-handers do not fit the traditional brain–behavior organization discussed here. Specifically, about 15 percent of left-handers show reversed brain organization (language in the right hemisphere) and another 15 percent reveal no lateralization (language in both hemispheres) (Rasmussen & Milner, 1977). In left-handers, inferences about lateralization of brain function must be approached with caution.

Lateralization of function is relative, not absolute. It is an oversimplification to use shorthand labels such as "language hemisphere" for the left hemisphere or "visuospatial hemisphere" for the right hemisphere. While it is substantially true that the left hemisphere processes language, the right hemisphere is capable of language comprehension for simple sentences. When it comes to understanding brain function, exceptions and qualifications are the rule.

An additional reason for avoiding a simplistic view of left- versus right-sided brain functions is that nearly all high level cognitive capacities require the synthetic interaction of the entire brain. The two cerebral hemispheres are joined together by a broad band of 200 million neurons collectively known as the *corpus callosum*. Because of this integrating brain structure it is nearly impossible for the cerebral hemispheres to act independently of one another. For example, the right cerebral hemisphere has some language comprehension and also provides the intonation pattern or rising and falling "music" of speech. Right cerebral hemisphere lesions may cause the patient to sound like a "talking computer" because of the loss of intonation patterns (Gardner, 1975). Hence, attributing language solely to the left cerebral hemisphere greatly oversimplifies the situation.

Having noted the appropriate caveats and qualifications, we are now in a position to utilize a tabular summary of the major findings on cerebral lateralization. Table 3.1 lists the findings on cerebral lateralization for major functional systems such as vision, hearing, language, and spatial processes. From a neuropsychological perspective, the most important lateralizations noted in Table 3.1 have to do with language, memory, and spatial processes. These are the cognitive processes for which psychologists have devised useful screening tests and procedures. For example, serious language difficulties such as *dysnomia* (inability to name common objects) or *dysgraphia* (acquired inability to write a simple sentence) usually are indicative of left cerebral hemisphere brain impairment. Memory difficulties also provide clues to lateralization, with verbal memory predominantly processed by the left hemisphere and pictorial memory by the right hemisphere. With regard to spatial processes, significant impairment of visuospatial abilities is more often than not an indicator of right hemisphere impairment (Wheeler & Reitan, 1962). These points are elaborated in the remainder of this chapter.

Aphasia is any loss of language function from brain injury or disease. Because the presence and laterality of cognitive impairment can be strongly inferred from responses to an aphasia screening procedure, clinicians commonly include simple language tasks in an assessment battery. (This issue is addressed in more detail in the chapter on screening tests for cognitive impairment.)

Screening tests for right cerebral hemisphere impairment often take advantage of the visuospatial specialization of this hemisphere. The ability to draw objects

TABLE 3.1   Summary of Findings on Cerebral Lateralization

Functional System	Left Hemisphere Dominance	Right Hemisphere Dominance
Vision	Processing of the right visual field Recognition of letters, words	Processing of the left visual field Recognition of faces Analysis of complex geometric patterns
Audition	Processing of right ear Processing of language-related sounds	Processing of left ear Processing of music and environmental sounds
Somato-sensory	Sensory input from the right side	Sensory input from the left side Tactile recognition of complex shapes
Movement	Motor output to the right side Complex voluntary movement, including speech	Motor output to the left side
Language	Speech, reading, writing, and arithmetic	Intonation and emotional patterning to speech
Memory	Verbal memory	Pictorial memory
Spatial processes		Analysis of geometric and visual space
Emotion		Comprehension and expression of emotion
Olfaction	Smell in left nostril	Smell in right nostril

Source: Reprinted with permission from R. J. Gregory. *Psychological Testing: History, Principles, and Applications* (2d ed.) (Boston: Allyn & Bacon, 1996).

or geometric shapes has an obvious spatial component but also includes perceptual activity and a motor response. Thus, difficulty copying simple geometric shapes—*constructional impairment*, as it is technically known—often is due to right cerebral hemisphere impairment. However, drawing geometric shapes also has an executive or motor component—the right hand must be commanded to go in specific directions—so left cerebral hemisphere damage also can cause constructional impairment.

The qualitative nature of errors in design copying provides the examiner with important clues as to the lateralization of cognitive impairment. Patients with right cerebral hemisphere impairment lose the overall gestalt of the construction task. Their drawings contain serious distortions in perspective or proportion. In contrast, patients with left-sided lesions may get the overall proportions correct, but they often leave out significant details. Their drawings are impoverished and incomplete (Lezak, 1995).

In a classic paper published decades ago, Warrington, James, and Kinsbourne (1966) conducted an exhaustive analysis of drawing errors in thirty-one persons with left cerebral hemisphere lesions and thirty-one persons with right-sided lesions. Their subjects were asked to copy simple line drawings such as a three-dimensional cube (Figure 3.3) and to provide freehand drawings of common scenes such as a house with a chimney. Independent judges found no significant difference in degree of drawing disability between the two groups. The authors concluded that failure in drawing may be indicative of more than one underlying disorder. In particular, it appeared likely that the right cerebral hemisphere supplies a perceptual and the left an executive component to the drawing task.

Even though there was no difference between left and right hemisphere cases in level of constructional impairment, several qualitative signs were found to be distinctive of each group (Warrington, James, & Kinsbourne, 1966). Specifically, the differences included:

■ An increased number of right angles among line drawings of a cube copied by left-sided cases, not found among copies produced by right-sided cases
■ A tendency for the left-sided group to widen and the right-sided group to reduce the angles constituting the points of a copied star
■ A greater tendency to asymmetry among the drawings of right- than of left-sided cases
■ A tendency for the left-sided cases to include fewer details in their freehand drawing of a house than did the right-sided cases. For example, right hemisphere cases would draw a house with roof, upstairs, windows, downstairs window, door, details on door, smoke, chimney, path, garden, etc., while left hemisphere cases would omit some of these items.

In summary, constructional impairment can be caused by more than one underlying disorder:

The types of error made by patients with right hemisphere lesions suggest that these patients have difficulty in incorporating spatial information into their draw-

FIGURE 3.3 **Typical Design-Copying Stimuli Used in the Assessment of Constructional Impairment**

ing performance, leading to disproportionate and faulty articulation of parts of the drawing, while the patients with left hemisphere lesions seemed to experience difficulty in planning the drawing process, leading to simplified versions of the model. (Warrington, James, & Kinsbourne, 1966, p. 82).

This topic is pursued further in Chapter 6 (Screening Tests for Cognitive Impairment), where drawing tasks useful in testing for constructional impairment are reviewed.

Functions of the Cerebral Lobes

Traditionally, the cerebrum of each hemisphere is divided into four major lobes or areas. The frontal lobe fills the forehead; the occipital lobe is at the back of the head; the temporal lobe is just beneath the temple; the parietal lobe is at the top of the head, just behind the frontal lobe.

The lobes of the cerebrum and some major functional areas of the cerebral cortex are depicted in Figure 3.4. On each side of the brain the four lobes are demarcated by two major fissures known as the lateral sulcus and the central sulcus. Within each lobe there are numerous minor sulci as well, such that each brain is subtly different from all others. The structural appearance of the lobes is roughly

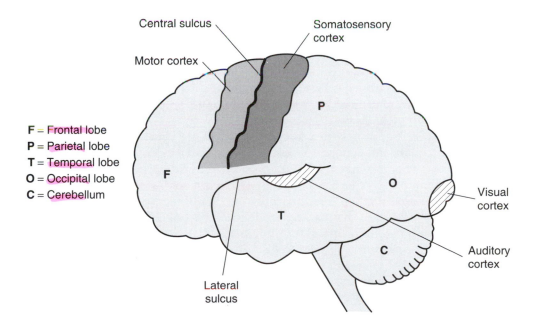

F = Frontal lobe
P = Parietal lobe
T = Temporal lobe
O = Occipital lobe
C = Cerebellum

FIGURE 3.4   Landmarks and Major Functional Areas of the Cerebral Cortex

the same for the left and right hemispheres, except for the slight enlargement of locations responsible for language in the left hemisphere and other minor configural differences, as discussed previously.

Luria (1973) has provided a model of brain function that is a useful starting point in the discussion of molar brain function at the level of the lobes. He describes three complex functional systems within the brain. The first system consists of subcortical structures such as the RAS that regulate the degree of cortical tone and control the sleep–wake cycle. This component has been discussed previously. The second unit is for obtaining, processing, and storing information arriving from the outside world. This unit consists of the lower and rearward portions of the cortex (parietal, occipital, and temporal lobes) and reveals numerous sensory functions. The third unit, the frontal lobes, is for programming, regulating, and verifying mental activity.

Within the second unit (parietal, occipital, and temporal lobes) are strips of committed cortex that serve primary sensory functions. These areas are committed in the sense that they have virtually no neural flexibility. That is, they are "hard wired" to do the initial primary processing of incoming sensory stimuli and they are incapable of doing anything else. As noted previously, the "hard wiring" is contralateral, or opposite-sided, with the left side of the body connecting to the right cerebral hemisphere, and vice versa. The complexities of the visual connections are discussed separately below.

Each of the sensory processing lobes within the second unit is also hierarchical in structure and function, consisting of two additional cortical zones built around the *primary* projection areas that receive the "raw" information from the external world (Luria, 1973). Specifically, the *secondary* or projection-association area is where incoming information from the primary zone is processed, and the *tertiary*, or overlapping, zone is where cross-sensory associations are made. For example, in Figure 3.4, incoming visual information is first processed in the primary visual area at the back of the brain, then interpreted in the adjoining secondary area (not labeled), and finally compared to auditory and tactile codes in the tertiary area, which includes the *angular gyrus*.

We turn now to a discussion of function and dysfunction within the parietal, occipital, and temporal lobes (Luria's second functional system), followed by a brief review of the frontal lobes (Luria's third functional system). A few cautionary comments are appropriate. First, the neat division of hemispheres into specific lobes is an oversimplification. Particularly in the case of the posterior lobes (parietal, occipital, and temporal) the boundaries are indistinct and the dysfunctions discussed here may be found in *any* diffuse lesion affecting the rearward portions of the brain. In fact, some authors prefer to discuss the *posterior association cortex* and its disorders instead of following the traditional lobe-by-lobe presentation. Nonetheless, I follow the traditional approach here. The second caution has to do with the impossible challenge of presenting a complex subject in a few manageable pages. Some degree of oversimplification is unavoidable. For a more thorough presentation on these topics, the reader is again referred to Kolb and Whishaw (1990) and Lezak (1995).

Parietal Lobes

The parietal lobes are involved in our perception of space and our awareness of the spatial orientation of our bodies. This is particularly true for the right parietal lobe, which plays an essential role in the perception of spatial relationships. The parietal lobes also mediate our awareness of what is happening on the surface of our bodies. Just to the rear of the central sulcus is the somatosensory area of the parietal lobe: It receives information about tactile sensations and the position of limbs. Adjacent body areas are represented by adjacent cortical areas. The relationship is upside down: face, lips, and tongue at the bottom, hand above that, body trunk at the top of the somatosensory strip. The feet are represented by the portion of the somatosensory strip that is tucked down in the median separating the two hemispheres. The amount of cortical area devoted to each body area depends on the functional importance of that body part. For example, feedback from the lips and tongue is crucial for speech. Consequently, the portions of the somatosensory strip devoted to these structures are relatively large. Neural connections to the somatosensory strip are predominantly opposite-sided. As a consequence, damage to the somatosensory strip on one side of the brain results in loss of sensation for the corresponding parts on the opposite side of the body.

The left parietal lobe incorporates an important junction where it adjoins the temporal and occipital lobes. This is the tertiary association area known as the angular gyrus, which is responsible for cross-modal association of visual, auditory, and tactile codes. Impairment of the left parietal lobe, particularly if it involves this tertiary association area, may result in high-level cognitive disorders including agraphia, an acquired inability to write, or *alexia*, a loss of reading skill. A reduction in these capacities (as opposed to their complete absence) would be called *dysgraphia* or *dyslexia*, respectively.

Generally, parietal damage on either side will impair the ability to draw. As noted in a previous section, left-sided damage results in an impoverished drawing; the person has trouble getting the drawing hand to go in the correct direction. In contrast, right-sided parietal damage results in a perceptual deficit; the person has trouble integrating the individual parts into a consistent whole, such that the overall gestalt of the drawing is lost.

Damage to the parietal lobes may cause *apraxia*, an inability to perform specific motor acts upon request. For example, a patient with apraxia might be unable to respond when asked "Show me how you use a key" or "How do you do a salute?" In some cases this disorder is a deficit of understanding in which the patient is unable to decode the meaning of the command. Another explanation, however, stresses the role of the left parietal lobe in keeping track of bodily movement and of the right parietal lobe in analyzing the spatial components. Because of the functions underwritten by the parietal lobes, it is obvious that any damage—but particularly bilateral damage—would make it very difficult for a patient to move his or her limbs through space.

Unilateral sensory neglect is another symptom occasionally observed in cases of parietal lobe damage. This is particularly likely in patients with right parietal lobe damage. These individuals may show neglect of left space and the objects within it. For example, their drawings may involve mainly the right half of the subject matter, while the left half will be omitted or impoverished. When eating, only the food on the right half of the plate will be consumed. When dressing, they might fail to put their left arm in the shirt sleeve. Left parietal damage only rarely leads to right sensory neglect, which underscores the not-so-subtle differences between left and right parietal lobe function.

Dyscalculia, difficulty in performing simple arithmetic calculations, is another symptom often associated with parietal lobe damage. Particularly when arithmetic problems are presented verbally, they have a distinct spatial component to them. For example, when computing 7 times 12 in one's head, it is necessary to visualize the numbers one above the other, then keep track of the spatial location of the subcomponents as the task is completed. This is very difficult for patients with parietal damage, particularly if it is right-sided.

A verbal task that is especially difficult for patients with left-sided parietal damage is understanding *relational language*. When told that "My mother's brother had a kidney removed," the patient may not know whether it was the mother or her brother who required surgery. More complex versions of relational language such as "What do you call your father's brother?" are especially troublesome for many patients with left parietal lobe damage.

Temporal Lobes

The temporal lobes are involved in memory, language, hearing, and social behavior. The memory functions are underwritten by the hippocampus, a bilateral structure beneath the surface of each temporal lobe. Damage to both hippocampi causes the severe deficit in short-term memory discussed previously. The language functions of the temporal lobe are localized mainly in the auditory association area of the left hemisphere, *Wernicke's area*. The role of Wernicke's area in the identification of words is discussed later. Here we will focus on the role of the temporal lobes in hearing and social behavior.

The primary *auditory cortex* occupies the upper and rearward portion of the temporal lobe and extends into the lateral sulcus and underneath the frontal and parietal lobes. Much of it is not visible from a side view of the brain. The left auditory cortex receives input primarily from the right ear, and vice versa. However, there is some same-sided input as well. While a lesion of the primary auditory zone in one temporal lobe does not produce a total loss of hearing in the opposite ear, there is an increase in the threshold of auditory sensation, particularly for sounds of short duration (Luria, 1973).

Surrounding the primary auditory cortex and occupying much of the temporal lobe is the secondary auditory cortex, which is important in the analysis of complex sounds and rhythmic acoustic structures. Damage to this area in the left hemisphere causes a disruption of language comprehension (discussed below). Damage to this area in the right hemisphere causes *amusia*, a characteristic difficulty in recognizing auditory patterns and rhythms. The comprehension of music is especially impaired. In addition, right temporal association area damage can result in a diminished ability to localize sounds in space. This symptom is one more illustration of the role of the right hemisphere in numerous different kinds of spatial processing.

The role of the temporal lobes in social behavior has to do with the modulation of biological drives such as aggression, fear, and sexuality. Just beneath the surface of each temporal lobe is the *amygdala*, a bilateral structure that is significantly involved in these motivational and emotional aspects of behavior. Lesions in one or both temporal lobes, particularly if they extend subcortically to encompass the amygdala, can lead to a variety of pathological behavior patterns. The symptoms may include compulsive and indiscriminant hypersexuality, anxiety and phobic responses, and preoccupation with religion and cosmology. A particularly striking correlate of temporal lobe impairment is social viscosity—a tendency to prolong social encounters and to harangue any available listener with endless details of the patient's life and world views (Bear, 1986).

One striking symptom related to temporal lobe lesions is *prosopagnosia*, an inability to recognize previously known faces and an inability to learn new ones. Patients may not recognize the faces of family members, close friends, and even themselves. Recognition by voice may compensate for the disability. Benson (1994) describes the case of a 70-year-old man who experienced a series of small strokes affecting the temporal and occipital lobes. The lesions left him unable to recognize his wife or daughter by sight, although he immediately recognized them by their voices. Bilateral lesions on the front, underside of the temporal lobes are especially likely to cause this disability (Tranel, 1992).

Occipital Lobes

The primary projection areas for vision are located in the occipital lobes. Each hemisphere sees the opposite side of the world, with the left half of the visual field going to the right hemisphere, and vice versa. Communication across the *splenium*, the rearward portion of the corpus callosum, allows the two hemispheres to share their information and produce a unified perception of the entire visual field.

Surrounding the primary visual projection areas are secondary zones that synthesize visual stimuli, code them, and form them into complex systems (Luria, 1973). Here is where a higher level of processing and storing of visual information occurs. While lesions of the primary zones lead to loss of the visual field, lesions of the secondary zones make it difficult for the patient to recognize what he or she is looking at:

> This is a description of a typical case of a patient with such a lesion. The patient carefully examines the picture of a pair of spectacles shown to him. He is confused and does not know what the picture represents. He starts to guess. "There is a circle...and another circle...and a stick...a cross-bar...why, it must be a bicycle?" (Luria, 1973, p. 116)

This is an example of *visual agnosia*, a difficulty in the recognition of drawings, objects, or faces. The visual agnosias are especially linked to lesions of the right occipital association cortex but may also result from impairment of the parietal and temporal lobes as well. In one case a patient could copy the picture of a train with great accuracy, but had no idea what he had drawn, an example of *object agnosia* (Benson, 1994).

Frontal Lobes

The frontal lobes are the units for programming, regulation, and verification of activity (Luria, 1973). It is here that persons create intentions, form plans, and regulate their behavior by comparing the effects of actions with the original intentions. The outlet channel for this unit is the motor cortex of the frontal lobes, just in front of the central sulcus and just across from the somatosensory strip, with which it cooperates in the regulation of bodily movements. The topical organization of the motor strip is very similar to that of the somatosensory strip. Lesions of the motor strip lead to paralysis of the corresponding body part on the opposite side.

Just in front of the motor strip is a secondary zone composed of premotor areas. These brain structures prepare the motor programs before they are sent to the motor strip for execution. Damage to the premotor areas can cause motor slowing on the opposite side. This diagnostic symptom is the principal justification for using simple motor tests such as finger tapping in screening for cognitive impairment.

Except for the language functions of the left frontal lobe (discussed below), it appears that the frontal lobes reveal fewer left-right differences than any other cerebral lobes. Consequently, the appearance of behavioral pathologies and deficits is more related to the extent of tissue damage than its lateralization. Lezak (1995) groups the behavioral disturbances associated with frontal lobe damage into five overlapping categories:

- *Problems of starting*, which include decreased spontaneity, decreased productivity, decreased rate of behavior, and diminished or lost initiative
- *Difficulties in making mental or behavioral shifts*, which include perseveration of activities and responses and rigidity or inability to try new strategies in problem solving
- *Problems in stopping*, which are often described as impulsivity, overreactivity, and difficulty in holding back a wrong or unwanted response
- *Deficient self-awareness*, resulting in an inability to perceive performance errors or to size up social situations appropriately
- *A concrete attitude* in which objects, experiences, and behavior are all taken at their most obvious face value (Goldstein, 1944)

Lesions in the orbital regions (the front, underside) of the frontal lobes have long been known to cause severe defects in social conduct. Such patients may be remarkably free of conventional neuropsychological deficits, yet their behavior is radically transformed by frontal lobe injury or disease. The previously model citizen now makes lewd comments, seeks out unsavory company, and gambles away his paycheck, to cite a few examples.

Left Hemisphere Language Functions

In 1861, the French anthropologist and surgeon Paul Broca observed that damage to a specific premotor area of the left frontal lobe was linked to a language disorder first called expressive aphasia and now known as *nonfluent aphasia* (see Figure 3.5). Persons with damage to Broca's area speak in a slow, labored manner and have difficulty enunciating words correctly. Although their speech makes sense, it is telegraphic. Nouns are usually expressed in the singular; and the small words that add color to speech—the adjectives, adverbs, articles, and conjunctions—frequently are omitted. These patients therefore find it nearly impossible to say "No ifs ands or buts," a phrase that is commonly used in screening for Broca's aphasia. Yet they reveal no difficulty understanding either spoken or written language.

In 1874, the German neurologist Carl Wernicke reported that damage to the upper and rearward portion of the left temporal lobe was linked to a language disorder first called receptive aphasia and now known as *fluent aphasia* (see Figure 3.5). The disorder was first named receptive aphasia because affected individuals appear unable to comprehend words. They apparently have no trouble perceiving the words, but they do not know their meaning. Yet the speech of these patients is fluent and shows proper articulation—hence the current designation of fluent aphasia. Even though their speech is fluent, affected persons produce bizarre word con-

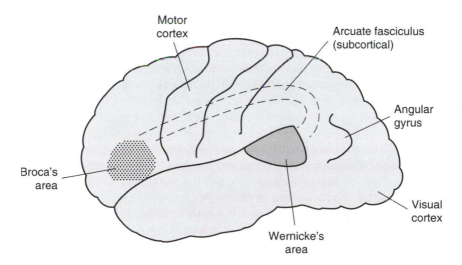

FIGURE 3.5   Primary Language Structures of the Left Hemisphere

structions and reveal errors in word usage. Their speech tends to be meaningless. For example, when asked to define "book," a patient with damage to Wernicke's area might respond "Book, a husbelt, a king of prepator, find it in front of a car ready to be directed." A "scarecrow" might be defined as "We'll call that a 3-minute resk witch, you'll find one in the country in three witches" (Williams, 1979, p. 105).

The Classical View of Aphasia

Building on the observations of Broca and Wernicke, Geschwind (1972) developed a structural model of language function that has received wide attention. Although the model is incomplete and slightly simplistic, it is nonetheless a useful starting point for understanding the effects of brain damage upon language functions. Goodglass (1993) describes the Geschwind approach as the "classical view" and notes that it is "disarmingly logical and compelling."

According to the model, Broca's area stores the "articulatory codes" or "programs" that specify the sequence of muscle actions required to pronounce a word. When these programs are transferred to the motor cortex, they activate the muscles of the tongue, lips, and larynx in the appropriate sequence to produce the desired spoken word.

Wernicke's area is where "auditory codes" and the meanings of words are stored. Hence, in order to speak a word, its auditory code first must be activated in Wernicke's area, then sent to Broca's area via a subcortical bundle of nerve fibers named the *arcuate fasciculus*. Upon reaching Broca's area, the auditory code activates the corresponding articulatory code, which in turn transmits the necessary "program" to the motor cortex for the production of the desired spoken word.

The understanding of language, whether written or spoken, always involves the activation of Wernicke's area. For example, to understand a word spoken by someone else, the word must be transmitted from the auditory cortex to Wernicke's area, where the spoken word is matched to its auditory code, which in turn brings forth the word's meaning. Written words are first registered in the primary visual cortex, then relayed through the secondary visual cortex to the angular gyrus. Here the visual form of the word is associated with its auditory code in Wernicke's area. Once the auditory code is called forth, its meaning is then available.

The value of the Geschwind model is that it helps explain several clinical syndromes involving discrete left hemisphere brain damage:

- Lesions to Broca's area will cause slow, labored, telegraphic speech, but the comprehension of spoken or written language will not be affected.
- Damage to Wernicke's area will have more serious and pervasive implications for language comprehension; namely, the patient will be unable to understand spoken or written communications. However, these patients will have fluent, but meaningless, speech (assuming Broca's area is intact).
- Damage to the angular gyrus will cause serious reading disability, but there will be little problem in comprehending speech or in speaking.
- Impairment limited to the left auditory cortex will result in serious disrup-

tion of verbal comprehension. However, these patients will be able to speak and read normally.

The Modern View of Aphasia

Recently, specialists in language and aphasia have emphasized the limitations of the classical view (Caplan, 1992; Goodglass, 1993). One problem with the classical approach is that it fails to account for subcortical components of language (Kolb & Whishaw, 1990). Perhaps more telling is that, in practice, few patients display aphasic symptoms that fall neatly into one or another of the categories proposed by Geschwind (1972) and his followers. Furthermore, many patients with left hemisphere lesions reveal language disorders that appear to contradict the simple guidelines proposed by Geschwind.

Rather than classifying patients according to unreliable syndromes of aphasia, the modern approach emphasizes a detailed analysis of symptomatology (Caplan, 1992; Goodglass, 1993). Perhaps the most important lesson to be learned for the generalist practitioner is that *any of several aphasic symptoms may signify cognitive impairment related to lesions in the left hemisphere language zone* (see Figure 3.5). Thus, the ability to localize impairment according to the Geschwind structural model is usually immaterial to the generalist practitioner. Of far greater consequence is recognizing when a peculiarity of language indicates a possible symptom of aphasia. Goodglass (1993) provides the following taxonomy of aphasic symptoms that may prove helpful in this regard:

- *Disorders of Motor Speech Implementation:* Examples include reduced voice volume, articulatory impairment known as dysarthria, increased voice onset time, loss of melodic contour in words and sentences, and recurrent stereotyped utterances.
- *Disorders of Word Retrieval:* These include unintended errors of word or sound choice (paraphasia), production of nonsense words, and severe word-finding difficulty (dysnomia).
- *Disorders of Syntax and Morphology:* Examples include the agrammatism of one-word sentences, telegraphic speech, and loss of the relational use of words.
- *Disorders of Auditory Comprehension:* These include problems in the processing of speech sounds, disorders of speech comprehension, and impaired word comprehension.
- *Disorders of Repetition:* The status of the ability to repeat spoken words and sentences is a crucial diagnostic indicator of the kind of aphasia affecting a patient.
- *Disorders of Reading:* Examples include impaired symbol recognition, lack of sentence comprehension, or complete inability to read.
- *Disorders of Writing:* These include the written equivalents of Broca's aphasia (writing reveals restricted output) and Wernicke's aphasia (writing is unintelligible jargon).

Many of the symptoms listed can be revealed by simple clinical procedures and brief screening tests for aphasia. More detail on assessment approaches and the varieties of aphasic symptoms is provided in Chapter 6.

Finally, a word of caution is appropriate with left-handers, who sometimes possess atypical organization for brain functions such as language. As a consequence of bilateral representation of language functions, the brain-behavior relationships noted here may not hold true for some left-handers. As a brief side note, one intriguing consequence of their anomalous brain organization is that left-handers sometimes show a surprising recovery from aphasia (e.g., after a stroke) due to the fact that language is redundantly represented in both cerebral hemispheres.

The Visual System and Defects in the Visual Field

It is worth repeating that the visual system obeys the general rule of contralateral control that applies to all sensory and motor systems. In particular, information from the right side of the body travels to the left cerebral hemisphere of the brain, and vice versa. As noted previously, the interpretation of this general rule is a little more complicated for vision. In particular, it is not true that the left optic nerve transmits information only to the right cerebral hemisphere and the right optic nerve only to the left cerebral hemisphere. In fact, each eye transmits information to *both* sides of the brain.

The correct application of the contralateral principle for visual information is that the left *visual field* is processed in the right cerebral hemisphere, and vice versa (Figure 3.6). When we fixate our eyes on a single location, the resulting image is projected onto the retina of each eye upside down and backward. Consequently, all information to the left of the fixation point (i.e., in the left visual field) is projected to the right side of the retina, and vice versa. The right half of each retina then transmits the image down its optic nerve where the two sets of fibers join at the optic chiasm. Both sets then transmit to the right *lateral geniculate body* and ultimately to the right visual cortex. Of course, the right visual field is processed in analogous (but reversed) manner and its information terminates in the left visual cortex. The retinas also send axons into the *superior colliculus*, where eye movements are controlled.

From a structural standpoint, the visual system can be likened to a complex cable transmission system that traverses the brain from front to back. Especially toward the rear of the brain, the cables "fan out" or radiate, occupying significant portions of the subcortical tissue. Therefore, lesions that are subcortical, and particularly those that are rearward and subcortical, will stand a good chance of disrupting or damaging the transmission system. This impairment in turn leads to a loss of the associated visual field.

Because the optic tract follows well-established pathways from eyes to occipital lobes, it is possible to correlate a variety of specific defects in the visual field with the precise location of an underlying lesion. For example, a tumor near the midline of the brain (e.g., from the pituitary gland) often will disrupt the half of

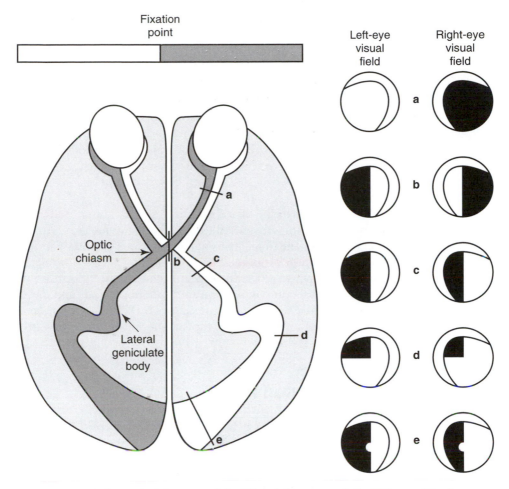

FIGURE 3.6 Schematic Diagram of the Visual System and the Effects of Lesions at Various Sites

each optic nerve that crosses over at the chiasm. The result is a peculiar deficit in which the left eye can only perceive stimuli to the right of the fixation point and the right eye can only perceive stimuli to the left of the fixation point, a symptom known as *bitemporal hemianopsia* (Figure 3.6b). Complete severance of the optic nerve in front of the optic chiasm causes total blindness in the same-sided eye (Figure 3.6a). In contrast, complete severance of the optic radiations behind the optic chiasm results in blindness in the opposite visual field of both eyes, a symptom known as *homonymous hemianopsia* (Figure 3.6c). Quadrantic deficits known as *quadrantanopsia* are a clear sign that the optic radiations have been partially compromised or impaired behind the lateral geniculate (Figure 3.6d). Extensive lesions in the general area of the visual cortex will sometimes produce a hemianopsia that appears to spare central vision, a so-called *hemianopsia with macular sparing* (Figure 3.6e).

Careful evaluation of the visual fields may provide valuable information about the presence, extent, and location of brain impairment. Particularly if a lesion is subcortical and in the rearward portion of the brain, correlated impairments in the visual fields will be evident. For example, when staring at a fixation point in the middle of concentric circles drawn on a chalkboard, a patient might fail to perceive a colored dot placed at the outer edge of one quadrant. The procedures for examining visual fields are fairly straightforward, but probably best left to the appropriate clinical or medical specialty (e.g., clinical neuropsychology or ophthalmology). Clinicians who suspect that a client manifests visual field loss should make an appropriate referral.

Not all disruptions of the visual system result in blatant blind spots, known as *scotomas*, or in the more substantial loss of visual field referred to as a cut in the visual field. Sometimes the defect consists not so much in nonawareness of a stimulus as in misrecognition of its meaning. Common pictures, faces, objects, even colors may lose their sense of familiarity. This class of symptoms known as *visual agnosia* is frequently seen in conjunction with blatant visual field defects. Persons with this disability have a problem recognizing drawings of common objects, particularly if the objects are drawn on top of one another or cut into pieces and rearranged.

Cognitive Impairment in Head Injury

In closing this chapter on brain-behavior relationships, we survey the diversity of consequences that can accompany head injury. The intention in these few paragraphs is not to make the reader an expert on the topic, but to introduce essential concepts so that practitioners will be sensitized to the variety of symptoms that may ensue from a blow to the head. Including very mild head trauma that apparently leaves no lasting sequelae, somewhere between 2 to 7 *million* Americans experience a head injury every year (Miller, 1987; Silver, Hales, & Yudofsky, 1992). Of these, 500,000 persons are admitted to hospitals and nearly 100,000 patients are left with permanent cognitive disabilities. Practitioners who engage in intellectual assessment need to be aware that even a "mild" head injury might be consequential and therefore warrant further evaluation or referral.

Brain trauma and resultant cognitive impairments can occur whenever a person's skull is rapidly accelerated or decelerated, such as from a blow to the head or impact with the windshield in an automobile accident. Terminology is confusing and inconsistent, but a few categories are accepted. A *concussion* is an acute impairment of brain function caused by a blow to the head in which brief loss (or alteration) of consciousness and transient memory disturbance are usually observed. The postconcussion syndrome is summarized in Table 3.2. A concussion is usually followed by full recovery, typically in a few days but occasionally postponed for

TABLE 3.2 The Postconcussion Syndrome

Physical Symptoms
Fatigue
Headache
Dizziness
Insomnia

Cognitive Symptoms
Attentional impairment
Memory difficulties
Concentration problems

Perceptual Symptoms
Ringing in the ears
Sensitivity to light
Sensitivity to noise

Emotional Symptoms
Irritability
Depression
Anxiety

Source: Adapted from L. Lishman (1988), "Physiogenesis and psychogenesis in the 'post-concussional syndrome.'" *British Journal of Psychiatry, 153,* 460-469.

weeks or longer. However, in some studies of persons with minor head injury about half of the patients still complained of memory loss, irritability, and depression *1 year later* (Schoenhuber, Gentili, & Orlando, 1988).

More serious than a concussion is a *closed head injury* that manifests damage to the brain even though the skull is intact. The damage may include any or all of the following: contusions or bruising of the brain tissue underneath the site of impact (*coup injury*); opposite-sided contusions from the rebound effect (*contrecoup injury*); diffuse axonal injury from shear-strain effects on neuronal pathways; damage to brain tissue from obstructed blood flow; hematoma or blood clot between the skull and the surface of the brain; and edema, or swelling, of the brain. In a *penetrating head injury* the skull is penetrated, which can lead to widespread damage from missile wounds and bone fragments forced into the brain.

The consequences of head injury are difficult to summarize because of the astonishing diversity of outcomes. Head injury can vary in its effects from a mild concussion with full recovery in 1 day to profound coma followed by months of hospitalization, years of rehabilitation, and a lifetime of disability. The nature and consequences of the trauma will not be the same in any two patients. In one patient, damage to the left-hemisphere language areas may lead to symptoms of aphasia. In another patient, damage to the frontal lobes may cause impairments in abstract reasoning, a loss of social skills, and one or more of the symptoms of frontal lobe injury summarized previously. Some patients will display visual field cuts as described above, particularly if the injury involved the occipital lobes. For example, one patient with an injury to the right, rearward section of his brain was unable to see anything to the left of his visual fixation point. The most common complaints after head injury are difficulties with attention, concentration, and memory. In addition to cognitive deficits, brain injury also can lead to impairments in physical, emotional, and social functioning. A brief compendium of potential neurobehavioral consequences is provided in Table 3.3.

TABLE 3.3   The Range of Potential Neurobehavioral Consequences in Traumatic Head Injury

Physical

Sensory and motor problems: reduced motor speed, impaired coordination, one-sided weakness, gait disturbance, one-sided paralysis

Visual impairments: reduced acuity, double vision, visual field cuts, and blindness

Neurological sequelae: headache and seizures, especially in early recovery.

Auditory problems: ranging from reduced acuity to deafness

Other: chronic fatigue, excessive sensitivity to light or noise, loss of smell

Cognitive

Attention: distractibility, disorientation, and reduced consciousness

Memory: impaired capacity to retain new information, global amnesia

Language: word-finding difficulty, slow and labored speech, expressive or receptive language disturbance

Visuospatial: facial recognition problems, perceptual-organizational impairments, spatial disorientation

Executive functioning: concrete thinking, poor judgment, planning difficulties, inability to set goals and monitor progress

Emotional

Mood changes: mild to severe irritability, lability of emotions

Psychiatric symptoms: mild to severe depression, suicidal thoughts and actions, suspiciousness to overt paranoia, episodic anxiety, post-traumatic stress disorder

Psychosocial

Isolation: job loss, divorce, loss of friends, alienation from family

Identity problems: loss of vocational identity, extensive dependence on others

Sexual adjustment: decreased libido or hypersexuality

Alcohol and drug use: increased use for self-medication, decreased tolerance to drug effects

The severity of brain injury is best judged by comprehensive medical, neurological, and neuropsychological evaluations. But simple observations are important, too. For example, a deep and lengthy coma following head trauma indicates a poor prognosis, and so does a prolonged period of post-traumatic amnesia. The astute practitioner will always inquire about these matters in the evaluation of patients who have experienced a head injury.

Coma is a continuum, not a dichotomous variable. A patient in deep coma will respond to nothing, whereas a patient in light coma may open her eyes on command and speak in a confused manner. The quantification of coma can be accomplished with a simple rating scale, the Glasgow Coma Scale, developed by Teasdale and Jennett (1974). This instrument is widely used in hospitals for the assessment of traumatic brain injury. It is scored by observing the patient and assigning the highest level of functioning on each of three subscales: eyes open, best verbal response, best motor response. The total score predicts later recovery with a reasonable degree of accuracy (Jennett, Teasdale, & Knill-Jones, 1975).

Another approach to the assessment of head trauma is to document the length of post-traumatic amnesia. Post-traumatic amnesia (PTA) refers to the number of minutes, hours, days, or weeks that transpire between the traumatic event and the point at which the patient's memory functions return to normal.

> PTA is not to be confused with coma and recovery from coma. PTA assumes that the patient is alert and functioning and has recovered from the comatose state but has persistent, severe deficits in retaining new information and processing new memories (i.e., anterograde amnesia). There also may be a retrograde amnesia for a period of time preceding the accident. (Bigler, 1990, p. 16)

Recovery from PTA is sometimes a striking event in which the patient suddenly realizes that normal memory has returned. Asking the head-injured patient and the family "When did normal memory return?" is always a wise practice.

The relevance of PTA is that a longer period predicts a poorer outcome. Although there is no strict dividing line, PTA lasting longer than 1 week is described as *very severe* and is almost always associated with serious cognitive deficits. At the other extreme, PTA of less than 5 minutes is described as very mild. This is common in concussion, from which full recovery is the rule. Beyond 5 minutes of PTA the probability of long-term impairment becomes more and more likely. PTA of even 5 minutes to an hour, described as *mild*, can be associated with lasting impairments (Jennett, 1984). A lexicon of PTA severity terms is summarized in Table 3.4.

Certainly it is incumbent upon any practitioner to ask clients suspected of head injury whether they experienced memory loss after the injury and, if so, how long did it last? The client who responds that he experienced significant amnesia may need referral for comprehensive medical and neuropsychological evaluation. Likewise, the practitioner needs to be sensitized that even a "mild" concussion months before may impact current assessment results. Whenever there is a suspicion of lasting consequences from a head injury, specialist referral for assessment and treatment is appropriate.

TABLE 3.4   **Duration of Post-Traumatic Amnesia (PTA) in Relation to Severity of Impairment**

Duration of PTA	Severity
less than 5 minutes	very mild
5 minutes to 1 hour	mild
1 to 24 hours	moderate
1 to 7 days	severe
more than 7 days	very severe

Final Comment

Now that the reader has received an introduction to brain–behavior relationships, we turn next to a presentation of tests and other instruments useful for appraising the functional capacity of the individual. Chapter 4 introduces the Wechsler Adult Intelligence Scale—III, the most widely used test of adult intellectual ability, and Chapter 5 discusses clinical issues related to the WAIS-III. Chapter 6 returns to the brain–behavior theme by introducing screening tests for cognitive impairment.

4 The WAIS-III: Introduction and the Meaning of IQ

This chapter and the next introduces the reader to the practice of individual intelligence testing, with emphasis on the Wechsler Adult Intelligence Scale—III (WAIS-III). The WAIS-III is a recent revision of the WAIS-R, which has served for decades as a rich source of information and hypotheses about intellectual functioning. Like its predecessor, the WAIS-III almost certainly will prove to be the most widely used of all the adult tests of intelligence. As Kaufman (1990) notes, the Wechsler test is the criterion of adult intelligence and "has no peer in the intelligence domain."

The focus of this chapter, then, is on the proper administration, scoring, and interpretation of the WAIS-III. Chapter 5 continues the coverage of the WAIS-III by delving into special issues and applications. Owing to the recency of the third edition, there will be reference to WAIS-R research in the discussion of test validity and other psychometric properties. Although the WAIS-III incorporates substantial revisions (including three new subtests), the heart of the test remains constant from the earlier edition. We can have confidence in the WAIS-III based on the strong continuity of this test with its predecessor.

While maintaining continuity with the WAIS-R (Wechsler, 1981), the WAIS-III introduces a number of substantial improvements (Tulsky, Zhu, & Ledbetter, 1997). These enhancements include:

- Updating and expanding the normative samples
- Extending the coverage to age 89
- Modernizing the item content and art work
- Using sophisticated analyses of item bias during test development
- Adding easy items to improve the assessment of mental retardation
- Decreasing reliance on timed performance
- Adding measures of fluid reasoning, working memory, and processing speed
- Developing four Index scores to supplement Verbal and Performance IQs
- Co-norming with the Wechsler Memory Scale—III
- Co-norming (for ages 16–19) with the Wechsler Individual Achievement Test (WIAT)
- Bolstering the psychometric analysis of reliability and validity

The product is an intelligence test unparalleled in its attention to detail and unrivaled in its clinical utility. The WAIS-III represents an important milestone in the history of psychological testing. An especially useful feature is its conceptual linkage to the Wechsler Memory Scale—III (WMS-III), a comprehensive test of memory. The WAIS-III and the WMS-III were developed together and co-normed on the same standardization subjects (Tulsky, Zhu, & Ledbetter, 1997). For practical reasons it is not realistic to cover the WMS-III here, but clinicians who take the time to master this lengthy instrument will be richly rewarded.

The value of the WAIS-III as an intellectual measure hinges substantially upon the validity and utility of the IQ construct. For this reason the chapter weaves back and forth between the particular (e.g., how to identify WAIS-III subtest strengths and weaknesses) and the general (e.g., how to think about the meaning of IQ). The starting point is a brief description of the WAIS-III and its fourteen subtests. This is followed by a detailed analysis of key issues in the administration, scoring, and interpretation of the test. The next chapter continues the coverage of the WAIS-III and includes a short survey of alternatives to it.

Brief Description of the WAIS-III

The WAIS-III is an individually administered test of intelligence that requires close interaction between examiner and client. The client answers oral questions, solves reasoning problems, and works at timed manual and perceptual problem-solving tasks. In most cases the instrument can be administered in about 60 to 90 minutes. The test is normed for use with persons 16 through 89 years of age.

The WAIS-III consists of fourteen subtests, but only eleven of these are needed to compute the traditional IQs (Verbal, Performance, and Full Scale). The IQ scores are normed to an average of 100 and standard deviation of 15 in the general population. The breakdown of subtests for the traditional IQ scores is as follows:

Verbal IQ

Vocabulary
Similarities
Arithmetic
Digit Span
Information
Comprehension

Performance IQ

Picture Completion
Digit Symbol-Coding
Block Design
Matrix Reasoning
Picture Arrangement

Of course, all eleven subtests serve as the basis for obtaining the Full Scale IQ. The apportionment of subtests in the WAIS-III is nearly identical to that found in the WAIS-R. The single exception is Matrix Reasoning, a new Performance subtest that replaces Object Assembly from the WAIS-R. On the WAIS-III, Object Assembly has been relegated to the status of an optional subtest, now rarely used.

In addition to the traditional Verbal-Performance breakdown, the developers of the WAIS-III also pursued an alternative model in which intelligence is partitioned into four domains: Verbal Comprehension, Perceptual Organization, Working Memory, and Processing Speed. Based upon factor analytic studies of intelligence, this model is a clinically useful *supplement* to the traditional approach. Two additional subtests (Symbol Search and Letter-Number Sequencing) were added to help capture the third and fourth domains. Summary scores in these four domains are called Index scores so as to distinguish them from IQ scores. The Index scores are normed to an average of 100 and standard deviation of 15 in the general population. The breakdown of subtests for the Index scores is as follows:

> Verbal Comprehension
>> Vocabulary
>> Similarities
>> Information
>
> Perceptual Organization
>> Picture Completion
>> Block Design
>> Matrix Reasoning
>
> Working Memory
>> Arithmetic
>> Digit Span
>> Letter-Number Sequencing
>
> Processing Speed
>> Digit Symbol-Coding
>> Symbol Search

The reader will notice that computation of the four Index scores is also based upon eleven subtests—nine subtests used for traditional IQ scores and two new subtests devised explicitly to enhance the fourfold model of intelligence. Thus, in order to derive traditional IQ scores *and* the four Index scores, the examiner needs to administer thirteen subtests. The fourteenth and optional subtest, Object Assembly, can substitute for other subtests under certain circumstances (Wechsler, 1997).

In general, the fourteen WAIS-III subtests follow a similar pattern of beginning with simple items and proceeding by carefully graded difficulty levels to harder and harder items. Exceptions to this pattern are the timed/speeded tasks of Digit Symbol-Coding and Symbol Search. These subtests are discontinued after the time limit of 120 seconds is reached. For all other subtests, administration is discontinued after the examinee fails a specified number of consecutive items (typically three to six items). Subtest scores normed to a mean of 10 and a standard deviation of 3 relative to same-age persons from the standardization sample. This means that the subtest scores used in the derivation of IQs and Index scores are *age-corrected*. This represents an important shift from the WAIS-R in which subtest scores for examinees of any age were based on comparison with results for the anchor group of individuals 20 to 34 years of age.

The three IQ scores and four Index scores are based on the distribution of results for all standardization subjects so as to produce an overall mean of 100 and standard deviation of 15. The standardization sample of 2,450 adults was chosen with great care and adequately represents a cross section of the American population along dimensions of age, sex, race/ethnicity, educational level, and geographic region. Very stringent selection criteria were applied so as to exclude persons with conditions that might affect performance on an intelligence test (e.g., uncorrected hearing loss, head injury, epilepsy, use of psychotropic medication).

WAIS-III scoring is almost completely objective, although some judgment is required for verbal items when allotting 0, 1, or 2 points raw score credit. Honest disagreements can occur when two examiners score the same test; however, this is seldom a significant factor in the overall score. Four of the Verbal subtests (Vocabulary, Similarities, Information, and Comprehension) require the greatest amount of judgment for scoring, yet even here perfect agreement occurs more than 90 percent of the time (Tulsky, Zhu, & Ledbetter, 1997). Clerical scoring errors are a more serious concern, as discussed in a later section.

WAIS-III Subtests

Consistent with David Wechsler's view of intelligence as both a global entity and also an aggregate of specific abilities, each subtest of the WAIS-III necessitates a slightly different combination of cognitive skills. We describe the subtests in their standard order of administration. The assessment begins with Picture Completion, a simple and nonthreatening measure intended to capture the interest of the examinee.

Picture Completion

The Picture Completion subtest measures the ability to recognize visually that some essential element is missing in a realistic color drawing of common objects or scenes. Picture Completion presupposes that the examinee has been exposed to the object or situation represented. For the more difficult items the examinee must be able to resist false leads and to identify the most essential part that is missing. Some of the items require judgments about practical and conceptual matters (e.g., new fallen snow will cover everything). In this respect, Picture Completion is sometimes considered to be a nonverbal analogue of Comprehension.

Vocabulary

In the Vocabulary subtest the examinee is asked to define as many as thirty-three words of increasing difficulty. Vocabulary is a direct measure of the ability to define what words mean. However, in an indirect way, a person's vocabulary is a measure of sensitivity to new information and the ability to decipher meanings based on the context in which words are encountered. Put simply, the acquisition of vocabulary requires high-level contextual inference. Contrary to the widespread view that vocabulary depends solely upon education, a person's vocabulary is, in fact, a strong index of general intelligence. Vocabulary usually has the highest loading on the general intelligence factor in factor analytic studies. It also displays a very high reliability (high .90s) and is usually considered the single best measure of overall intelligence on individual IQ tests.

Digit Symbol-Coding

Known as Digit Symbol on the WAIS-R, the name of this subtest has been revised slightly so as to indicate that a coding process (digits to symbols) is required. The examinee must associate one written symbol with each of the digits 1 through 9 and quickly draw the appropriate symbol underneath a long series of 133 digits. This is a speeded measure with a time limit of 120 seconds. This subtest calls for on-the-spot learning of an unfamiliar task. Digit Symbol-Coding also measures visual-motor dexterity, persistence in the face of a boring task, and clerical speed. Kaufman (1990) lists the following influences upon scores:

- Anxiety
- Compulsive concern for accuracy and detail
- Distractibility
- Learning disabilities
- Persistence
- Working under time pressure

Similarities

The examinee is asked questions of the type "In what way are shirts and socks alike?" The ability to distinguish essential from nonessential similarities in objects, facts, and ideas is at issue in the Similarities subtest. Indirectly, this subtest measures the incidental assimilation of likeness in objects, facts, and ideas. The examinee must also have the ability to judge when a likeness is essential rather than trivial. Hence, Similarities is a test of verbal concept formation. Like the Comprehension subtest, Similarities is adversely affected by negativism ("They're not alike") and overly concrete thinking.

Block Design

The examinee is asked to construct a copy of geometric designs using blocks that are all white on two sides, all red on two sides, and half red/half white on the remaining two sides. The more difficult items on Block Design require the analysis of spatial relations and the rigid application of logic. The first few items can be solved by simple trial and error. Along with Matrix Reasoning (discussed below), this measure mandates a greater amount of reasoning and problem solving than most of the other subtests, in which memory and prior experience are significantly weighted. Block Design also requires spatial visualization ability and the capacity to work under pressure. It is generally recognized as an excellent index of perceptual organization on the WAIS-III.

Arithmetic

Successful performance on Arithmetic obliges the examinee to apply very basic computational skills of addition, subtraction, division, percentages, and the like to story problems. The problems are presented orally and have a time limit, so this measure also taps auditory concentration and freedom from distractibility. Kaufman (1990) lists the following influences upon Arithmetic subtest scores:

- Attention span
- Anxiety
- Concentration
- Distractibility
- Learning disabilities
- School learning
- Working under time pressure

Matrix Reasoning

Matrix Reasoning is a new subtest on the WAIS-III. It was added to enhance the assessment of fluid intelligence, a type of largely nonverbal reasoning ability. The WAIS-R had been criticized for failing to include measures of this domain. *Fluid intelligence* refers to the "ability to perform mental operations, such as manipulation of abstract symbols" (Sternberg, 1995, p. 437). This subtest is a nonverbal measure of inductive reasoning based on figural stimuli. In order to correctly answer items on Matrix Reasoning, examinees must identify a recurring pattern or relationship between figural stimuli drawn on a card in a square pattern or along a straight line. On each of the twenty-six cards, one stimulus is missing. Based on the discernment of patterns and relationships, the examinee must identify the missing stimulus and select it from five choices at the bottom of the card. The items embody pattern completion, classification, reasoning by analogy, and serial reasoning. Matrix Reasoning is considered an excellent measure of the fluid intelligence construct identified by Cattell and others (Carroll, 1997; Cattell, 1943, 1971; Cattell & Horn, 1978).

Digit Span

In the Digit Span subtest the examiner reads a series of digits at one per second, then asks the examinee to repeat them (Digits Forward) or to repeat them in reversed order (Digits Backward). The easiest item is two digits in length whereas the most difficult is nine digits for the Digits Forward portion and eight digits for the Digits Backward portion. This is a measure of immediate auditory memory for numbers, which is one aspect of *working memory* (Tulsky, Zhu, & Ledbetter, 1997, pp. 4–6). Facility with numbers, good attention, and freedom from distractibility are needed. Digits Backward engages fundamentally different cognitive abilities than does Digits Forward. The examinee must form an internal visual engram from the orally presented numerical sequences and then mentally inspect from end to beginning to do well on the Digits Backward section. Both Digits Forward and Digits Backward are measures of working memory, but the former is an example of a *simple span* task (because it deemphasizes the manipulation of the material), whereas the latter is an example of a *complex span* task (because it requires the mental reordering of the information).

Information

Factual knowledge of persons, places, and common phenomena is tested on the Information subtest. It measures the amount of general information absorbed from books, school, media, and significant persons. The items query general knowledge normally available to individuals reared in the United States or Western Europe. Kaufman (1990) identifies the following influences upon Information scores:

- Alertness to the environment
- Cultural opportunities
- Foreign language background
- Intellectual curiosity and striving
- Interests
- Learning disabilities
- Outside reading
- Richness of early environment
- School learning

Picture Arrangement

In Picture Arrangement, nonverbal cartoon strips that tell a story are laid down out of order. The examinee's task is to put them together in the correct order to make a sensible story within a generous time limit (2 minutes for the difficult items). This subtest measures sequential thinking and the ability to see relationships between social events. To some extent, social sophistication and a sense of humor are needed for successful performance—some of the cartoon stories reveal humorous themes. Other factors tapped by Picture Arrangement include creativity, cultural opportunities, exposure to comic strips, and working under time pressure (Kaufman, 1990).

Comprehension

In the Comprehension Subtest the examinee is queried on the proper interpretation of common social and cultural conventions. The questions are of the type "Why are votes often taken by secret ballot?" For the most part, this subtest is a measure of comprehension of everyday social and cultural situations. Thus, it measures degree of social acculturation, especially in the spheres of moral and ethical judgments. However, a high score does not mean a person will choose "right" action. Kaufman (1990) lists the following influences upon Comprehension scores:

- Cultural opportunities
- Development of conscience or moral sense
- Negativism ("People shouldn't pay taxes," "You don't need a marriage license")
- Overly concrete thinking

The two hardest items require the examinee to interpret common proverbs of the form "What does this saying mean? 'A bird in the hand is worth two in the bush.'" The interpretation of proverbs on this subtest is curious in that these items call on a different set of experiences than the mainstay "social intelligence" items. Proverbs may help detect overly concrete thinking, but they also appear to assess an intellectual component unlike that measured by the other Comprehension questions (Kaufman, 1983).

Symbol Search

In the new subtest Symbol Search the examinee sees a paired group of target stimuli (simple geometric shapes) and a larger group of search stimuli. Then, under pressure of a 120-second time limit, the examinee indicates, by marking a Yes or a No box, whether either target symbol appears in the search group. This subtest is considered an excellent measure of cognitive processing speed. Together with Digit Symbol-Coding, it contributes to the Processing Speed Index score.

Letter-Number Sequencing

In the new subtest Letter-Number Sequencing the examiner orally presents a series of letters and numbers that are in mixed-up order. The subject must reorder and repeat the list by saying the numbers first in ascending order and then the letters in alphabetical order. For example, if the examiner says "S-3-B-4-Z-1-C," the examinee should respond, "1-3-4-B-C-S-Z". Good attention, concentration, and freedom from distractibility are needed. Together with Arithmetic and Digit Span, this subtest contributes to the Working Memory Index score.

Object Assembly

Object Assembly is an optional subtest that can be used as a substitution for any spoiled Performance subtest for examinees 16 through 74 years of age. In practice, it is rarely administered. Drawings of common objects have been cut into several pieces. These must be assembled correctly by the examinee. Object Assembly measures the ability to form visual concepts quickly and then translate them into rapid hand responses. On the WAIS-III, Object Assembly has been relegated to optional/replacement status because it reveals lower reliability than most other subtests (.70 in the standardization sample) and shows a weak association with general intellectual ability.

Administration of the WAIS-III

The *WAIS-III Administration and Scoring Manual*, hereafter referred to as the *Administration and Scoring Manual*, provides detailed coverage of general testing conditions and specific subtest considerations (Wechsler, 1997). It is not the purpose of this brief section to supplant the instructions found in that source. The aspiring practitioner must read this manual carefully. Trainees also must receive extensive supervised experience in WAIS-III administration to develop competence in the testing of intelligence. The discussion that follows assumes that prospective examiners of intelligence have read the *Administration and Scoring Manual* and have received, are receiving, or will receive appropriate, supervised experience.

This section will supplement the *Administration and Scoring Manual* by highlighting certain problematic areas of WAIS-III administration that arise when the inexperienced examiner sits down with a referral to administer the test. The following points are entirely consistent with standard procedures as outlined in the manual. It is hoped that practitioners will find these recommendations helpful when learning the subtleties of competent test administration.

The Need for Reasoned Flexibility

Examiners should follow carefully the standardized procedures for administration and scoring found in the *Administration and Scoring Manual*. A competent and standardized approach to the execution of the test is essential if the practitioner hopes to obtain valid and useful results. Nonstandard testing procedures usually introduce measurement error and decrease the accuracy and validity of the test results. Standardized procedures are so important that they are highlighted separately in *Standards for Educational and Psychological Testing* (1985, 1997), a reference manual published jointly by the American Psychological Association and other groups:

> In typical applications, test administrators should follow carefully the standardized procedures for administration and scoring specified by the test publisher. Specifications regarding instructions to test takers, time limits, the form of item presentation or response, and test materials or equipment should be strictly observed. Exceptions should be made only on the basis of carefully considered professional judgment, primarily in clinical applications.

Even though standardized procedures typically are essential, there are instances in which flexibility in testing is desirable, indeed, even necessary. As suggested in the APA Standards, adjustments in test administration should be reasoned and deliberate. An analogy to the spirit of the law versus the letter of the law is relevant here. An overly cautious examiner might capture the letter of the law, so to speak, by adhering literally and strictly to testing procedures outlined in the publisher's manual. But is this really what the test publisher intended? Is it even how the test was actually administered to the standardization sample? Most likely, publishers would prefer that examiners capture the spirit of the law even if, on occasion, it is necessary to adjust testing procedures slightly.

Consider the following situation, which arose when a practitioner administered the first arithmetic item to an anxious and overly concrete college student. The first question resembled "How much is three dollars plus five dollars?" The nervous student quickly replied "Three dollars is three dollars and five dollars is five dollars." Following the test manual literally, the examiner should record zero credit, reverse course, and administer easier items intended for persons with limited intelligence. However, the question was intended to test arithmetical skills, not concrete thinking. For this reason, the examiner asked the question again (with the stopwatch still running), changing the emphasis slightly: "How much is three dollars *plus* five dollars?" The subject guffawed loudly and answered immediately, "Eight dollars—I didn't realize it was an arithmetic question."

Experienced examiners routinely make deliberate and reasoned adjustments that heed the spirit in which a test was developed. These slight deviations are no cause for alarm. Minor adjustments do not invalidate the established norms—on the contrary, the appropriate adaptation of procedures is necessary so that the norms remain valid. After all, the examiners who helped standardize the test did not act like heartless robots when posing questions to persons in the standardization sample. Examiners who desire to obtain valid results must likewise employ a careful, deliberate flexibility in testing procedures.

The Importance of a Clipboard

The typical scenario in intellectual assessment is for examiner and examinee to sit across from one another at a table. In WAIS-III testing the examiner then encounters the delicate situation in which the client might observe the recording of item scores on the Record Form. The *Administration and Scoring Manual* explicitly cautions that the Record Form should never be readable to the examinee, but also warns against self-conscious efforts to conceal the materials. The easiest way to meet these conflicting demands of test administration is to place the Record Form on a clipboard. The clipboard is then angled over the edge of the table, resting on the examiner's lap, with the Record Form out of the subject's view.

How to Provide Support

A common error for the beginning tester is to say "Good!" after every correct response from the client. This sounds like a desirable practice—until the client starts to fail subtest items. The examiner's lack of response then conveys a powerful message of failure. A better testing practice is to say nothing after the completion of each item, or to offer a simple nod or a noncommittal "OK, here's another one."

The *Administration and Scoring Manual* specifies clearly that the examiner should be supportive and reassuring. The best time to convey such support is between test items or after an entire subtest is completed. Acceptable forms of feedback would include the following kinds of statements:

- "Remember that the questions [problems] go from easy to hard and nobody is expected to get them all correct."
- "A lot of people find that question [problem] to be difficult—let's try another one."
- "You did very well on that subtest—let's try something different now."

The examiner should keep in mind that although it is appropriate to reassure the examinee, it is not acceptable to divulge the correct answer or to provide feedback that an answer is right or wrong. When the examinee asks "What's the answer to that one?" an appropriate response is:

- "I'm sorry, it is standard policy with this test that we can't reveal the answers."

If the examinee wants to know "Why?" the answer is:

- "There is always some chance that you might take this test again in the future."

Stopwatch Protocol

Examiners need a stopwatch for timing responses on several of the subtests. The necessity for accurate timing poses an interesting predicament that is not discussed in the manual. Whether examinees voice their concerns or not, they want to know if they are being timed. Furthermore, they want to know whether the time limit is generous or stringent, and their presumptions about this matter surely will affect their performance. Many examinees will ask, "Is this subtest being timed?" The examiner's predicament is how to answer this question without conveying the wrong message.

The *Administration and Scoring Manual* provides no guidance on this topic. The examiner could simply respond "Yes" and then raise the stopwatch to shoulder level in the manner of an official at a track meet. Surely this would be a mistake, since it would convey that speed is more important than accuracy. At the other extreme, the examiner could respond "Yes, but there is more than enough time, so don't be concerned about it." This, too, would be a disservice, as it would convey that speed is unimportant. What is the examiner to do?

An approach that is consistent with the general tone of the *WAIS-III Administration and Scoring Manual* is recommended here. The appropriate response to examinee concerns about timing is to be honest but nondirective. The examiner might reply, "Yes, this subtest is timed—work quickly, but not at the expense of accuracy." Within the constraints of standardized procedures, a truthful approach to assessment is always appropriate.

Special Considerations in Digit Span

Although Digit Span appears to be pristinely simple to administer, the reality of hands-on testing is otherwise. Considerable practice is needed to master the crucial dictum that *digits should be spoken at the rate of one per second*. This seems a snail's pace to the unpracticed ear. The untutored examiner therefore may read the digits much faster, as fast as two digits per second. This is not just a minor variation from standard procedure; it is a serious error. Reading digits at a rate faster than one per second renders them substantially easier to recall. The best way to learn the appropriate pacing for Digit Span is to practice reading items in synchrony with the changing display of a digital watch. Once this rhythm is internalized, the examiner will be able to read digits at one per second with great ease.

Another concern with Digit Span administration is whether the examiner should make eye contact during the subtest. The *Administration and Scoring Manual* is completely silent on this question. Based on research with college and high school students, Goldfarb and others (1995) concluded that eye contact is actively averted by examinees and may impair performance slightly. Although the presumed impact is not large, the authors advise against making eye contact during the administration of this sensitive subtest.

Impact of the Examiner

The impact of examiner characteristics such as race, sex, and age has been the object of extensive study that we will not review here. The interested reader is referred to Sattler (1988, ch. 5) for information on this topic. The reason for not reviewing this body of research is that the findings are inconclusive and contradictory. For example, some studies find that female examiners obtain slightly higher IQs than male examiners, whereas other studies conclude that the sex of the examiner makes little or no difference.

Although the external characteristics of the examiner may have little impact, his or her behavior during testing is another matter. Clinical experience suggests that the demeanor of the examiner could shape a significant difference in the performance of the client. An excessively austere, formal, cold tester might obtain IQs that are several points lower than scores obtained by a friendly tester who takes time to establish rapport. How much of a problem this is when testing adults has not been well studied. The research with children suggests that occasionally it could be a serious problem.

A study by Gregory, Lehman, and Mohan (1976) has direct bearing on this issue. They sought to determine the effects of low-level lead exposure on IQ by administering the WISC to 193 children ages 5 to 10. Children were assigned to five different graduate student testers on a quasi-random, first-come-first-served rotational basis. The groups of children tested by each of the psychometricians did not differ in average age, lead level, or social class. Moreover, the sample sizes were substantial, ranging from 30 to 45. Hence, the average tested IQs of the five groups should have been highly similar.

However, the differences between testers were distressingly large, with average IQs varying by as much as 14 points. Ranked from low to high, the average scores for the five groups were 90, 94, 95, 96, and 104. As principal investigator for this part of the research project, the author had the opportunity to oversee the individual testers, who were also his graduate students. The impression was that the testers at each extreme were portraying different forms of subtle incompetence related to the warm-cold variable in testing. The tester whose subjects had an average IQ of 90 was very formal, precise, cold, and hurried. In fact, he examined the most children by far (45, compared to 37 for the next most prolific tester) and was usually finished with an individual child much sooner. At the other extreme was the tester whose subjects had an average IQ of 104. He went beyond good rapport to offer support and encouragement that bordered on leading the examinees to the correct answer. His test sessions lasted twice as long, and he demonstrated the error of being too solicitous.

The moral of this story is that testers have temperaments. Cold testers may obtain uniformly lower IQs from their examinees. Warm testers who are overly solicitous may err in the opposite direction, giving subtle cues as to the correct solutions or answers. For example, the examiner might encourage examinees on the Block Design with advice to "get the blocks in the corners and go forward from there." Or the examiner might nonchalantly offer specific advice on an Information question such as "I'll bet you studied this one in your literature course." This kind of overly helpful encouragement is just as inappropriate as acting in a cold, robotic manner toward the examinee. Examiners should provide a warm, supportive atmosphere for testing, but they must do so within the bounds of standardized procedure as described in the *Administration and Scoring Manual*.

Scoring the WAIS-III

The *Administration and Scoring Manual* provides excellent guidelines for scoring individual responses and subtests on the WAIS-III. The mechanics of computing the IQs and Factor Index Scores are also well defined and straightforward. I do not intend to duplicate these scoring instructions, which every examiner must learn through supervised experience. Rather, the purpose of this brief section is to highlight certain pitfalls encountered by examiners when scoring the WAIS-III.

Many students of testing scoff when scoring errors are described as a significant threat to the validity of intelligence testing. There is almost an implicit assumption that if a person can read and also add a column of two-digit numbers, scoring errors will be nonexistent. To prick this balloon of hubris, I routinely issue a challenge to each group of students in my intellectual assessment courses. All students are given the identical unscored Wechsler protocol, with the prediction that at least one of them will make a gross clerical scoring error when calculating test scores for the examinee. Each class is challenged to be the first in the professor's 25-year career to obtain IQs within a point or two of the correct values. The one- or two-point leeway is given to clarify that subtle scoring disagreements (as when scoring the individual items on Vocabulary) are not the issue. Actually, such scoring disagreements have a trivial effect on overall IQs, and it is largely a waste of instructional time to focus on them.

Not one class in 25 years has successfully met this challenge. Every year, at least one graduate student has made a gross clerical scoring error affecting overall IQ by 10, 20, even 50 points. A recent set of scores for fifteen graduate students is depicted in Table 4.1. For this protocol the actual VIQ was 88, but scores of 87–89 could be considered arguably correct (e.g., based on liberal versus conservative interpretations of ambiguous answers). Two examiners (A and E) made clear-cut scoring errors that yielded misleadingly high VIQ scores of 95. Other examiners were off by smaller amounts.

A more serious problem is encountered on PIQ, where blatant scoring errors caused the same two examiners (A and E) to report inflated scores. The correct PIQ was 79, but these two examiners calculated scores of 106 and 116, respectively. Of course, if these errors remained undetected they would result in totally unrealistic expectations for this examinee in regard to performance intelligence. The errors also boosted the Full Scale IQs reported by these examiners as well. The correct Full Scale IQ was 83, whereas their findings were 100 and 104, respec-

TABLE 4.1   **WAIS-III IQ and Index Scores from the Same Test Protocol for 15 Graduate Students**

IQ or Index	Examiner														
	A	B	C	D	E	F	G	H	I	J	K	L	M	N	O
Verbal IQ	95	90	87	85	95	89	87	88	88	88	86	86	89	**88**	87
Performance IQ	106	80	72	78	116	80	79	78	78	78	79	79	78	**79**	79
Full Scale IQ	100	85	81	80	104	84	82	82	82	82	81	81	83	**83**	82
VCI	89	91	89	88	96	91	88	89	89	89	84	84	91	**91**	110
POI	80	84	69	80	120	84	82	80	80	80	82	82	80	**82**	82
WMI	92	92	92	92	92	92	92	92	92	92	94	94	92	**92**	92
PSI	99	99	99	99	109	99	99	99	99	99	99	99	99	**99**	99

Note: VCI = Verbal Comprehension Index; POI = Perceptual Organization Index; WMI = Working Memory Index; PSI = Processing Speed Index.

The correct scores are VIQ 88, PIQ 79, FSIQ 83, and VCI 91, POI 82, WMI 92, PSI 99, as reported by Examiner N.

tively. In sum, an examinee with low average ability was reported to be of slightly above average intelligence.[1]

It might be tempting to assume that this example is an isolated, freakish event that occurs only among naive, untutored graduate students. Not so, according to Ryan, Prifitera, and Powers (1983). They asked nineteen psychologists and twenty graduate students to score the WAIS-R protocols from two vocational counseling clients. Regardless of the scorer's experience level, mechanical scoring errors produced summary scores (Verbal, Performance, and Full Scale IQs) varying by as much as 4 to 18 IQ points. For example, the correct Full Scale IQ for one examinee was 110, whereas the practicing psychologists (all Ph.D.s) provided scores ranging from 107 to 115, and the graduate students obtained scores ranging from 108 to 117.

This is only one study from a dozen or so that could be cited to illustrate the ubiquity of scoring errors on the Wechsler scales (Kaufman, 1990; Slate & Hunnicutt, 1988). Scoring errors occur frequently and detract from the accuracy of intelligence test results. This is a chronic problem that does not improve merely because an examiner acquires more experience. The only appropriate response to clerical scoring errors is to declare loudly that their existence is a serious, widespread problem. Examiners must exercise great care when scoring protocols.

---

[1] This is perhaps a more benign error than the reverse (reporting a low IQ for an examinee with high ability), but the consequences still could be unpleasant for the person tested. For example, counselors might expect more from this individual than is realistic.

Reliability of the WAIS-III

By way of quick review, reliability is the attribute of consistency in measurement. Reliability is important in intellectual assessment because an unreliable (inconsistent) measure cannot be trusted. Although reliability does not guarantee validity, it is a necessary precursor. Put another way, reliability constrains validity. An unreliable measure is doomed to invalidity.

Two broad approaches prevail in the assessment of reliability. The first is to administer the test twice to the same group of persons and compute a correlation coefficient between the two sets of scores (test-retest). This index is known as a *stability coefficient* or a *test-retest reliability coefficient*. An alternative approach is to obtain scores from a single administration, split each scale in half, and compute a correlation coefficient between the two sets of half scores, adjusting for reduced scale length by the Spearman-Brown formula (Crocker & Algina, 1986). This index is known as a *split-half reliability coefficient* (which is one form of an internal consistency coefficient). For both approaches, reliability can range from 0.0 (none) to 1.0 (perfect).

What is an acceptable level of reliability for a psychological measure? Most sources concur that the reliability of a test, scale, or measure should be at least .90 for decisions about individuals (Gregory, 1996; Salvia & Ysseldyke, 1988). Although tests or scales with reliability lower than .90 can be useful in research or when combined with other measures, basing a decision on such a measure is risky because it is an imprecise index of individual differences.

Table 4.2 summarizes the available estimates of reliability for WAIS-III IQs, Index scores, and subtest scores. These values were derived from data in the *WAIS-III—WMS-III Technical Manual*, hereafter called the *Technical Manual* (Tulsky, Zhu, & Ledbetter, 1997). The split-half data are the mean values for the thirteen age groups in the standardization sample of 2,450 persons between 16 and 89 years of age. The test-retest data are the means of the coefficients for four pooled age groups (16–29, 30–54, 55–74, 75–89). These values were derived from 394 examinees tested twice, with a mean retest interval of about 35 days.

The reader will notice that the reliability of the traditional WAIS-III IQs is exceptionally good. Composite split-half reliabilities averaged across all age groups are: Verbal IQ .97, Performance IQ .94, and Full Scale IQ .98. Stability coefficients on test-retest are: Verbal IQ .96, Performance IQ .91, and Full Scale IQ .96. With the exception of the stability coefficient for Performance IQ, all of these reliability indices are in the mid- to high-.90s. We can conclude, then, that inferences about intellectual functioning based on these global scores can be made with respectable accuracy and confidence.

Reliability results are somewhat more variable for the four Index scores. Verbal Comprehension reveals very good reliability values (.96 for internal consistency and .95 for stability). However, the other three indices (Perceptual Organization, Working Memory, and Processing Speed) display reliability outcomes that are less sturdy, especially for test-retest stability (correlations of .88, .89, and .89, respectively). Thus, inferences about intellectual functioning based on the

TABLE 4.2   **Average Subtest Reliabilities for WAIS-III IQs, Index Scores, and Subtests**

Subtest/Scale/Index	Split-Half	Test-Retest
Vocabulary	.93	.91
Similarities	.86	.83
Arithmetic	.88	.86
Digit Span	.90	.83
Information	.91	.94
Comprehension	.84	.81
Letter-Number Sequencing	.82	.75
Picture Completion	.83	.79
Digit Symbol-Coding	.84[a]	.86
Block Design	.86	.82
Matrix Reasoning	.90	.77
Picture Arrangement	.74	.69
Symbol Search	.77[a]	.79
Object Assembly	.70	.76
Verbal IQ	.97	.96
Performance IQ	.94	.91
Full Scale IQ	.98	.96
Verbal Comprehension Index	.96	.95
Perceptual Organization Index	.93	.88
Working Memory Index	.94	.89
Processing Speed Index	.88	.89

[a] Represents a test-retest value, split-half is not appropriate for speeded tests.

Source: Based on data from D. Tulsky, J. Zhu, and M. Ledbetter. *WAIS-III WMS-III Technical Manual* (San Antonio, TX: Psychological Corporation, 1997).

Index scores can be made with less accuracy and confidence than those based on the traditional IQ scores (except for Verbal Comprehension, which rivals Verbal IQ and Full Scale IQ in regard to robust reliability).

In contrast to the global IQs and the Index scores, the reliability of the specific subtest scores indicates a need for caution when making inferences about individuals. The only subtests with stability coefficients in excess of .90 are Vocabulary

(.91) and Information (.94). Four subtests reveal split-half reliabilities in excess of .90: Vocabulary, Digit Span, Information, and Matrix Reasoning. For the remaining subtests, reliability values range from the low .70s to the mid .80s.

Most practitioners know that WAIS-III IQ scores possess excellent reliability. However, few practitioners appreciate the generally modest reliability of the individual subtests. Only two subtests, Vocabulary and Information, reveal consistently strong reliability values in split-half and test-retest studies. Only for these subtests can we be confident that the specific underlying abilities have been measured with high accuracy. At the other extreme are Picture Arrangement, Symbol Search, and Object Assembly, which reveal marginal reliabilities (below .80).

The reliabilities shown in Table 4.2 are as good as can be expected, given that the WAIS-III aims to be a short and practical instrument. Nonetheless, these reliabilities are generally modest, which bespeaks the need for caution in the use of subtest scores. First, it is unwise to make individual decisions based on subtest scores alone (with the possible exceptions of Vocabulary and Information). Second, WAIS-III subtest patterns should be interpreted conservatively; that is, a certain pattern of subtest scores may suggest a hypothesis about cognitive functioning, but additional findings will be needed to confirm it. We return to these topics later in this chapter.

Validity: The Meaning of Full Scale IQ

The validity of a test is judged by the extent to which it measures what it claims to measure. The WAIS-III and similar tests provide a global IQ score as an index of intelligence. A crucial question, then, is whether the global IQ construct is valid as a measure of intelligence.

A huge corpus of research could be cited in support of the validity of the IQ construct. We will examine a few key trends here. For more details the interested reader is referred to several distinguished scholars who have compiled and reviewed the relevant studies. Matarazzo (1972) surveyed the early research, whereas Jensen (1980) provided additional theoretical notes; Brody (1985) published an insightful chapter titled "The Validity of Tests of Intelligence." Beyond a doubt, these reviewers would agree with Kaufman (1990) that "...the IQ construct, as measured by contemporary intelligence tests, is valid when defined within the societal context and when the IQ's limitations are kept fully in mind." We will consider some of the limitations of IQ in a later section.

The validity of the IQ construct as a measure of intelligence rests on four foundations. We will examine this issue briefly in relation to the WAIS-R and the WAIS-III. For adolescents and adults it has been demonstrated convincingly that Wechsler IQ scores:

- Correlate robustly with other IQ scores
- Strongly predict academic achievement
- Correlate solidly with educational attainment
- Relate modestly to occupational level

Detailed discussion of these points can be found in the sources just cited. A few key findings for each point follow.

Intercorrelation of IQ Tests

Scores from mainstream IQ tests always show strong, positive correlations with one another. The only (apparent) exceptions involve studies with individuals from a restricted range of ability—which artificially reduces the correlation coefficient. With studies using heterogeneous groups of individuals the correlations among scores on different IQ tests are always strong and positive. What makes this finding remarkable is that it holds true even when the tests appear to have minimal overlap in their intellectual requirements. For example, the WAIS-R contained few items that require reasoning about abstract symbols, yet Full Scale IQ correlated in the range of .5 to .8 with Raven's Progressive Matrices, a pure measure of high-level abstract reasoning (Burke, 1985; Raven & Summers, 1986).

Time and again in the history of testing it has been shown that IQ test scores always correlate positively and substantially. This holds true for tests developed in different historical epochs, on different continents, according to different theoretical approaches, and with different stimulus materials. This remarkable finding speaks powerfully to the validity of the IQ construct as a measure of intelligence. The ubiquity of the IQ × IQ correlation supports the existence of a general factor of intelligence as a real characteristic of human beings, not just an artifact invented by IQ test developers.

Validation studies with the WAIS-III also reveal strong correlations of Full Scale IQ with global scores on other measures: .93 with the WAIS-R, .88 with the WISC-III, .64 with the Standard Progressive Matrices (Raven & Summers, 1986), and .88 with the Stanford-Binet: Fourth Edition (Thorndike, Hagen, & Sattler, 1986). In sum, Full Scale IQ such as from the WAIS-III and similar instruments would appear to capture an important underlying quality of individuals, a general factor of cognitive ability that shows significant variation from one person to the next.

IQ and Academic Achievement

The very first individual test of intelligence was designed to identify children who would not benefit from regular public school instruction. Binet's pathbreaking test appeared in 1905 in Paris and was eminently successful in meeting its pragmatic purpose. The capacity of successor tests such as the WAIS-III to predict academic achievement (and especially academic failure) is a powerful argument for the validity of the IQ construct.

The extent to which Full Scale IQ is a useful predictor of adaptive school behavior depends to some extent on the age of the person being tested. Jensen (1980) reviewed the voluminous literature and found the typical range of correlations between IQ and grades to be .6 to .7 for the elementary grades, .5 to .6 for high school, .4 to .5 for college, and .3 to .4 for graduate school. Kaufman (1990) cites an overall value of .5 for the correlation between IQ and performance in school.

The lower correlations at the higher educational levels arise from a number of causes, among them the low reliability of college grades, and admission policies that tend to eliminate low–IQ students altogether. These inverse relationships—the higher the educational level the lower the relationship between IQ and grades—should not be interpreted to mean that intelligence becomes any less important at more advanced levels of education. In fact, the converse is probably true. Most likely, low–IQ individuals rarely qualify for advanced education. If they did, the correlations between IQ and grades would be substantial. Regardless of how we interpret the subtleties of the IQ × achievement relationship, the strength of the connection is a crucial argument for the validity of the IQ construct.

The developers of the WAIS-III included an analysis of IQ × achievement patterns by using a standardized achievement test, the Wechsler Individual Achievement Test (WIAT). The WIAT is a standardized measure of academic achievement that includes eight subtests designed to assess different aspects of reading, mathematics, language, and writing. Correlations between WIAT scores and WAIS-III IQs for 142 normally functioning adults 16 to 19 years of age are reported in Table 4.3. These relationships are very solid, mostly in the .60s and .70s, confirming that IQ bears a strong relationship to school achievement. It is intriguing that the WIAT scores uniformly correlate more strongly with VIQ than with PIQ. Apparently, Verbal IQ is more important for school-based achievement than is Performance IQ.

TABLE 4.3   Correlations between WAIS-III IQs and WIAT Subtest Scores

WIAT Subtest	WAIS-III IQ		
	VIQ	PIQ	FSIQ
Basic Reading	.73	.53	.69
Math Reasoning	.82	.69	.82
Spelling	.69	.53	.66
Reading Comprehension	.72	.58	.71
Numerical Operations	.71	.62	.72
Listening Comprehension	.74	.53	.71
Oral Expression	.45	.37	.45
Written Expression	.52	.43	.52

Source: Based on data from D. Tulsky, J. Zhu, and M. Ledbetter. *WAIS-III WMS-III Technical Manual* (San Antonio, TX: Psychological Corporation, 1997).

Wechsler emphasized practical utility when he developed his intelligence scales. It should come as no surprise, then, that a very important use of intelligence tests is the prediction of academic achievement. To be more specific, IQ tests can be used to identify students at high risk for academic failure. The early diagnosis of potential school failure can alert teachers and parents to the need for preventive intervention, tailored to the strengths and weaknesses revealed by an IQ test.

IQ and Educational Attainment

To the extent that the WAIS-III is a good measure of intelligence, we should expect to find a strong relationship between educational attainment and Full Scale IQ (Kaufman, 1990). This expectation follows from two reasonable assumptions:

1. More intelligent persons will tend to seek a higher level of education.
2. Education will boost intelligence.

Apparently, analyses of the relationship between WAIS-III IQ and educational attainment have not yet been published. However, the relevant research has been conducted on the precursor to the current edition, the WAIS-R. A strong relationship between WAIS-R IQ and education is, in fact, exactly what Matarazzo and Herman (1984b) found when they analyzed the total years of schooling against IQs for the 1,880 individuals used in the standardization sample. For the 500 subjects 25 to 44 years of age, the correlation between years of school completed and Full Scale IQ was .63, whereas for the 730 subjects 45 to 64 years of age, the correlation was .62. For all 1,880 subjects, WAIS-R IQs were strongly linked to years of education completed (Table 4.4).

TABLE 4.4   Mean IQs by Years of Education for the WAIS-R Standardization Subjects

Years of Education	VIQ	PIQ	FSIQ
0–8	86.5	89.2	86.8
9–11	96.1	97.8	96.4
12	100.1	100.2	100.1
13–15	107.7	105.7	107.4
16+	115.7	111.2	115.3

Source: Based on data from J. D. Matarazzo, and D. O. Herman (1984), "Relationship of Education and IQ in the WAIS-R Standardization Sample," *Journal of Consulting and Clinical Psychology, 52,* 631–634.

IQ and Occupational Attainment

Wechsler IQ and occupational attainment also are broadly linked. In general, skilled and professional occupations ought to require higher levels of intelligence than unskilled or entry-level occupations (although there will certainly be individual exceptions). Relevant research with the WAIS-III has not been published, but extensive analyses are available for the prior version of this test. Reynolds and colleagues (1987) examined WAIS-R IQ in relation to occupational data for standardization subjects 20 to 54 years of age. Younger subjects were excluded because the occupational data pertained to their parents, whereas older subjects were excluded because most were not in the labor force. The findings revealed a 25-point average IQ difference between the most skilled workers (professional and technical) and the least skilled workers (laborers). These results strongly support the validity of the IQ construct (Table 4.5).

The Meaning of Full Scale IQ

The Wechsler Adult Intelligence Scale—III is based on the premise that intelligence is a general attribute that reveals itself in many spheres of intellectual functioning. WAIS-III Full Scale IQ is thus a single summary score that expresses the combined subscores from a broad spectrum of mental abilities.

TABLE 4.5   Mean IQs by Occupational Group for the WAIS-R
Standardization Subjects

Occupational Groups (Typical Workers)	Mean Full Scale IQ
Professional and Technical (physicians, lawyers)	112.4
Managers and Administrators (sales workers, supervisors)	103.6
Skilled Workers (craftsmen, foremen)	100.7
Semiskilled Workers (service, farmers)	92.3
Unskilled Workers (laborers, farm workers)	87.1

Source: Based on data from C. R. Reynolds, R. Chastain, A. Kaufman, and J. McLean (1987), "Demographic Characteristics and IQ among Adults: Analysis of the WAIS-R Standardization Sample as a Function of the Stratification Variables," *Journal of School Psychology, 25,* 323–342.

Wechsler did not have a well-developed theory of intelligence and he refused to regard it unitarily. In fact, he thought of intelligence as a whole array of abilities that included such personality factors as persistence and drive. Beyond this broad rationale he had no rigorous theory behind his tests. Instead, he preferred to take the practical approach of sampling abilities that he thought to be important, and which psychometricians generally regarded as reflecting "intelligence."

Wechsler's views inevitably reflected the culture in which he was reared. For this reason, WAIS-III Full Scale IQ is first and foremost an imperfect index of ability to succeed at tasks valued by Western society and culture. Of course, this interpretation of global IQ has a number of qualifications and limitations, discussed below. Nonetheless, it is important to stress that Full Scale IQ is useful because it is an index of the ability to handle important intellectual demands made by Western society and culture.

The attainment of a particular Full Scale IQ therefore can be viewed as improving the odds that a person can manage the intellectual prerequisites of various occupations and endeavors. Table 4.6 presents an idealized chart that relates IQ to social, educational, and occupational attainment. This chart is partly based on published Wechsler test research (Kaufman, 1990; Matarazzo, 1972) and partly based on the author's experience examining test scores for a large variety of persons from many professions.

The scores in Table 4.6 are averages only, and there will be considerable spread above and below these points for the specific groups. Remember, too, that a particular IQ is a "soft" prerequisite, and not a sufficient condition for the attainment of a specific educational or occupational goal. That is, an IQ of 125 does not guarantee that one can obtain a Ph.D.; it only signifies that one of several prerequisites has been amply met. In addition, note that these data are descriptive, not prescriptive. There is nothing inherent in this information to justify excluding a person with an IQ of 97 from college admission. On the other hand, what the information does illustrate is that such a college freshman will function at a distinct disadvantage compared to classmates, will find the corresponding educational demands to be notably taxing, and will have a significantly increased risk of failing to graduate.

Of course, IQs never should be used rigidly as part of any decision-making or advice-giving process. Many persons with unremarkable IQs accomplish quite remarkable things in life. I know one recent college graduate who is highly successful as a physical education instructor in a small rural town. When tested because of borderline grades in her junior year at college, her Full Scale IQ was 91. This kind of outcome highlights the need to prognosticate with probabilities, not certainties.

Full Scale IQ and the Band of Error

The concept of band of error also compels examiners to soften their predictions and acknowledge the uncertainty inherent in comparing any single individual to a descriptive scheme such as Table 4.6. Even though the WAIS-III possesses general-

TABLE 4.6   IQ Levels and Typical Social, Educational, and Occupational Attainments

IQ	Criteria
125–130	Mean of persons receiving medical, doctorate, and law degrees; mean for technical degrees such as chemistry and engineering
115–120	Mean of college graduates; mean for professional positions such as teachers, managers, and policemen
105–110	Mean of high school graduates; 50:50 chance of graduating from college
100	Average for the general population; about half of all persons score in the 90 to 109 range
90–95	Mean of persons from inner city, low income, and rural settings
85–90	Mean of unskilled laborers and persons employed for simple assembly line work
75–80	About 50:50 chance of reaching high school; need special education services; difficulty coping with modern technological society
65–70	Mild mental retardation likely; may achieve social and vocational adequacy with special training and supervision
55–60	Mild mental retardation definite; partial independence in living arrangements; may achieve fourth grade academic level
45–50	Moderate mental retardation likely; function well in a sheltered workshop; need supervised housing
35–40	Severe mental retardation likely; little or no communication skills; sensory and motor impairments; trainable in basic health habits
Below 25	Profound mental retardation likely; minimal functioning and incapable of self-maintenance; need constant nursing care and supervision

Source: Reprinted with permission from R. J. Gregory (1994a), "Classification of Intelligence." Reprinted with permission of Macmillan Library Reference USA, a Simon & Schuster Macmillan Company, from R. J. Sternberg, Ed. in Chief: ENCYCLOPEDIA OF HUMAN INTELLIGENCE, Vol. 1, pp. 260–266. Copyright © 1994 by Macmillan Publishing Company.

ly high reliability, it still has a standard error of measurement of approximately 2.0 to 2.5 points for Full Scale IQ, depending on the age group (Tulsky, Zhu, & Ledbetter, 1997). Thus, a person's true IQ may be several points above or below the measured IQ. The best a psychometrician can do is state the odds that the true IQ will be included within some range above and below the obtained score. Averaging across all the age ranges, a person's true IQ will be within ±5 points of his/her measured IQ more than 95 percent of the time. To stress that IQs are not perfectly reliable, many examiners bound the obtained score by a 5-point band of error. An obtained Full Scale IQ of 91 would be reported as 91 ± 5, which means that the true IQ is found between 86 and 96 (with 95 percent likelihood).

One final point about the utility of Full Scale IQ needs to be mentioned. Global IQ is generally more meaningful for low scores than for high scores. To the degree that the Full Scale IQ drops below 100, intelligence plays a more and more important role in determining behavioral adequacy, vocational adjustment, and academic achievement. For example, individuals with IQs of 50 are seriously handicapped in their capacity to meet the educational and occupational demands of our society, no matter how much drive and persistence they possess. In contrast, at the higher levels of IQ, nonintellectual factors such as motivation, persistence, and emotional stability will play important, even decisive, roles in determining achievement. A person with an IQ of 150 could be a highly accomplished genius, or an occupational sloth who seeks out only menial jobs. An example of the latter is William James Sidis, a brilliant child prodigy who was admitted to Harvard College at the age of 11, but who later attempted to lead a solitary, unassuming existence, drifting from one poorly paid job to another (Montour, 1977).

Profile Interpretation with the WAIS-III

Up to this point, this text has emphasized that the intelligence construct, as embodied in WAIS-III Full Scale IQ, is useful in understanding an individual's capacity to function in modern societies, especially with regard to academically related pursuits. We turn now to a more specific explanation of how the test is used for this goal. In particular, the WAIS-III practitioner needs a strategy for profile interpretation—making sense of the component IQs, Index scores, and subscale scores.

The WAIS-III provides a large number of scores useful for interpretation: three IQ scores, four Index scores, and up to fourteen subtest scores. In profile interpretation, the practitioner analyzes the level, shape, and scatter of a test profile in relation to established interpretive guidelines. The objective is to determine the distinctive cognitive capabilities of the individual. The emphasis in profile interpretation is one of personalization (Gregory, 1994b): What do these unique scores tell us about the cognitive functioning of this particular person?

Profile interpretation is used to *generate* hypotheses, not necessarily to confirm them. Whether a hypothesis can be confirmed will depend upon the availability of other information: "The most appropriate use of profile analyses is the generation of hypotheses that are, in turn, either corroborated or refuted by other evaluation results, background information, direct behavioral observations, or additional evaluation" (Tulsky, Zhu, & Ledbetter, 1997, p. 205). Profile interpretation is a form of detective work, a clinical skill developed through experience and supervision.

A sensible strategy in profile interpretation is to proceed from the global to the specific. In general, the examiner first interprets Full Scale IQ and then proceeds to a discussion of major component scores such as Verbal IQ, Performance IQ, and the four Index scores. Finally, for some examinees a detailed analysis of subtest scores might be appropriate.

Competent profile interpretation requires substantial training and abundant clinical skill. A basic orientation to the topic is provided here. For more detail the reader should consult Kaufman (1990), who devotes three lengthy chapters to the topic.

Full Scale IQ

The logical starting point for profile interpretation is the Full Scale IQ. This is the overall summary score that estimates an examinee's general level of intellectual functioning. Full Scale IQ is an aggregate score based on both VIQ and PIQ. It is usually considered to be the best representative of g, or global intellectual ability. Reporting the Full Scale IQ is a four-step procedure:

1. Listing the score
2. Reporting the band of error
3. Providing the percentile rank
4. Describing the intellectual category

Listing the score is very straightforward (e.g., "On the WAIS-III, Mr. Jones obtained a Full Scale IQ of 107..."), but the other elements of reporting the IQ require clarification.

Practitioners should always report a band of error in conjunction with listing the IQ. Bracketing the Full Scale IQ with a band of error is essential to convey that IQ is a range and not a fixed number. The usual band of error is ±5 IQ points, which provides a 95-percent confidence interval (or greater) for the WAIS-III. Using a band of error indicates that the measurement of intelligence is empirically based but nonetheless fallible and inexact. The wording might resemble any of the following:

- On the WAIS-III, Mr. Jones obtained a Full Scale IQ of 107 ±5 points. Thus, there is a 95-percent likelihood that his true IQ is in the range of 102 to 112.
- Mr. Jones's Full Scale IQ is in the range of 102 to 112 (95-percent likelihood) with a best estimate of 107.
- On the WAIS-III, Mr. Jones obtained a Full Scale IQ of 107, which is accurate to ±5 points (95-percent confidence).

The last example may be preferable because of the direct acknowledgment that IQ is only an estimate and not a perfect measurement.

The percentile rank expresses the percentage of persons in the standardization sample who scored below the obtained score of the examinee. The percentile rank is easy to compute and intuitively appealing to laypersons and professionals alike. For many persons, knowledge of the percentile rank conveys information that is more useful than the IQ score. For example, everyone knows that a Full Scale IQ of 120 is well above average, but just how special is it? In an age when IQs of 160, 180, and 200 are routinely bandied about in the popular media, a score of "merely" 120 appears pedestrian. The lay public does not know that IQs above 150 are astonishingly rare—at least as measured by the WAIS-III and similar individual tests of intelligence. Thus, an examinee might feel disappointed upon hearing that his or her IQ is "only" 120. Here is an instance when reporting the percentile rank will prove beneficial, as this information helps place the score in perspective. In fact, an IQ of 120 corresponds to a percentile rank of 91; that is, it exceeds 91 percent of the general population. This is indeed a special score indicating a high level of intellectual ability.

The *Technical Manual* provides a partial table for converting IQ scores to percentile ranks. This table is based on theoretical values for a normal distribution, which are very close to the actual values from the standardization sample. An expanded version of this information appears in Table 4.7.

In addition to reporting the IQ score and the corresponding percentile rank, another way to convey global test results is by attaching a qualitative label to the findings. Are the results broadly within the "average" range? If not, should they be described as exceptional in some way, for example, "superior" if well above average, or "borderline" if well below average? A qualitative and diagnostic label provides a shorthand way to convey essential information.

Unfortunately, the classification practices recommended in the *WAIS-III Administration and Scoring Manual* leave something to be desired. One problem is that low IQs receive pejorative and potentially misleading labels. Here is the correspondence between IQs and qualitative, diagnostic labels recommended for the WAIS-III (Tulsky, Zhu, & Ledbetter, 1997):

130 and above	Very Superior
120–129	Superior
110–119	High Average
90–109	Average
80–89	Low Average
70–79	Borderline
69 and below	Extremely Low

This descriptive schema suffers from several shortcomings, especially at the extremes (Gregory, 1994a). At first glance, the "Superior" and "Very Superior" designations for those with IQs of 120+ and 130+ seem harmless enough. However, might not these labels contribute to the common bias that IQ is somehow a measure of personal worth? The problem is that the examinee (and perhaps the examiner as well!) might conclude that a score of 133 designates a superior *person*. Of course, no label can be completely neutral and value-free. Yet it is certainly possible to avoid the smugness of "Superior" and "Very Superior."

The classification for IQ scores below Low Average also presents a problem. The designation of "Borderline" for IQs of 70 to 79 is not only offensive; it is also potentially misleading. After all, borderline personality disorder is

TABLE 4.7   WAIS-III IQs and Corresponding Percentile Ranks

IQ	Percentile Rank	IQ	Percentile Rank
135+	99	99	48
131–134	98	98	45
128–130	97	97	43
126–127	96	96	40
125	95	95	37
123–124	94	94	35
122	93	93	32
121	92	92	30
120	91	91	28
119	90	90	26
118	89	89	24
117	87	88	22
116	86	87	20
115	84	86	18
114	83	85	16
113	81	84	15
112	79	83	13
111	77	82	12
110	74	81	10
109	72	80	9
108	71	79	8
107	68	78	7
106	66	76–77	6
105	63	75	5
104	60	73–74	4
103	58	70–72	3
102	56	66–69	2
101	53	65	1
100	50	<65	<1

now a prominent diagnosis within the *Diagnostic and Statistical Manual of Mental Disorders, Fourth Edition (DSM-IV)* used for psychiatric nomenclature (American Psychiatric Association, 1994). A naive reader might confuse a classification of "borderline" intelligence with the diagnosis of borderline personality disorder.

On the plus side, the label of "Extremely Low" for IQs below 70 is an improvement over the label of "Mental Retardation" used with the WAIS-R. Modern conceptions of mental retardation emphasize the need to evaluate both intelligence *and* adaptive skills in making a diagnosis. By providing a label of mental retardation based on IQ only, the WAIS-R classification schema played into the hands of those who would prefer to make the diagnosis based on a simple test result. The WAIS-III avoids this mistake.

So what is the WAIS-III examiner to do? I recommend that practitioners use the classification system developed by Kaufman and Kaufman (1983). Although their schema was devised for a different test (the Kaufman Assessment Battery for Children), the relevance to global score ranges for all major intelligence tests is immediate and obvious. The Kaufman system for designating intelligence with qualitative labels is as follows:

130 and above	Upper Extreme
120–129	Well Above Average
110–119	Above Average
90–109	Average
80–89	Below Average
70–79	Well Below Average
69 and below	Lower Extreme

Here is a specific example of how the various components of reporting the Full Scale IQ might be combined into a narrative statement:

- On the WAIS-III, Mr. Jones obtained a Full Scale IQ of 121, which is accurate within ±5 points. This score exceeds 92 percent of the general population and corresponds to a designation of Well Above Average.

The final task in the interpretation of IQ is to personalize the results in relation to the referral question(s) that prompted the assessment in the first place. What does the score *mean* in the life of the examinee? The starting point for this interpretation must be knowledge of the relationship between IQ and social, educational, and occupational outcomes. This kind of information can be gleaned from many sources, including published studies on the significance of IQ (e.g., Table 4.6). However, the practitioner must avoid simplistic and confident assertions. Test interpretations are more truthful when they are conditional and probabilistic. After all, tests are imperfect, and factors other than IQ may influence individual attainment.

Perhaps a few examples will clarify this approach. We consider first the case of Brian T., a 24-year-old male who completed high school in a special program for slow learners (Gregory, 1987). He was referred by a local rehabilitation office for basic intellectual and psychological assessment to determine his eligibility for services. This individual made a good first impression but obtained a WAIS-R IQ of only 75, which placed him at the 5th percentile with a Well Below Average classification of intelligence. What should the examiner say to the rehabilitation office with regards to prospects for this client? The following brief narrative illustrates how test results for this client might be described:

> On the WAIS-R, a well-validated test of general intelligence, Brian obtained a Full Scale IQ of 75, placing him at the 5th percentile for the general population. This corresponds to a Well Below Average classification of intelligence. Regarding his intellectual ability, Brian leaves a much stronger impression in one-to-one social conversation than is portrayed by objective testing. He also has a much higher self-assessment of his skill level than is realistic in light of his test scores. He is clearly a slow learner who takes longer to master job skills than others might expect. The test results indicate the need for continued emphasis upon simple and repetitive job skills such as might be encountered in assembly line work or fast-food preparation. Although Brian believes he is ready for higher levels of employment, he is likely to experience great frustration in dealing with vocational situations that require novel problem solving, abstract reasoning, or academic facility.

A second example pertains to Jack C., a college student referred for assessment because of mediocre grades. This individual was clearly motivated to do well in school but was receiving mostly Cs and a few Ds in a geology curriculum. On the WAIS-III he obtained a Full Scale IQ of 97, which corresponds to the 43rd percentile and an Average designation. The brief narrative that follows indicates, in part, how his test results might be reported:

> Jack was referred by Student Services because he is struggling in his current major of geology, receiving mostly Cs and a few Ds. The purpose of the testing is to help determine the reasons for his academic difficulties. On the WAIS-III he obtained a Full Scale IQ of 97, which is just slightly below the national average of 100 but still within the Average range of intelligence. However, college students typically average about 115 on individual intelligence tests, which suggests that Jack is at a comparative disadvantage within an academic setting. Success in his chosen major is certainly possible, but it will require strong motivation and earnest effort, coupled with such practical prescriptions as a reduced courseload and tutoring for his more difficult classes.

As these examples illustrate, the proper interpretation of global IQ depends on the insight, experience, and wisdom of the practitioner. Guidelines for interpretation can be found in this book and other sources. However, simplistic formulas will not suffice. In the end, making sense of IQ hinges upon the experience and training of the examiner.

Discrepancy Analysis: Verbal IQ and Performance IQ

After analyzing and reporting the Full Scale IQ, the examiner turns to the Verbal IQ and the Performance IQ. In interpretating these scores, it will prove helpful if the examiner understands their history and origin. For this reason, we begin with a few historical notes.

The WAIS-III (1997) is a fourth generation test with a lineage that can be traced back through the WAIS-R (1981), the WAIS (1955), and the Wechsler-Bellevue Scales (1939). In one sense the WAIS-III is a break from tradition because it incorporates three new subtests and permits a four-factor solution for the partitioning of intelligence (discussed below). Yet what stands out with the most recent revision is its continuity with previous editions. In particular, the WAIS-III maintains the familiar dichotomy of Verbal IQ and Performance IQ, a constant feature of the test since its inception in the 1930s (Wechsler, 1932).

In constructing the Wechsler-Bellevue, Wechsler (1939) used a purely rational "armchair" strategy when assigning the various subtests to a Verbal IQ scale or a Performance IQ scale. His justification was that certain subtests seemed to "hang together" in that they required mainly verbal abilities, whereas a second group of subtests required perceptual-manipulative skills. It is a tribute to the genius of Wechsler that his original dichotomy of Verbal IQ and Performance IQ remains a useful method of analysis even after six decades of practice and three revisions of the test. Verbal IQ and Performance IQ are not arbitrary designations. The six verbal subtests do, indeed, stand apart from the five performance subtests. The VIQ score and the PIQ score each emphasizes a different aspect of general intelligence.

The VIQ score on the WAIS-III can be considered a measure of acquired knowledge, verbal reasoning, and facility with verbal materials. All of the items found on the subtests in this scale are presented verbally, and the examinee must verbalize his or her response. In a very fundamental way, facility with verbal skills is at the heart of the Verbal IQ.

The PIQ score on the WAIS-III can be considered a measure of fluid reasoning, visual-spatial processing, attentiveness to detail, and visual-motor integration. Whereas the VIQ subtests require the application of prior knowledge to verbal stimuli, the PIQ subtests require examinees to respond efficiently to nonverbal stimuli. In a very fundamental way, facility with perceptual-analytical skills is at the heart of the Performance IQ.

The reader is cautioned, however, that the validity and success of the Verbal-Performance dichotomy does not mean that each component should be individually interpreted for every examinee. The practitioner needs to provide a separate discussion of Verbal IQ and Performance IQ only when they differ meaningfully from one another. A *meaningful* difference is one that is both statistically significant and relatively infrequent in the standardization sample. Information on the statistical significance of VIQ-PIQ differences is found in table B.1 in the *WAIS-III Administration and Scoring Manual* (Wechsler, 1997, p. 205). For most age groups a difference of 8–9 points is significant at $p < .05$. But a statistically significant difference can be quite common and therefore not necessarily meaningful. To be meaningful, a difference also needs to be distinctive, that is to say, relatively infrequent. Information on the frequencies (cumulative percentages) of VIQ-PIQ differences is found in table B.2 of the same manual (p. 206). This table reveals that even seemingly "large" and statistically significant differences of 15 points or more are really quite common—found in nearly 18 percent of the standardization sample. Only when a VIQ-PIQ difference exceeds 25 points does it become truly infrequent—found in only 2 percent of the standardization sample.[2] These findings mandate a conservative approach to profile analysis, as outlined below.

A cautious approach is warranted because seemingly "large" differences between VIQ and PIQ are really very common. For example, differences of 10 points or greater are practically normative—these are found in 37 percent of the standardization sample! Even a difference of twice that magnitude—20 points or greater—is seen in about 7 percent of these examinees. It is the experience of many psychometricians that moderate differences of this magnitude are often overpathologized. The following conservative guidelines are recommended.

When the difference is less than 10 points, the practitioner should focus on the interpretation of the Full Scale IQ and leave it at that—separate discussion of Verbal IQ and Performance IQ will add little to the explanation of the test findings. However, when the difference is 10 points or more, it becomes increasingly important for the examiner to discuss relative cognitive strengths and weaknesses. Differences of 10 to 20 points might be described as moderate, whereas differences of more than 20 points might be designated as extreme.

A moderate difference of 10 to 20 points should be viewed as useful information, but not necessarily as evidence of an underlying problem (e.g., cognitive impairment). For example, a Full Scale IQ of 120 might be based on a Verbal IQ of 130 and Performance IQ of 110. The most important thing to emphasize in this case is that the Full Scale IQ will be misleading. In this example the global score hides a major strong point and a relative weakness. A client with these test scores would likely fare better studying English (emphasis on verbal abilities) than pursuing architecture (emphasis on perceptual-analytical abilities). In an individualized way that answers important referral questions, the test interpreter needs to discuss the implications of the relatively stronger Verbal IQ and the relatively weaker Performance IQ.

If the direction of the disparity is reversed, the practical task of the clinician remains the same: Identify the implications of the relative strength/weakness portrayed in the higher PIQ and lower VIQ. For example, an individual with the same Full Scale IQ of 120 but the reversed pattern of Verbal IQ 110 and Performance IQ of 130 probably would find architecture an easier discipline than English. In sum, moderate Verbal-Performance IQ discrepancies (in the range of 10 to 20 points) clearly signal relative intellectual strengths and weaknesses that the clinician should attempt to explain and interpret.

When the VIQ-PIQ difference exceeds 20 points or so, a hypothesis of cognitive impairment becomes increasingly viable. Although a moderate VIQ-PIQ difference of 10 to 20 points raises a suspicion of underlying cognitive impairment, standing on its own a disparity of this magnitude does not provide strong evidence of such a problem. However, to the extent that VIQ-PIQ discrepancies exceed 20

[2] A more refined breakdown (by overall IQ level) for frequencies of VIQ-PIQ differences is also found in appendix D of the *Technical Manual* (Tulsky, Zhu, & Ledbetter, 1997, pp. 299–309).

points, there is an increasing suspicion of an underlying pathological process. For differences of 25 points or greater, the suspicion of impairment is very strong: these are found in only about 2 percent of the normative sample. The most serious concern is that a large discrepancy in either direction may signify a neuropsychological impairment or perhaps even a neurological disorder. Of course, the WAIS-III should never be used in isolation for reaching this kind of conclusion. The next chapter outlines additional approaches for helping to confirm or disconfirm a suspicion of cognitive impairment.

In addition to the possibility that the client exhibits cognitive impairment, many other hypotheses are feasible in explaining moderate and extreme VIQ-PIQ score discrepancies. For example, "action-oriented" people who have difficulty with impulse control, reflection, and concentration may yield discrepantly higher Performance IQs (Allison, Blatt, & Zimet, 1988). Conversely, individuals who are experiencing a serious depression often yield distinctly higher Verbal IQs on the WAIS-III. The reason is straightforward: Severe depression is accompanied by motor slowing that reduces scores on the timed performance scales. In fact, even mild depression yields a reduction on these portions of the Wechsler scales (Wolff & Gregory, 1992). In these cases the VIQ-PIQ discrepancy is probably temporary and likely will abate once the depression has been treated.

The relationship between Verbal IQ and Performance IQ also reflects social class, educational attainment, and ethnic background. Individuals from higher social classes and those with advanced education often show a pattern of VIQ > PIQ, whereas the opposite is likely to be true of unskilled persons and those with less education. Native American examinees frequently produce WAIS-R profiles with PIQ substantially higher than VIQ. The same is likely to be true of the WAIS-III (although data are not yet available). Finally, a study by Levinson (1958) found that Jewish individuals are likely to show a very strong Verbal greater than Performance pattern, although the reasons for this are unclear. The research involved a group of sixty-four traditional Jewish American male adults in their early 20s. The average results were Verbal IQ 126, Performance IQ 105, and Full Scale IQ 118.

The following example illustrates the way a very large difference between VIQ and PIQ might be interpreted. The client was a 36-year-old postal worker with no prior history of neurological problems.

> On the WAIS-III, Joan S. obtained a Full Scale IQ of 108, a score that exceeds about 71 percent of the general population and corresponds to the Average range of intelligence. However, there was a large difference between her VIQ of 121 and her PIQ of 95. The VIQ-PIQ difference of 26 points is statistically significant at well below the $p < .05$ level, and is found in less than 2 percent of the standardization sample. Because the difference is both statistically significant and rare, it is reasonable to hypothesize that Joan S. exhibits an impairment of nonverbal intellectual functioning in comparison to her verbal intellectual functioning. Further testing is recommended to determine the possible cause(s) of this impairment.

Index Scores on the WAIS-III

As noted above, the WAIS-III also embodies an alternative model of intelligence in which four Index scores are provided. The Index scores are supplementary to the traditional clinical approach (Verbal IQ and Performance IQ) discussed above. The advantage of the Index scores is that they were derived by factor analytic methods and therefore furnish a breakdown of intelligence that is "purer" and more refined. All of the Index scores are normed to the familiar mean of 100 and standard deviation of 15.

The Verbal Comprehension Index (VCI) is composed of Vocabulary, Similarities, and Information. The VCI score is a measure of verbal reasoning and verbal acquired knowledge. This is similar to the Verbal IQ score but does not include the subtests sensitive to attention (i.e., Digit Span and Arithmetic). Thus, VCI is a more direct measure of verbal comprehension than is VIQ.

The Perceptual Organization Index (POI) is composed of Picture Completion, Block Design, and Matrix Reasoning. The POI score is a measure of fluid reasoning, visual-spatial problem solving, and attentiveness to detail. This is similar to the Performance IQ score but is less dependent on speed. Thus, POI is a more refined measure of fluid reasoning and visual-spatial problem solving than is PIQ.

The Working Memory Index (WMI) is composed of Arithmetic, Digit Span, and Letter-Number Sequencing. What these subtests have in common is that the examinee must attend to verbally presented information, process the information in memory, and formulate a response. A relatively low score on WMI may signify that the examinee has an attentional or memory difficulty, particularly with verbally presented materials. Additional reasons for a relatively low score might include a high level of anxiety, a strong degree of distractibility, poor number facility, or difficulties with sequencing (Kaufman, 1990, 1994).

The Processing Speed Index (PSI) is composed of Digit Symbol-Coding and Symbol Search. The PSI score is a measure of the examinee's ability to process visual information quickly. The *Technical Manual* notes: "Comparisons between the PSI and POI scores can reveal possible effects of time demands on visual-spatial reasoning and problem solving" (Tulsky, Zhu, & Ledbetter, 1997, p. 187). The PSI is also highly sensitive to a wide variety of neurological and neuropsychological conditions (see below).

Once the examiner has administered the WAIS-III and obtained the Index scores, how is this information to be used? If all four scores are similar, there is little to be gained from an analysis of the Index scores, which merely convey the same thing as captured in the Full Scale IQ. But discrepancies between selected pairs of Index scores may provide valuable clues about intellectual functioning. The *Technical Manual* (pp. 207–209) suggests the following comparisons:

1. The VCI-POI difference provides a comparison similar to the VIQ-PIQ difference, but the former is "purer" in the sense that it is less influenced by attention, working memory, or processing speed. Thus, the VCI-POI difference indicates relative strength or weakness in verbal abilities versus perceptual-spatial skills.

This difference may have implications for academic or vocational functioning, as noted above.

2. The VCI-WMI difference furnishes a comparison of acquired knowledge and verbal reasoning skills versus the capacity to hold and process information in memory. An examinee who scores relatively high on VCI and relatively low on WMI might display memory weaknesses with regard to verbally presented materials. This discrepancy is pertinent to academic difficulties. In particular, individuals with this pattern are intellectually bright but they do not learn well in the traditional lecture format that prevails in most educational institutions.

3. The POI-PSI difference provides a comparison of visual-spatial and fluid reasoning skills versus the ability to process nonverbal information quickly. An examinee who scores relatively high on POI and relatively low on PSI might display sound reasoning skills with nonverbal materials but function poorly under time pressure. In academic settings, this discrepancy might indicate the need for testing accommodations with timed exams (e.g., additional time).

When is one Index score relatively higher than another? Regarding this question, once again we encounter the distinction between a statistically significant difference and a meaningful difference (i.e., one that also shows a low frequency of occurrence). A disparity in scores that is statistically significant at $p <$ .05 might occur with high frequency in the normative sample. It makes little sense to "interpret" cognitive patterns as if they were anomalous when they are found in large proportions of the population. In order for a difference to be meaningful, it should be both statistically significant and also occur with low frequency in the normative sample. Then there is something to talk about, something to analyze and interpret.

Tables B.1 and B.2 of the *Administration and Scoring Manual* (Wechsler, 1997, pp. 205–207) furnish the relevant information on statistical significance and frequency of occurrence for differences between pairs of Index scores. Compared to the data for VIQ-PIQ differences discussed above, what these tables reveal is that score differences for pairs of Index scores need to be even larger to reach significance. The same is true for score differences needed to disclose a low frequency of occurrence. The reason is simple: The Index scores are based on two or three subtests, whereas the IQ scores are based on five or six subtests. Aggregate scales are usually more reliable when they are based on a larger number of subtests.

Whereas a contrast of IQ scores permits only one comparison (Verbal IQ versus Performance IQ), the four Index scores allow for six comparisons (VCI-POI, VCI-WMI, POI-PSI, VCI-PSI, POI-WMI, WMI-PSI). The criteria for a statistically significant difference and an infrequent difference differ slightly from one comparison to another (and they also differ slightly by age group). Certainly the skilled practitioner will consult the tables in the manual when making comparisons between Index scores. Nonetheless, a few general guidelines are proposed here. Differences of less than 15 points between pairs of Index scores are probably unremarkable and do not deserve further attention. Differences of 15 to 25 points are moderate and provide useful information about cognitive strengths and weaknesses. These moderate differences *may* also signify cognitive impairment. Extreme differences of more than 25 points raise a suspicion of cognitive impairment.

The following example illustrates how a large difference between Index scores might be interpreted. In this case the disparity was VCI > WMI, one of the more important comparisons between pairs of Index scores. The client was a 23-year-old college student referred because of academic difficulties:

> David F. obtained a score of 121 on the Verbal Comprehension Index, which indicates that his verbal comprehension skills are well above average. In contrast, he obtained a score of 94 on the Working Memory Index, a measure of working memory. Although this score is in the average range, it is well below his level of functioning in verbal comprehension. The 27-point discrepancy is both statistically significant ($p < .05$) and uncommon in normally functioning persons (found in less than 4 percent of the normative sample).
>
> A reasonable hypothesis for David is that memory skills for verbally presented materials are significantly weak in comparison to verbal comprehension skills. This disparity indicates that he would benefit from tape recording his course lectures for playback at a later time. He has sufficient ability to comprehend the course content, but he may experience a problem when committing verbally presented materials to memory.

Profile Analysis with Individual Subtests

In addition to interpreting the IQ scores and Index scores, it may be useful for the practitioner to evaluate discrepantly high or low scores obtained on individual subtests. Simple pattern analysis can be used to identify relatively strong or weak performances on the WAIS-III components. Inferences about discrepant subtests might be helpful in understanding the cognitive functioning of the examinee. For example, an examinee whose overall WAIS-III performance was average but who obtained an unusually low score on Similarities might have a serious problem with concrete thinking. But when is a Similarities score "unusually low"? This section recommends a simple and objective approach for making this kind of determination.

Most practitioners know that each of the subtests has an average score of 10 and a standard deviation of 3 within a specified age group. What few testers fully appreciate, however, is the generally modest reliability of the individual subtests. As discussed earlier in the section on reliability, only two subtests—Vocabulary and Information—reveal consistently strong reliability values in split-half and test-retest studies. For these subtests the practitioner can be confident that the specific underlying abilities have been measured with high accuracy. At the other extreme are Picture Arrangement and Symbol Search, with marginal subtest reliabilities that range from .67 to .77 . As noted, these subtest reliabilities are as good as can be expected, given that the WAIS-III aims to be a short and practical instrument. However, the generally modest level of subtest reliabilities carries with it an important and often overlooked implication, namely, *WAIS-III subtest scores and patterns should be interpreted with caution and conservatism.*

The most rigorous approach to identifying relative strengths and weaknesses on subtest scores is to consult table B.3 in the *Administration and Scoring Manual* (Wechsler, 1997, pp. 208–209). This table gives cutoff values at the .15 and .05 level for comparing each subtest score with the average of other groups of subtests. It also provides information on the differences obtained by various percentages (1%, 2%, 5%, 10%, and 25%) of the normative sample. Procedures for identifying strengths and weaknesses on the subtests are described in the *Administration and Scoring Manual* (pp. 60–61) and in the *Technical Manual* (p. 207). These procedures are technically and statistically correct, but they are somewhat elaborate and also slightly ambiguous. For example, the examiner is given no advice on whether individual subtests should be compared to their respective subgroup (e.g., Verbal subtests) or compared to all subtests administered.

I advocate a simple and unambiguous strategy for determining significant fluctuations within WAIS-III subtest scale scores. The system was first described by Kaufman (1990). It has the virtues of being simple and of reducing the examiner's dependency on the details of table B.3. The steps to follow in determining significant strengths and weaknesses in the scaled-score profile are as follows:

1. Examine the difference between Verbal IQ and Performance IQ to determine whether their respective subtests need to be examined separately or in combination with one another. If the difference between Verbal IQ and Performance IQ is less than 10 points, compare all subtests together (2a). If the difference is 10 or more points, interpret these components separately (2b).

2a. If the VIQ-PIQ discrepancy is less than 10 points, the examiner should compare each of the subtest scores to the mean of all the subtests (computed from the eleven to fourteen subtest scores). The mean is rounded to the nearest whole number.

2b. If the VIQ-PIQ discrepancy is 10 points or more, the examiner should compare each Verbal scaled score to the mean of the Verbal subtests (computed from the six or seven verbal subtest scores) and each Performance scaled score to the mean of the Performance subtests (computed from the five, six, or seven performance subtest scores). In each case the means are rounded to the nearest whole number.

3. The rule of ± 3 is then used to identify significant strengths and weaknesses. Subtests with scaled scores 3 or more points above the relevant mean indicate significant strengths and can be labeled with an "S", whereas subtests with scaled scores 3 or more points below the relevant mean indicate significant weaknesses and can be labeled "W". All other subtests are indeterminate; that is, they are interpreted as neither strengths nor weaknesses.

Table 4.8 provides two examples of the procedure. In the first example the examinee obtained a Verbal IQ and a Performance IQ that differ by 27 points and therefore the Verbal and Performance subtests are considered separately. In the sec-

TABLE 4.8   Two Examples of the Rule of ±3 for Subtest Strengths and Weaknesses

Verbal IQ = 121, Performance IQ = 94, Full Scale IQ = 109[a]

Verbal Subtests	Scaled Score	Performance Subtests	Scaled Score
Vocabulary	15	Picture Completion	11
Similarities	13	Digit Symbol-Coding	9
Arithmetic	12	Block Design	8
Digit Span	9—W	Matrix Reasoning	5—W
Information	16—S	Picture Arrangement	13—S
Comprehension	15	Symbol Search	12
Letter-Number	13		
M = 13.29 (rounded to 13)		M = 9.67(rounded to 10)	

Verbal IQ = 102, Performance IQ = 100, Full Scale IQ = 102[b]

Verbal Subtests	Scaled Score	Performance Subtests	Scaled Score
Vocabulary	13—S	Picture Completion	11
Similarities	10	Digit Symbol-Coding	9
Arithmetic	10	Block Design	8
Digit Span	7—W	Matrix Reasoning	10
Information	12	Picture Arrangement	13—S
Comprehension	11	Symbol Search	12
Letter-Number	10		
M = 10.46 (rounded to 10)			

[a] In the first example the VIQ-PIQ difference is 27 points and therefore Verbal and Performance subtests are considered separately.

[b] In the second example the VIQ-PIQ difference is 2 points and therefore each subtest is compared to the mean of all thirteen subtests.

ond example the VIQ-PIQ discrepancy is minimal at 2 points and all subtests are therefore combined in the analysis.

Once the strengths and weaknesses are identified, the examiner should review the abilities measured by the subtests (listed in an earlier section of this chapter) to determine the associated talents or comparative deficits. Take note that the pattern of strengths and weaknesses is relative to the individual. It is conceivable that an examinee might show a weakness on a subtest and yet perform above average when compared to the general population. Conversely, some persons with mental retardation might show strengths on some subtests and yet still be well below average. In describing strengths and weaknesses, the examiner needs to integrate this information with the referral questions and discuss the functional implications.

Final Comment

Effective use of the WAIS-III requires more than the basic skills of test administration, scoring, and interpretation. In addition, practitioners should be familiar with the limitations of the test so that they can provide useful feedback to examinees. Furthermore, practitioners will need expertise pertaining to a variety of special circumstances, including the use (and potential misuse) of short forms, the effects of retesting, and the assessment of persons with possible neurological impairment. We pursue these and other distinctive WAIS-III topics in the next chapter.

5 The WAIS-III: Clinical Issues and Alternative Tests

In this chapter we continue coverage of the WAIS-III by reviewing special topics and concerns. Where appropriate, the WAIS-R receives passing mention as well. The focus is on the real-world implications of test results, especially when the findings indicate low intelligence or possible cognitive impairment. In addition, we survey circumstances that warrant extra caution in test interpretation. These situations include the use of short forms and the common practice of readministering the WAIS-III. The final purpose of this chapter is to present alternatives to the Wechsler tradition of adult intellectual assessment.

We begin by pursuing an issue that cuts across all of the topics listed above: What are the limitations of the WAIS-III? The WAIS-III is an outstanding instrument but it is only one sample of intellectual behavior. As such, the test exhibits certain limitations and manifests the potential for misuse. The same is true for its predecessor, the WAIS-R. The potential for abuse is especially true in the assessment of minority individuals—a topic highlighted below. The chapter begins on a cautionary note.

Limitations of the WAIS-R and the WAIS-III

The WAIS-III is a relatively new test as of this writing, so it is too soon to identify the subtle weaknesses that most instruments eventually reveal. Certainly the WAIS-III appears to be a significant improvement over the WAIS-R. Like its predecessor, the WAIS-III is a valuable source of information on the intellectual functioning of adults. Indeed, it is the cornerstone of the assessment battery for almost every referral question in which intellectual status is involved. In the hands of a competent examiner this test is often the single most important test that can be administered. Results for the WAIS-III form the nucleus of data from which constructive recommendations can be made.

In spite of their many strong points, both the WAIS-R and the WAIS-III possess significant limitations. This section outlines weaknesses peculiar to the WAIS-R and also discusses limitations common to both instruments. The WAIS-R suffers from significant psychometric weaknesses that have been corrected in the WAIS-III. For both instruments there are certain social contexts in which the tests should be used with caution. Finally, as with any tool, there is always the risk that either test can be applied for destructive purposes, whether through carelessness or design. This latter point is not so much a fault of the tests as it is a defect in human character. Nonetheless, in the eyes of the public the harmful consequences reside in the tests per se, so it is appropriate to treat these mixed issues as if they were of one fabric.

As a general overview to the sections that follow, it will be argued that the Wechsler tests do possess flaws and can be misused, but that these shortcomings are not debilitating and do not justify the abandonment of intelligence testing. Rather, examiners must understand the limitations of the instruments and must be sensitive to the potential for misuse. In the main, these problems can be overcome by the selection of appropriate supplementary measures and by the use of caution and conservatism when interpreting test results.

Problems inherent to the Wechsler adult scales fall into one of five categories. The first three are limited to the WAIS-R, whereas the last two are common to any test of intelligence, including the WAIS-R and the WAIS-III. The first WAIS-R problem pertains to certain technical peculiarities in the test data of the younger subjects in the standardization sample. The second WAIS-R weakness stems from the archaic practice of using a reference group of subjects 20 to 34 years of age to determine scaled scores for all adults. The narrow conception of intelligence on the WAIS-R and, in particular, its failure to measure reasoning with novel stimuli is the third weakness. These weaknesses have been amended on the WAIS-III.

We also consider two limitations inherent to any test of intelligence, including the WAIS-R and the WAIS-III. One consideration is the need for caution when testing minority subjects. The last concern is the possibility of harmful social and educational consequences.

Peculiar WAIS-R Norms for 16–17- and 18–19-Year-Olds

Kaufman (1983) has made the point that there are unexplainable and surprising results in the standardization data for the WAIS-R. To cite one example, the samples of 16- to 17- and 18- to 19-year-olds performed strikingly lower than the 20- to 24-year-old group. The 20- to 34-year-old subjects (N = 500) were used as the "benchmark" group for whom the averaged scale scores would equal 10 (and SD = 3). Scaled scores for all other age groups were computed in comparison to this large reference group.

The scaled scores for the 16- to 17- and 18- to 19-year-olds were surprisingly low, particularly for the Verbal IQ subtests. For example, the 16- to 17-year-olds obtained an averaged scaled score on Vocabulary of 7.8, while the 18- to 19-year-olds fared only slightly better at 8.1. These scores are substantially lower than the 9.5 observed for 20- to 24-year-olds and 10.4 found for 25- to 34-year-olds. The "jump" is large and discontinuous, which does not make psychometric sense. This becomes particularly evident when data from the WAIS are examined. Here there is a smooth progression of average scaled scores as progressively older subjects from the standardization sample are examined. The relevant data for the WAIS-III also reveal a smooth progression of scores across the age groups.[1]

A related problem is the absence of a difference in the overall performance of the two teenage samples on the WAIS-R. This is particularly puzzling in light of background information: Nearly 60 percent of the 18-to 19-year-olds had 12 or more years of schooling, compared to only 3 percent of the 16-to 17-year-olds. Yet, the sum of the eleven scaled scores was, on average, an insignificant half point higher for the older sample.

It is clear that something is wrong with one or more of the young standardization samples. Most likely, there was some unknown bias in the sampling of one or both of the teenage groups that caused the results to be distorted. The central implication for psychometricians is that the validity of WAIS-R IQ data for subjects under 20 is less well established than for the remaining age groups. Fortunately, this anomaly of subtest scores has been rectified on the WAIS-III.

Inappropriate Reference Group for Determining Scaled Scores on the WAIS-R

The WAIS-R continued the tradition of the WAIS by using a reference group 20 to 34 years of age to determine scaled scores for all adults. The problem with this practice is that subtest scaled scores have a fixed mean of 10 (SD = 3) *only* for the reference group, whereas for other age groups the parameters become inconsistent from subtest to subtest and from group to group.

Consider the pattern for Block Design, for which the average score peaks at age group 20–24 (M = 10.3, SD = 2.8) then shows a steady decline in mean and standard deviation right through the last age group of 70–74 (M = 6.4, SD = 2.2). In contrast, Vocabulary scaled scores rise steeply from ages 16–17 (M = 7.8) to 25–34 (M = 10.4) then slowly descend to 9.2 by ages 70–74. Digit Symbol shows the greatest age effect of all: The average score is close to 10.0 for the younger age groups under 35 but drops precipitously for older subjects. For ages 70–74 the average scaled score is a mere 4.9. As Kaufman (1983) noted, in view of the different growth curves for the separate abilities, it is not meaningful to examine profile fluctuations for a 17-year-old or a 50-year-old when their scaled scores are derived from a reference group ages 20–34. This is a grave problem that limits test interpretation, especially for older persons ages 70–74.

A partial solution to this shortcoming is to use the *age-corrected* scaled scores provided in appendix D (Scaled Score Equivalents of Raw Scores by Age Group) of the *WAIS-R Manual* (Wechsler, 1981). Certainly, these scaled scores should be used

---

[1] Because the WAIS-III subtest scores are age-corrected from the very beginning, the average for each age group is always 10. Nonetheless, it is possible to examine age trends by looking at the raw scores needed to obtain an average subtest score. These raw scores follow a smooth trend; that is, they do not have a discontinuous "jump" for subjects in the younger age groups.

for any intratest analyses involving subtest scatter. However, this is not a totally sat-isfactory solution. This procedure adds another eleven scores to the fourteen stan-dard scores (eleven subtests, three IQs), thereby increasing the likelihood of a cleri-cal error and rendering the test protocol unwieldy (Kaufman, 1983). Fortunately, the developers of the WAIS-III recognized the need to determine scaled scores sepa-rately for each age group. On the WAIS-III, subtest scores are age-corrected from the very beginning.

Narrow Conception of Intelligence on the WAIS-R

The WAIS-R embodies a heavy emphasis upon verbal abilities that pervades near-ly all the subtests. This emphasis is quite obvious in the case of Verbal IQ subtests such as Vocabulary, Comprehension, and Similarities, for which the verbally facile maintain a clear advantage. What is less clear is that this advantage extends to sev-eral of the Performance IQ subtests as well. For example, the examinee needs ade-quate verbal comprehension in order to decipher the underlying story in Picture Arrangement. Even such purely spatial tasks as Block Design can be successfully approached on a verbal level. Many practitioners have overheard examinees talk-ing out loud, saying things like "I need a half-red block with the red part in the upper left-hand corner here." Hence, even spatial tasks can be transformed to self-monitored verbal instructions.

Note also that the examinee must listen to lengthy verbal instructions before beginning Picture Arrangement, Block Design, and Digit Symbol. This offers no dif-ficulty to a high-functioning individual who "catches on" to the underlying task demands immediately. But for a person with low intellectual ability, his or her fail-ure to fully comprehend the verbal instructions might preclude effective testing on these performance items. In sum, the WAIS-R assesses a narrow slice of intellectual functioning that overemphasizes verbal skills at the expense of spatial thinking, pattern recognition, figure completion, and the like. In contrast, the WAIS-III is less guilty of overlooking the assessment of nonverbal skills—the addition of Matrix Reasoning helps redress the imbalance.

The narrow focus of the WAIS-R can be further highlighted by reference to Gardner's theory of multiple intelligence. Gardner (1983, 1993) has identified seven forms of intelligence, only two of which are measured to any extent by the WAIS-R. The two that are valued most highly in modern Western culture and which are therefore incorporated in the WAIS-R are the linguistic and the logical-mathemati-cal intelligences. But there are five other kinds of intelligence that are every bit as important, according to Gardner: spatial, musical, bodily-kinesthetic, and two forms of personal intelligence—interpersonal, knowing how to deal with others, and intrapersonal, knowledge of self. From this expanded list the WAIS-R touches briefly on spatial intelligence (Block Design) but completely ignores the remainder.

While both logical-mathematical and linguistic intelligences are important in the Western world today and appropriately emphasized on the WAIS-R, this is not necessarily true in every culture or setting. In Japanese society, for example, inter-personal intelligence—the ability to work well in groups and to arrive at joint decisions—is highly valued. Thus, the WAIS-R is a good measure of those dimensions of intelligence generally valued in Western industrialized societies, but due to its narrow emphasis on verbal thinking, the test neglects the many alternative modes of intelligence outlined by Gardner and others.

Another problem with the WAIS-R is that the test requires very little on-the-spot learning. A content analysis of the WAIS-R reveals that it is almost totally a measure of things previously learned. In general, the examinee is not asked to learn anything new and apply it to ensuing problems as the test progresses. Stated more directly, there is little on-the-spot learning needed. The WAIS-R is a very poor direct measure of learning capacity, insofar as it asks the subject mainly to apply previously learned information and skills. The only significant exception to this basic dictum is Digit Symbol. On this subtest, optimal performance requires the immediate learning of associations between digits and corresponding symbols. The faster these associations are made, the less the examinee has to consult the master list of digits and symbols, and the greater the number of items completed.

Of course, acquired knowledge must depend to some extent on the capacity to learn. In this sense, the capacity to learn is measured indirectly on the WAIS-R. For example, vocabulary tests, which are the prototypical example of things already learned, do correlate to a very high degree with reasoning tests, which are a more direct measure of learning capacity. This demonstrates that it is unwise to judge from armchair speculations just what intelligence tests measure.

Yet there is good evidence from both content comparisons and correlational research with other tests that a significant dimension of intelligence, a dimension that might be labeled "capacity for in situ learning," is substantially lacking on the WAIS-R. This point is illustrated by contrasting the WAIS-R with another measure of cognitive ability, the Category Test (Reitan & Wolfson, 1993). While these two tests have some overlap in the abilities measured, the correlation coefficient between the two is only $r = -.54$ (negative because the Category Test is scored for errors) in a heterogeneous sample of adults (Swiercinsky, 1978). This correlation is far lower than the $r = .8$ to .9 commonly observed between such mainstream intelligence measures as the WAIS-R and the Stanford-Binet. Thus, while the Category Test measures intelligence of some sort, it must tap different abilities than does the WAIS-R.

The Category Test was developed by Halstead (1947) and refined and validated by Reitan (Reitan & Wolfson, 1993). It was designed to measure the capacity to deduce general principles from experience with specific stimuli. The examinee views a series of 208 individual slides of geometric shapes (e.g., three small squares and one large square all in a single row) and must pull one of four toggle switches, numbered 1 through 4. The purpose is to identify an underlying principle or concept (e.g., the ordinal position of the odd stimulus) that will allow for correct answers, which are signaled by a bell. The examinee is allowed only one response per slide; incorrect answers result in an unpleasant buzzer sound.

There are seven different subtests, the first six of which have their own underlying principle. The seventh subtest is a mixture of items from the first six and consequently has no single underlying principle. The concepts or principles illustrated by the first six subtests are generally very straightforward and involve paying attention to such things as the number of stimuli, the position of missing elements, or the proportion of a figure that is shaded. Reitan and Davison (1974) have provided a lengthy discussion of the specific principles and concepts used in the Category Test.

The Category Test measures the examinee's ability to generate hypotheses and to validate or discard them on the basis of experience. The client must be able to induce general hypotheses from specific examples and to learn from ongoing experience whether the hypotheses are correct or not. Successful performance requires a systematic and flexible approach to problem solving.

The test is normally used as part of neuropsychological test batteries and is up to 85 or 90 percent effective overall in distinguishing between brain-impaired persons and normal, nonpsychiatric subjects (Reitan & Wolfson, 1993). While the Category Test is usually considered a "brain impairment" measure, it is clear from the item content and task demands that it requires high levels of on-the-spot learning capacity for successful performance. The Category Test can be used as an alternative or supplement to traditional intelligence tests for normal persons. For this reason, it is a good choice when the examiner wants a pristine measure of capacity to learn that is not so directly anchored in acquired knowledge and skills as is the WAIS-R.

The case of Samuel M. illustrates the point that the WAIS-R is a weak test of on-the-spot learning and that certain referral questions mandate the use of supplementary cognitive measures such as the Category Test. Samuel was referred because of achievement problems in law school. In spite of adequate motivation and a strong undergraduate background, he was failing certain key courses in law school, which would, at a minimum, postpone his career as a lawyer. He sought testing to determine the source of his problems. The examiner first administered the WAIS-R and was pleased to find that his Full Scale IQ was 119, acceptable although not outstanding for a law student. However, the Verbal IQ was much higher at 129, while the Performance score was unimpressive (for a law student) at 110. This pattern is sometimes observed in overachievers who, by sheer force of memory, application, and motivation, have developed their vocabulary and verbal skills to a very high level, in spite of having only an average endowment of fluid intelligence (Cattell, 1971).

Desiring to obtain a fuller picture of his cognitive capacities, the examiner also administered the Category Test and was surprised to discover that Samuel's abilities on this test were mediocre. He made forty-seven errors. Although precise norms are not available for college students, undergraduates average about thirty errors and law students typically would make far fewer errors than that. In sum, although Samuel's score was technically in the "normal" range, compared to his competitors in law school he was operating at a distinct disadvantage in courses that required new learning. Although this information had few implications for remediation, at least Samuel was able to approach law school devoid of any misconceptions that it should be as easy for him as for the other students.

Need for Caution When Testing Minorities with the Wechsler Tests

The Wechsler adult tests were developed and revised by David Wechsler and associates over a period of dozens of years. As decisions were made about the structure of the test, the content of the items, the use of timed or untimed formats, it was unavoidable that the choices would reflect the values of its developers. The test developers were products of their culture, and inevitably these persons highlighted the abilities and ways of behaving that were encouraged and valued in their personal development. It is little mystery, then, that the WAIS-III and its predecessors mirror the values of the majority American culture and that persons reared within that culture will be more comfortable with the test. In contrast, persons reared in a different culture—especially African Americans, Hispanics, and working-class whites—may find the test to be an alien experience and therefore perform at a competitive disadvantage. In this respect, the Wechsler tests can be said to be *culture-loaded.*

Whether this is a shortcoming of the instruments depends largely on the context in which the test results are to be used. Stated differently, there are situations in which "culture loading" is relevant to the criterion and therefore a desirable feature in a test. For example, when an individual moves out of the culture or subculture in which he or she was reared and intends to function, compete, or succeed within mainstream American culture, a traditional test of individual intelligence such as the WAIS-III may provide useful information precisely because its structure and content reflect the values of that group.

But there are situations in which a test developed in the majority American culture may give dangerously misleading results. Mercer (1979) has pointed out that traditional IQ tests tend to identify disproportionate numbers of minority students as needing special education placement. Yet many of these children and young adults function at an appropriate and normal level within their own social system or subculture. In effect, they are "retarded" only six hours out of the day. Even though the tests are good at predicting who will function competently within a traditional school system, they perform substantially less well in forecasting social adaptation within the minority community. Seen from this standpoint, the Wechsler scales (and many other traditional tests) reflect a narrow focus—one in which competence is defined by the values of middle-class America.

As an antidote to the psychomedical model of intelligence that reigned in the 1970s and to counteract abuses in the evaluation of sociocultural minorities, Mercer (1979) developed SOMPA, the System of Multicultural Pluralistic Assessment. SOMPA differed from earlier approaches to assessment in that it attempted to integrate three different approaches to assessment: medical, social, and pluralistic. The underlying assumption of SOMPA is that minority examinees tend to score low on the traditional tests because they are ignorant of the ways of the majority culture. In addition, medical problems are more prominent and must be evaluated in any comprehensive assessment approach. Finally, persons must be assessed relative to others who have had similar life experiences.

A philosophical and almost axiomatic assumption of SOMPA is that tests should assess individuals only against others in the same subculture. This pluralistic component recognizes that different subcultures have different life experiences. Only within subcultures do individuals share common experiences. Although the concept is controversial, SOMPA was developed according to the principle that norms for tests should be specific to individual subcultures.

SOMPA is a complex and controversial approach to assessment that applies mainly to children (Mercer, 1994). A brief discussion of it has been provided here because the issues raised by SOMPA are generally pertinent to the assessment of minorities. The main point is that the WAIS-III and other tests were developed by upper-middle-class psychologists (mainly white) and the instruments therefore embody the values of the majority American culture. When using them with minority individuals, the examiner should use great care that traditional tests do not, inadvertently, become a justification for unfairly denying or restricting privileges.

This point was recognized many years back by Anastasi (1958). Her arguments are relevant today:

> Thus, for the middle-class white American child the usual intelligence test bears a close resemblance to his everyday school work, which is probably the most serious business of his life at the time. He is therefore easily spurred on to exert his best efforts and to try to excel his fellows. For an American Indian child, on the other hand, the same test cannot have such significance. This type of activity has no place in the traditional behavior of his family or tribe. (Anastasi, 1958, p. 552)

Of course, this contention pertains not just to children but to adults as well and extends to all minorities. Cultural differences, whether observed in Native Americans, Hispanics, African Americans, or recent immigrants to the United States, most likely exert subtle influences on what a test *means* to the examinee. These differences in meaning easily can be translated to subtle and largely invisible differences in motivation. The result is misleadingly low scores for some minority individuals.

The effect of cultural variables on Wechsler test results has been ingeniously demonstrated by Terrell, Terrell, and Taylor (1981). They identified African American college students with high and low levels of mistrust of whites; half of each group was then administered the WAIS by a white examiner, the remainder by an African American examiner. The high-mistrust group with an African American examiner scored significantly higher than the high-mistrust group with a white examiner (average IQs of 96 versus 86, respectively). In addition, the low-mistrust group with a white examiner scored significantly higher than the low-mistrust group with an African American examiner (average IQs of 97 versus 92, respectively). In sum, cultural mistrust among African Americans was associated with significantly lower IQ scores, especially if a white examiner was used.

The authors concluded that personality characteristics among some African Americans reduce their motivation to fully demonstrate their mental ability on standardized cognitive tasks. As Anastasi (1982) notes, data bearing on this type of cultural effect are meager, and there is certainly room for additional research. At a minimum, the existing results are a sufficient basis for advocating caution when tests like the WAIS-III are used with minority individuals.

One last point is so obvious that it will be mentioned only briefly. The WAIS-III can be a dangerously misleading test for any examinee whose everyday language is not English. This is particularly pertinent to many Hispanic individuals whose primary language in the home is Spanish. Even for Hispanics who are reasonably fluent in English, it should be obvious that the English-version WAIS-III can be an unfair and misleading test. Fortunately, a Spanish version of the WAIS-III should be forthcoming soon.

Potential for Harmful Social Consequences

Any tool that possesses constructive applications, such as the WAIS-III, also can be used for destructive purposes. As mentioned above, this is not so much a problem with the test per se as it is a problem with human character. Ill-informed, careless, or malicious persons can employ almost any information destructively. Just so with WAIS-III IQ test results.

With adults, harmful social consequences from individually administered IQ tests tend to fall into one of two categories. The first is excessive reliance upon the WAIS-III and similar tests to make significant decisions about access to social privileges or, the reverse, removal from society to an institution. The second is insensitive feedback to the examinee that leads to a deflated self-concept.

As an example of the first type of destructive effect from IQ testing, consider the case of Daniel Hoffman (Sattler, 1988), who was initially placed in a class for the mentally retarded when he was 5 years and 9 months of age because his Stanford-Binet IQ was 74. The psychological examiner did not interview the mother or take a social history. If these additional sources of information had been obtained, it would have been discovered that his only real handicap was a speech impediment. In previous testing with a more appropriate instrument, the Merrill-Palmer Scale of Mental Tests, his IQ was a near normal 90. However, this information was never revealed to the school system tester because of the hurried way in which the initial assessment was completed.

In sum, Mr. Hoffman was given an incomplete assessment and placed in inappropriate classes on the basis of inadequate testing. Compounding the harm, he was not retested for 11 years, even though the earlier report recommended retesting in 2 years, and even though it is axiomatic to any well-trained psychologist that IQ is notoriously unstable in the early childhood years. The final irony is that, after receiving inadequate educational opportunity for 11 years because of a childhood IQ test, an adult IQ test was later used to *restrict* Daniel Hoffman's access to a training program that he enjoyed:

> In a curious twist of fate, testing, which resulted in the assignment of Mr. Hoffman to special education, also played an important role in removing him from a special

workshop program during his late teenage years. Mr. Hoffman had made poor progress during his school years, and there had been no significant change in his severe speech defect. At the age of 17 years, he entered a shop training school for retarded youths. After a few months in the program, he was given the Wechsler Adult Intelligence Scale and obtained a Verbal Scale IQ of 85, a Performance Scale IQ of 107, and a Full Scale IQ of 94. His overall functioning was in the Normal range. On the basis of these findings, Mr. Hoffman was not permitted to remain at the Occupational Training Center. On learning of this decision, he became depressed, often staying in his room with the door closed. (Sattler, 1988, p. 2)

At least three errors were made in Hoffman's case. First, a single IQ test score was used in isolation to make an important placement decision. This is always an unwise practice in that IQ scores are not only a restricted source of information, but they also can be highly misleading in individual cases. Test results should always be placed in the context of the person's social history and moderated by as much additional information as possible. The second error was the failure to do periodic retesting. Even with adults, whose intellectual capacities are more stable than those of children, it is wise periodically to retest individuals when IQ test data have been used to make placement decisions. Not only does this help monitor any changes in cognitive capacity; it also serves to redress any errors made in initial placement.

Finally, IQ test data never should be used rigidly to determine eligibility for special placement or programs. For example, no remedial program ever should have a mandatory criterion that Full Scale IQ must be below some specific cutoff (e.g., 90) for eligibility. Such human factors as self-confidence, psychological readiness, and impact on self-concept need to be considered when granting or restricting access to special programs.

A different category of misuse is insensitive feedback about test results. Appropriate and constructive feedback takes time and clinical sensitivity, so it is understandable that many professionals will fail here. Furthermore, there is no single method for giving feedback that will always have the desired outcome of informing individuals about their intellectual abilities and simultaneously protecting or boosting their egos. Giving constructive feedback is therefore a difficult skill to learn, one that requires experience and insight about how others will react.

Providing Feedback about WAIS-III Scores

Of course, some examinees will always feel deflated about their test results, no matter how sensitive the practitioner is when interpreting the test data for them. However, the more typical cause of such depressive changes in self-concept is that the examiner has managed the feedback session poorly. For example, the psychologist can make incorrect or incomplete statements about the implications of IQ test data, resulting in unintended harm to the examinee.

An error of commission occurs when the examiner gives categorical and unqualified predictions about potential for achievement, as embodied in statements like: "You don't have a chance of obtaining a bachelor's degree, and I don't think you should waste your money trying." A more honest statement, and one that is much more tactful, might be: "Obtaining a bachelor's degree probably will be very difficult for you, although not necessarily impossible. The final choice is up to you, but you might want to have a backup plan or consider other forms of educational improvement."

More is involved here than simple tact when breaking bad news to a person whose IQ is lower than expected. Perhaps a more important point is that the results might be misleading or just outright invalid. Even persons with very low IQ occasionally do mock the tests and accomplish astonishing things. Every statement about potential for achievement should be accompanied by at least a hint of qualification. Most psychologists learn this humility the hard way, by discovering that their predictions about future achievement don't always come true. Far better that novice practitioners realize their limitations from the very beginning.

Another facet of insensitive feedback is that the examiner may fail to challenge the client's incorrect stereotypes about IQ tests. Many persons deify IQ tests and consider them a measure of personal worth. This is especially true in college settings, where intellectual prowess is considered a major ingredient of academic success. In such instances it is appropriate to provide the client with a lengthy preamble about the limitations of IQ tests before discussing any specific results. A "pat" speech will not do. The examinee's views should be elicited and challenged when appropriate. The following points should be discussed at length:

- Most people make too much out of IQ test scores. They are not a measure of personal worth. Nor, for that matter, are they very good at predicting future success. For example, overall scores may help predict within broad limits who can succeed at college. However, there are always exceptions to the general trends. Many persons with intelligence test scores that are well below average still earn college degrees.

- The WAIS-III and similar tests address a narrow slice of intellectual abilities. They do not measure creativity, intuition, musical talent, athletic ability, or social intelligence. They are not the whole picture.

- At best, the scores are accurate to ±5 points. There is some subjectivity involved in scoring, and there are both lucky and unlucky guesses. Hence, the current score is only an estimate.

- There is room for change. IQ test performance does not necessarily remain static. Some people will show modest improvement over the years; others may decline slightly. Scores are not "fixed in concrete."

- Many things in addition to intelligence are important in leading a good life, and IQ tests measure none of them. Humor, motivation, honesty, decency, and compassion cannot be captured by any test score. Nor, for that matter, can good looks, luck, or having selected the right parents.

Although guidelines can be offered, there is no single hard and fast formula for giving feedback to examinees. One sticky point about which professional opinions have shifted in recent years is whether to provide actual IQ scores and the like. I believe that it is almost always appropriate to reveal IQ scores, Index scores, scaled scores, and percentiles—after discussing the above list of qualifications. The reason for doing this is simple: When we refuse to provide scores to examinees, we only contribute to the mystique that surrounds IQ testing and guarantee that the tests will continue to be deified by some and vilified by others.

Retesting with the WAIS-III

Does prior exposure to the WAIS-III cause an artificial increase in the scores of an examinee? This is an important question because examiners may administer the test more than once to some referrals. The common practice of retesting arises for many reasons, some valid and others misguided. For example, a clinician might not trust the recent testing of other practitioners and therefore administer the test again. Another reason has to do with lawsuits. Whenever litigation is involved—such as documenting the effects of head injury from a car accident—opposing attorneys will requisition independent assessments. In other cases, clinicians may suspect that a client has improved (or declined) and desire to document the change by administering the test again.

A review of the research substantiates the commonsense expectation that taking the same Wechsler test twice generally will cause scores to increase on the second administration. Most of the relevant studies are with the WAIS or the WAIS-R, but the trend of the findings is almost certain to apply to the WAIS-III as well. Catron (1978) studied the extreme case of *no* interval between test and retest, in which the WAIS was given twice in back-to-back testing sessions. Despite the fact that fatigue and boredom could have negatively influenced their second effort, thirty-five college males showed significant increases in Verbal, Performance, and Full Scale IQs of about 3, 14, and 8 IQ points, respectively.

Using a longer retesting interval of 2 to 7 weeks, Wechsler (1981) found similar but slightly smaller gains with the WAIS-R. He used two samples of subjects, those 25–34 years of age (N = 71) and those 45–54 years of age (N = 48). With Verbal IQ the gain was about 3 points, and with Performance IQ it was 7 or 8 points (depending on age group). Full Scale IQ showed a 6- or 7-point increase. Using a 2-week retest interval, Axelrod, Brines, and Rapport (1997) observed an increase of 8 points in Full Scale IQ for sixty-four college students.

Retesting results reported in the *WAIS-III Technical Manual* are similar to previous findings, although slightly more attenuated. Perhaps this is because of the longer interval between test and retest (an average of 35 days). Using four age groups (16–29, 30–54, 55–74, and 75–89) and large samples (88 to 104 persons in each age range), the increases were: VIQ 2.0 to 3.2 points, PIQ 3.7 to 8.3 points, and FSIQ 3.2 to 5.7 points. The mean gains and average gains by age group for subtests, IQs, and Index scores are reproduced in Table 5.1. One intriguing trend observed in this table is that the older subjects (ages 55–74, and 75–89) showed smaller increases in test scores than did the younger subjects. Why this would happen is unclear. In the discussion that follows, we examine average trends for the combined sample of 394 subjects.

The pattern of gains on the subtests appears to follow commonsense expectations. For example, it is likely that Information items missed the first time would be

TABLE 5.1   Mean Gains in WAIS-III Subtests, IQs, and Index Scores

Subtest/Scale/Index	Gain by Age Group				Mean Gain
	16–29	*30–54*	*55–74*	*75–89*	
Vocabulary	.2	.1	.2	.4	.23
Similarities	.6	.3	.4	.7	.50
Arithmetic	.6	.3	.3	.5	.43
Digit Span	.5	.4	.4	−.1	.30
Information	.6	.6	.5	.6	.58
Comprehension	.4	.1	.1	.3	.23
Letter-Number	.1	.7	.3	.5	.40
Picture Completion	2.3	2.4	1.6	.9	1.80
Digit Symbol-Coding	1.2	1.1	.8	.6	.93
Block Design	1.0	.7	.2	.3	.55
Matrix Reasoning	.1	.3	.2	−.1	.13
Picture Arrangement	1.2	1.2	1.2	.7	1.08
Symbol Search	1.0	.5	.5	−.2	.45
Object Assembly	2.3	1.6	1.0	.9	1.45
Verbal IQ	3.2	2.0	2.1	2.4	2.43
Performance IQ	8.2	8.3	5.7	3.7	6.48
Full Scale IQ	5.7	5.1	3.9	3.2	4.48
Verbal Comprehension Index	2.5	2.1	1.9	3.2	2.43
Perceptual Organization Index	7.3	7.4	4.0	2.7	5.35
Working Memory Index	2.9	3.1	2.2	1.3	2.38
Processing Speed Index	6.0	4.6	3.8	1.3	3.93

Source: Based on data in D. Tulsky, J. Zhu, and M. Ledbetter, *WAIS-III WMS-III Technical Manual* (pp. 58–61) (San Antonio, TX: Psychological Corporation, 1997).

a source of curiosity to individual examinees, perhaps causing them to discuss the questions among friends. This is precisely what Steisel (1951) found in a test-retest study with college females. This would explain the modest increase in scaled scores for that subtest (.58 scaled score points, on average).

In contrast, few persons are really curious about the meanings of words they don't know. There likely would be little followup on the meaning of high-level words not defined correctly. It seems reasonable, then, that Vocabulary scores would increase only minimally (.23 scaled score points, on average).

The questions on Similarities are unusual and therefore perhaps easy to remember. It seems reasonable that examinees might ruminate about specific items that they missed on the first testing. It is rare that we are asked questions such as "In what way are fingers and toes alike?" Such questions are likely to leave examinees pondering the essential likeness of pairs of items for hours or days afterward. This might explain the average increase of .50 scaled score points on this subtest.

Of course, the relatively large increases on most of the Performance subtests present no mystery at all. Most of these subtests are timed. The one Performance subtest that is not timed, Matrix Reasoning, showed virtually no increase at all (.13 scaled score points). The remaining subtests revealed retesting effects ranging from about a half point to nearly 2 scaled score points. For these subtests, prior exposure to specific stimuli resulted in a large boost in performance level on retesting.

Note particularly that Picture Completion increased by nearly 2 scaled score points on the retest. In selected cases, increases of this magnitude could make a previously abnormal pattern of subtest scores look normal or transform a previously normal profile into one with "suspicious" subtest scatter. For this reason, examiners should use extra caution when undertaking subtest pattern analysis with persons who have been tested recently on the WAIS-III.

Matarazzo and Herman (1984a) analyzed the frequency of different magnitudes of gain or loss in the eleven WAIS-R subtests for each of the 119 subjects who were retested in the original standardization (Wechsler, 1981). As an overall generalization, most individuals showed very small changes from test to retest on the eleven subtests, and the vast majority of the changed scores were modest increases of 1 or 2 scaled score points. However, a few subtests revealed interesting departures from this general pattern of subtest stability. For example, 13 of the 119 subjects displayed scaled score *declines* of 2 or more points on Digit Span. In contrast, 24 of the 119 subjects showed increases of 4 or more points on Picture Arrangement. These normative data provide support for Matarazzo's conservative rule of thumb that a change of 3 to 5 scaled score points from test to retest in a single subtest score "...constitutes adequate clinical potential for the practitioner *to begin to search for extratest corroborative evidence of pathology*" (Matarazzo & Herman, 1984a, p. 361). Note that such a change merely justifies searching for evidence of pathology, as opposed to proving its existence.

Cautionary Note: Declines on Retest

Matarazzo and Herman (1984a) also examined the individual raw scores for the 119 subjects in Wechsler's (1981) original test-retest study for the WAIS-R. They note that the mean gains of 3 points in VIQ, 8 points in PIQ, and 6 points in FSIQ are almost identical to the median gains of 2, 8, and 5 points, respectively, found in an earlier literature review of ten test-retest studies on the WAIS (Matarazzo, Carmody, & Jacobs, 1980). More importantly, they plotted the frequency of different magnitudes of gain or loss in VIQ, PIQ, and FSIQ from initial test to retest for all 119 subjects. Although the majority of the 119 increased their score on retest, a substantial percentage showed *declines* on retest, in particular, 20 percent for VIQ, 8 percent for PIQ, and 7 percent for FSIQ.

While it was true that very few persons showed decreases of more than 5 points, it is mildly surprising that any examinees displayed a loss at all. After all, the advantage of having seen *all* the items previously would seem to overwhelm any fluctuations due to the ± band of error associated with IQ measurement. In spite of this armchair expectation, a full 20 percent of the subjects declined in Verbal IQ. Such a counterintuitive finding is critically important information for the clinician. The prevailing expectation that, in the short run, retest scores will always be higher is simply incorrect.

A hypothetical case will serve to illustrate the importance of this finding. Suppose a head-injured client was retested after 6 weeks and displayed a "drop" of 3 IQ points. It is tempting to assume that since he should have shown an increase of 6 points (the average gain on retest), the decline of 3 points actually represents a 9-point change for the worse. If real, such a decline might represent a worsening of the underlying medical condition and might be sufficient cause for a medical referral. The impact of the Matarazzo and Herman (1984a) data is to make us more cautious when interpreting fluctuations of this magnitude. Certainly, it would be important to consult additional information and data sources before jumping to negative conclusions.

The relevant table from Matarazzo and Herman (1984a) provides the examiner with a reference point for determining how much of a gain or decline can be expected with normal subjects who are retested after 2 to 7 weeks on the WAIS-R. For example, declines of 5 or more points in FSIQ are rare, occurring in only 2 of 119 subjects. However, declines of 3 or more points in FSIQ are observed for 5 percent of the sample (6 of 119 subjects). Similar tables for the WAIS-III are not yet available.

Retest Gains after Longer Intervals

There is seldom any practical reason for the examiner to engage in immediate retesting of a referral. Nor, for that matter, is retesting normally done in the few weeks used in the test-retest studies of the WAIS-III. What is more common in clinical practice is that examinees are retested months or years later. For example, in monitoring the progress of a head-injured patient, it is not unusual to repeat entire test batteries, including the WAIS-III, every 4 to 12 months. In these cases, what compensation should we make for the effects of retesting?

The published research on this important question is surprisingly scant. There are many studies using short intervals (days or weeks) and a few developmental studies such as Maas and Kuypers (1975) that used long intervals (years to decades). Few studies engage the retest intervals that are most commonly observed in clinical practice: 6 months to a few years.

An important study by Catron and Thompson (1979) provides guidelines for retesting after 1 week to 4 months. The nineteen subjects in each of four experimental groups were tested twice with the WAIS after retest intervals of either 1 week, 1 month, 2 months, or 4 months. Intentional rehearsal or checking of missed items was discouraged by *not* telling the subjects what they would be doing in the second session.

Average gains in Verbal IQ ranged from 5 points at 1 week to 1 point at 4 months. As expected, Performance IQ gains were substantially greater. For example, for the one week retesting interval, the average gain was a whopping 11 points. A totally unexpected finding was that Performance IQ showed large gains even with the longest retesting interval of 4-months—in which scores increased an average of 8 points.

How long might we expect such gains to last? A study by Gregory and Gilbert (1993) provides a disturbing answer to this question. Using twenty-eight college students as subjects, they readministered the WAIS-R after an average interval of 10 months and found that the 8-point gain in Performance IQ persisted. In fact, combining the findings of Catron and Thompson (1979) with those of Gregory and Gilbert (1993) and extrapolating the resulting trends (Figure 5.1), we arrive at the astonishing conclusion that gains in Performance IQ persist for years. In other words, in normal subjects a single exposure to the Performance subtests causes an artificial increase in Performance IQ for at least 10 months, probably a few years, perhaps more!

Of course, these findings pertain only to high-functioning individuals, and the results may not generalize beyond the kind of subjects involved in these studies. Nonetheless, the results are so striking that we should view apparent increases in Performance IQ with some skepticism. An "improved" score might be nothing more than an exposure effect, not a true increase in the underlying abilities sampled by these subtests. The relevance of retesting effects is illustrated by the following case study.

Case Study: Relevance of Practice Effects for Test Interpretation

Paul C. was a 35-year-old accountant who was evaluated for possible cognitive impairment. He had been in a car accident in which he sustained a closed head injury that required hospitalization for several days. There was clearly some dam-

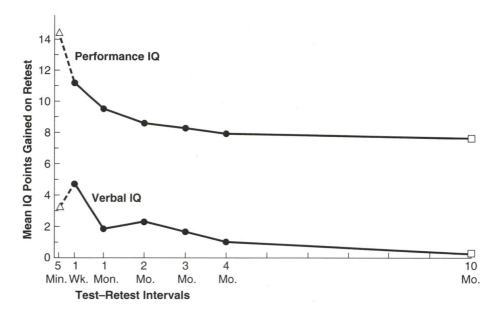

FIGURE 5.1   Retest Gains on Wechsler Verbal and Performance IQ Scores after Four Retest Intervals

Source: Based on Catron (1978), Catron and Thompson (1979), and Gregory and Gilbert (1993).

age to the cranial nerves controlling eye movements, judging from the eye patch he wore to manage his chronic double vision. In addition, he had sustained some cognitive deficits that impaired his functioning as an accountant. In particular, he couldn't do the accounting tasks expected of him unless he retreated to a quiet room with no distractions. Even then, his impression was that it took him longer than usual to balance accounts. These tasks had presented no problem to him prior to the car accident.

In discussing his symptoms and prior history, Paul revealed that he had sought vocational counseling and had been administered a WAIS-R just 14 months before his recent accident. Such rare occurrences of accidental baseline testing are a practitioner's dream come true, insofar as they provide a reference point for interpreting current testing. The first order of business was therefore to readminister the WAIS-R, with the intent of comparing the pre-accident test protocol with current post-accident data. Surely, this comparison would constitute the "acid test" of the extent to which the head injury had compromised his cognitive functions.

Much to the examiner's initial surprise, there was little difference between the two WAIS-R protocols separated by a 15-month retesting interval (Table 5.2). Verbal IQ was down very slightly, and Performance IQ was the same. The Full Scale IQs were nearly identical scores of 124 pre-accident and 121 post-accident. The clinician's initial reaction was that the two sets of scores were indistinguishable, considering the various sources of unavoidable measurement error such as lucky ver-

TABLE 5.2   Pre- and Post-Accident WAIS-R Scaled Scores and IQs
for Paul C., Age 26

Test	Pre-Accident	Post-Accident
Information	16	15
Digit Span	11	11
Vocabulary	15	14
Arithmetic	12	12
Comprehension	14	13
Similarities	16	16
Picture Completion	12	14
Picture Arrangement	15	15
Block Design	10	9
Object Assembly	10	10
Digit Symbol	12	11
Verbal IQ	125	122
Performance IQ	113	113
Full Scale IQ	124	121

sus unlucky guesses, differences between testers in scoring criteria, and time of day the tests were administered (evening the first time, morning the second).

However, an alternative interpretation certainly is possible. Assume for the sake of argument that retesting effects on Performance IQ are still substantial at 15 months followup. If it is legitimate to extrapolate the trend from Figure 5.1, such effects will be on the order of 8 IQ points at 15 months. If this is correct, then Paul's "corrected" post-accident WAIS-R scores would be Verbal IQ 122, Performance IQ 105, and Full Scale IQ 116. The difference between Full Scale IQs in this hypothetical discussion is now 8 points, which could be a "real" effect due to cognitive impairment from the head injury.

Of course, the difference in IQs on the two occasions might also arise from various sources of measurement error. The point of this philosophical discussion is to illustrate that the paucity of data on the effects of retesting introduces a problem of interpretation for psychometricians who readminister the WAIS-R after intervals of a year or more.

Short Forms of the WAIS-R and WAIS-III

Psychometricians have devised numerous short forms of the WAIS-R as a means of saving time. Beyond a doubt, short forms of the WAIS-III will be forthcoming soon. However, at the present time, practitioners who desire a short form Wechsler test must rely upon the WAIS-R. We consider here the issues raised by short forms and review prominent applications.

Regarding the WAIS-III and forthcoming short forms, the *Administration and Scoring Manual* offers the following essential advice:

> Short forms should be used only for a quick estimate of intellectual functioning or for screening purposes. They should not be used in isolation for diagnosis or classification. In general, they should not be used in examinations with a legal, judicial, or quasilegal purpose (e.g., a statutorily mandated diagnosis or determination of a disability). (Wechsler, 1997, p. 36)

The manual also cautions the practitioner against transferring short-form formulas devised with the WAIS-R to the WAIS-III. Short forms must be revalidated with each new edition of a test.

Perhaps the majority of all adult IQ tests administered in clinical practice are abbreviated slightly to one degree or another. In a minimally shortened WAIS-R administration the practitioner merely drops one subtest and prorates the remaining results. This type of assessment closely resembles the original WAIS-R; the prorated IQ (Verbal or Performance) is generally quite accurate. While the examiner saves only a few minutes by dropping a single subtest, this may prove vital to the completion of an assessment.

The term *short form* is generally reserved for substantially reduced test forms that require only a fraction of the usual administration time. One use for short forms is rapid intellectual screening of clinical referrals. For example, in a psychiatric hospital a short form IQ test can be used to determine whether individual psychotherapy might be an appropriate treatment approach. Because a patient with a very low IQ likely would respond better to behavioral techniques instead of talking psychotherapy, there is a need for intellectual testing. However, all that is desired in this case is a rough estimate of intellectual functioning, not a full and detailed report of strengths and weaknesses, vocational implications, and so on. For this purpose a short-form IQ test would be useful.

Examiners need to know that a price is paid for cutting corners and that short forms should not be used routinely merely because they save time and increase the "cost effectiveness" of consulting (translation: same fee for less time). Wechsler (1958) emphasized this when he argued that the WAIS is a clinical tool that can yield more than just an overall IQ. He held the view that personality was difficult to disentangle from intellect; he regarded the WAIS as a clinical, projective tool that could reveal facets of temperament, humor, and character as well as intellectual functioning. Of course, a foreshortened Wechsler test reduces the opportunity to observe the full range of such personality factors, and he therefore frowned on short forms.

Zimmerman and Woo-Sam (1973) have expressed a most telling point about the dangers of short forms. Discussing short forms of the WAIS (the WAIS-R was not yet available), they noted:

> There might be added to these objections another critical point: once a brief form of the WAIS is given, the results are usually entered somewhere as a WAIS, rarely as a "brief-WAIS" score. Later, some critical decision might be made using this score with the same assurance as if it were based upon a carefully and fully administered

individual test of intelligence. Where in the full administration there is almost always a detailed summary of results, including valuable material as to the ability of the subject to respond adequately to the various aspects of the examination, the brief WAIS is often rather slap-dash and fails to note the absence of critical information. (p. 178)

As a solution to this problem, Zimmerman and Woo-Sam (1973) suggest that the examiner use one of several available screening tests instead of the WAIS-R. The Shipley Institute of Living Scale (SILS) might be recommended for this purpose (Zachary, Crumpton, & Spiegel, 1985). The SILS is a two-part test consisting of vocabulary and abstractions. The test can be administered by a clerk in 10 to 20 minutes and hand-scored in seconds. With conversion tables a reasonably accurate estimate of Wechsler IQ can be obtained. Another useful test devised expressly as a screening tool is the Kaufman Brief Intelligence Test (K-BIT), which consists of vocabulary and matrices problems. These tests are reviewed briefly at the end of this chapter. The essential point is that using tests such as the SILS for purposes of simple screening would then leave the WAIS-III inviolate as a clinical instrument.

When to Use WAIS-R and WAIS-III Short Forms

If short forms are not a panacea for the overworked clinician, when is it appropriate to use them? Kaufman (1990) lists the following justifiable reasons for using short forms:

- Only a global evaluation of IQ is needed in the context of a personality assessment (as discussed previously).

- The examinee was administered a full IQ test in the past few years and a quick check of current status is desired.

- Large numbers of examinees must be screened for potential educational or neurological impairment.

- The available time is limited by practical constraints such as the need to assess several areas of functioning.

- The testing is for research, for which individual scores are less important than group comparisons.

The research literature on short forms is substantial, so it is not feasible to discuss this topic exhaustively. For a thorough review the reader is referred to Kaufman (1990), who devotes a full chapter to short forms and cites several dozen empirical studies. The coverage here is limited to just a few recommended short forms.

The dozens of proposed short forms can be divided into three types:

1. Split-half approaches in which the individual subtests are scaled down in length, for example, using only the odd-numbered items

2. Skip-item methods in which results on the first subtest, Information, are used to justify skipping easy items on subsequent subtests
3. Prorating approaches in which specified subtests are administered, e.g., four complete subtests to estimate IQ

While the first two methods may have applications in special circumstances, they raise serious concerns about validity and therefore should be avoided. The problem with split-half and skip-item approaches is that, by omitting items within subtests, they change the nature of the test and therefore potentially compromise the validity of the results.

Consider the previously popular Satz and Mogel (1962) short form, in which examinees receive only every second Block Design item and every third Picture Completion item, and so forth, from which total scaled scores are estimated. The problem with this approach is that examinees may not do as well on the more difficult items because they did not experience the shaping process provided by the easier items. Retrospective comparisons in which Satz-Mogel estimated IQs are derived from full WAIS-R protocols miss the point. What we don't learn from these studies is how examinees would have done on *just* the Satz-Mogel form. This question is amenable to research, but none has been provided.

The same criticism applies to modified forms of the WAIS-R that justify omission of easy items based on sufficiently high scores on the initial Information subtest (Cella, 1984; Vincent, 1979). In a modified WAIS-R an examinee who answers the first ten Information items correctly is subsequently credited for the unadministered first five items on Comprehension, the first ten items on Arithmetic, and so on. The true WAIS-R IQ and the modified WAIS-R IQ show an impressive correlation of .99, but this statistic is based on retrospective analysis of full WAIS-R protocols. Unanswered is this question: How would the examinees have scored if *only* the modified WAIS-R had been administered? Until these kinds of questions are answered, practitioners are advised to steer clear of split-half and skip-item short forms of the WAIS-R or WAIS-III.

Recommended WAIS-R Short Forms

The general strategy for shortening the WAIS-R recommended here is to administer two to seven subtests and compute a prorated IQ from these scaled scores. Whether the practitioner chooses a short form consisting of two, three, four, or seven subtests will depend upon the accuracy of measurement desired. Short forms consisting of two subtests tend to be accurate within ±7 IQ points about two-thirds of the time, whereas short forms consisting of seven subtests reduce the potential measurement error to ±4 IQ points. Intermediate short forms of three and four subtests possess intermediate accuracies of about ±6 and ±5 IQ points, respectively.

Based on the criteria of brevity, reliability, and accuracy, the short forms recommended here include the two-, three-, and four-subtest versions developed by

Kaufman, Ishikuma, and Kaufman-Packer (1991) and the seven-subtest form developed by Benedict and colleagues (Benedict, Schretlen, & Bobholz, 1992; Schretlen, Benedict, & Bobholz, 1994). The essential characteristics of these four approaches are listed in Table 5.3.

As noted previously, the choice of a short form depends on the level of accuracy desired by the practitioner. A very short form—a two-subtest version—might be appropriate for research applications, whereas a four-subtest version could be acceptable in the evaluation of examinees for general intellectual level (e.g., in counseling applications). The seven-subtest version, which reduces testing time by more than half, can be used as part of a comprehensive neuropsychological test battery (Schretlen, Benedict, & Bobholz, 1994).

For the two-, three-, and four-subtest short forms, computing the estimated WAIS-R IQ is a straightforward matter of accessing the relevant prediction equation with *age-corrected* scaled scores. For example, using the four-subtest short form, Full Scale IQ is estimated with this formula:

$$\text{est. IQ} = 1.6(A + S + PC + DSy) + 36$$

TABLE 5.3   **Summary of WAIS-R Short Forms**

Version: Subtests	Testing Time	Reliability	Accuracy*
Two Subtests: Information, Picture Completion	12 min	.90	±7
Three Subtests: Information, Picture Completion, Digit Span	15 min	.91	±6
Four Subtests: Similarities, Picture Completion, Arithmetic, Digit Symbol	18 min	.93	±5
Seven Subtests: Similarities, Picture Completion, Arithmetic, Digit Symbol, Information, Block Design, Digit Span	35 min	.97	±4
Full WAIS-R	75 min	.97	

*Accuracy is ±1 SEest and refers to the accuracy with which the Full WAIS-R IQ is predicted by the short forms.

Source: Based on A. Kaufman, T. Ishikuma, and J. Kaufman-Packer (1991), "Amazingly Short Forms of the WAIS-R," *Journal of Psychoeducational Assessment, 9,* 4–15. Also based on D. Schretlen, R. Benedict, and J. Bobholz (1994), "Composite Reliability and Standard Errors of Measurement for a Seven-Subtest Short Form of the Wechsler Adult Intelligence Scale—Revised," *Psychological Assessment, 6,* 188–190.

Thus, an examinee whose *age-corrected* scaled scores were Arithmetic 10, Similarities 12, Picture Completion 14, and Digit Symbol 12 (sum of 48) would receive

est. IQ = 1.6(10 + 12 + 14 + 12) + 36

which works out to be 113. Repeating once again, for the two- to four- subtest versions the practitioner *must* use age-corrected scaled scores.

For the seven-subtest short form, the practitioner uses the ordinary, *non–age-corrected* scaled scores on the WAIS-R. These values are plugged into preliminary equations that yield the prorated sums of Verbal scaled scores and Performance scaled scores, as follows:

sum Verbal scaled scores = 2I + 2S + DSp + A

sum Performance scaled scores = 2PC + 2BD + DSy

With these sums in hand the examiner then consults table 20 of the *WAIS-R Manual* (Wechsler, 1981) to compute Verbal, Performance, and Full Scale IQs in the usual manner. The details of deriving estimated IQs from short forms are given in Tables 5.4 and 5.5.

WAIS-R Short Forms: Final Comment

Even though short forms should not be routinely used, they do serve a valid function when a rough screening for overall intellectual level is desired. In this context,

TABLE 5.4 Equations for Estimating IQ from Two-, Three-, and Four-Subtest Short Forms of the WAIS-R

Subtests	Equation	Standard Error of the Estimate
I—PC	Est. IQ = 2.9 X_c + 42	7.3
I—DSp—PC	Est. IQ = 2.1 X_c + 37	6.0
A—S—PC—DSy	Est. IQ = 1.6 X_c + 36	4.7

I = Information, PC = Picture Completion, DSp = Digit Span, A = Arithmetic, DSy = Digit Symbol

Note: The examiner must use *age-corrected* scaled scores for these computations.

Source: Reprinted with permission from A. Kaufman, T. Ishikuma, and J. Kaufman-Packer (1991), "Amazingly Short Forms of the WAIS-R," *Journal of Psychoeducational Assessment, 9,* 4–15.

TABLE 5.5   **Worksheet for Computing Sums of Verbal and Performance Scaled Scores from a Seven-Subtest Short Form of the WAIS-R**

	Scaled Score		Weighted Score
Information	_____	× 2 =	_____
Similarities	_____	× 2 =	_____
Digit Span			_____
Arithmetic			_____
		Total: _____	= Sum of Verbal Scaled Scores
Picture Completion	_____	× 2 =	_____
Block Design	_____	× 2 =	_____
Digit Symbol			_____
		Total: _____	= Sum of Performance Scaled Scores

Note: The examiner must use the ordinary, *non–age-corrected* scaled scores for these computations. Table 20 in the *WAIS-R Manual* then provides the estimated Verbal, Performance, and Full Scale IQs.

Source: Based on D. Schretlen, R. Benedict, and J. Bobholz (1994), "Composite Reliability and Standard Errors of Measurement for a Seven-Subtest Short Form of the Wechsler Adult Intelligence Scale—Revised," *Psychological Assessment, 6*, 188–190.

I recommend the four-subtest version described above, as it provides a reasonably accurate estimate of IQ and lets the examiner sample skills from both the verbal and performance domains.

Short forms also can be justified if the examiner is facing severe time constraints beyond his or her control, such as when a client from a distant rural site must catch a bus in 45 minutes. Even a two-subtest short form, such as Vocabulary plus Block Design, is better than no test at all. The danger in short forms is that they can be for the benefit of the examiner and at the expense of the client. Some diagnostic information is always lost with a short form, and the shorter the form the greater the loss. Examiners who routinely administer short forms should look long and hard at their rationale for this unacceptable practice.

Assessment of Mental Retardation

In the early part of the twentieth century it was not unusual for mental retardation to be regarded by the general public as a definite entity—either present or absent for a given person. The dichotomous diagnosis of mental retardation (present versus absent) was usually made on the basis of an IQ test alone. A score that was below a certain cutoff (about 70 on the Stanford-Binet or Wechsler scales) was deemed a sufficient basis for positive diagnosis.

In contrast to this earlier simplistic viewpoint, the modern outlook recognizes that mental retardation is not a specific disease, but rather, is a vague, complex, and heterogeneous concept. The group of people to whom the concept refers differ greatly among themselves in terms of identifying characteristics, causes, prognosis, and treatment implications. Modern conceptions also stress that low intelligence is only one of three crucial components in the diagnosis of mental retardation.

The most authoritative source for a practical working definition is the American Association on Mental Retardation (AAMR). The most recent AAMR manual (AAMR, 1992) defines mental retardation as follows:

> *Mental retardation* refers to substantial limitations in present functioning. It is characterized by significantly subaverage intellectual functioning, existing concurrently with related limitations in two or more of the following applicable adaptive skill areas: communication, self-care, home living, social skills, community use, self-direction, health and safety, functional academics, leisure, and work. Mental retardation manifests before age 18. (p. 1)

This definition specifies three concurrent criteria for the diagnosis of mental retardation:

- Significantly subaverage intellectual functioning
- Deficits in adaptive skills
- Onset before age 18

We discuss each of these criteria in more detail below.

Significantly Subaverage Intellectual Functioning

The requirement of significantly subaverage intellectual functioning refers to the person's level of general intelligence, as determined from an individually administered test such as the WAIS-III or Stanford-Binet: Fourth Edition. The practical criterion is a Full Scale IQ more than 2 standard deviations below the average, which translates to below 70 for the WAIS-R (standard deviation of 15) or below 68 for the Stanford-Binet: Fourth Edition (standard deviation of 16). The upper IQ range for the diagnosis is considered a guideline only. When clinical judgment concurs, the cutoff score can be extended to approximately 75.

Group tests are specifically prohibited as an appropriate basis for diagnosing mental retardation, because of their questionable validity with low-functioning individuals. Likewise, poorly standardized instruments that lack appropriate norms should not be used for this diagnostic purpose.

Deficits in Adaptive Skills

The adaptive skills criterion represents a significant historical shift away from sole reliance on low IQ in the diagnosis of mental retardation. There must now be demonstrable impairment in adaptive behavior as well. The deemphasis of low IQ is justified eloquently in an earlier position statement by the Division on Mental Retardation of the American Psychological Association (Ellis, 1975). The statement emphasizes that behavioral inadequacy is the foremost problem of the mentally retarded, low IQ notwithstanding:

> The term mental retardation is applied to persons who exhibit behavioral inadequacy that appears early in life and persists. There are many causative factors involved: disease, injury, inheritance, cultural environment, or combination of these. Patterns of inadequacy differ from individual to individual, with low intelligence as a common denominator. Those more severely affected frequently suffer physical and health problems as well. However, mental retardation is, in the main, a behavioral problem. The individual's behavior cannot cope with everyday problems; normal adaptation does not occur.

In general, the adaptive deficits in mental retardation derive from limitations in practical intelligence and/or social intelligence. The ten areas of relevant adaptive behavior include:

- Communication
- Self-care
- Home living
- Social skills
- Community use
- Self-direction
- Health and safety
- Functional academics
- Leisure
- Work

A deficit in two or more of the ten subelements is needed for the diagnosis.

Deficits in adaptive skills usually are established by means of appropriate standardized instruments, although the AAMR manual affirms that the final determination is always a matter of professional judgment. For most of the twentieth century the Vineland Social Maturity Scale (Doll, 1953) was the only instrument available for this purpose. Beginning in the 1970s, rival instruments emerged. Appropriate measures for this purpose include the AAMR Adaptive Behavior Scales (ABS; Nihira, Leland, & Lambert, 1993), the School version of the ABS (Lambert, Nihira, & Leland, 1993), the Scales of Independent Behavior—Revised (Bruininks et al., 1996), the Comprehensive Test of Adaptive Behavior (Adams,

1984), and the latest version of the Vineland, the Vineland Adaptive Behavior Scales (Sparrow, Balla, & Cicchetti, 1984).

These instruments rely upon informants (typically parents or caregivers) to answer structured questions about specific behavioral competencies. From answers to dozens of questions, standard scores (mean of 100) are derived for adaptive skill domains, for example, communication, daily living skills, socialization, and motor skills. Proceeding from individually scored items such as "gives complete address, including city and state, when asked," the examiner obtains summary scores and adaptive behavior composite scores that are conceptually similar to IQs. Reschly (1987, 1990) provides an excellent review of adaptive behavior assessment instruments.

Onset before Age 18

The third necessary criterion for the diagnosis of mental retardation is onset before age 18. During the early formative years the growth of intelligence is paramount. The developing individual is therefore more likely to experience serious and long-term impairment if normal brain functions are not established because of adverse genetic, constitutional, or environmental factors.

The criterion of onset during the developmental period was included to help distinguish mental retardation from other disorders that result in low IQ or adaptive failures. For example, an acutely psychotic individual might reveal severe deficits in adaptive behaviors and require institutional care. Such an individual might even have an IQ below 70 if tested during the "florid" phase of the disorder. However, these disorders usually are not evident during the developmental period. Mandating that the low IQ and adaptive skill deficits must both arise during the developmental period helps to differentiate mental retardation from disabling psychiatric disorders.

Another example would be the college student who receives a severe head injury in an automobile accident. It is not unusual for severe head injuries to result in IQs depressed well below 70 and adaptive abilities impaired in the extreme. However, a diagnosis of mental retardation is not appropriate because the disability was incurred after the developmental period. This is not just academic hair-splitting with definitions. A head-injured patient with low IQ and adaptive deficits may require a different rehabilitative approach and might have a better long-term prognosis than a mentally retarded individual with identical low IQ and adaptive deficits.

A final point about definition is that a diagnosis of mental retardation describes only the current functioning of the individual. There is no implication that a mentally retarded individual is inexorably stuck in that diagnostic category. An individual may meet the criteria for mental retardation at one point in life but not another. Individuals may change status especially if they receive appropriate support and training. In addition, changes in the expectations of society may force changes in individual diagnoses. Mental retardation is a relative concept that is culturally defined; it is not something that resides within the character of the individual who receives that label.

Levels of Mental Retardation

The most recent AAMR manual embodies a substantial revision of previous terminology that recognized four levels of retardation: mild, moderate, severe, and profound. Previously the diagnostic nomenclature focused on the shortcomings of the retarded person, whereas the updated manual introduces a hierarchy of "Intensities of Needed Supports." The purpose of this revision is to redirect attention to the rehabilitation needs of the individual. The four levels of needed supports are: intermittent, limited, extensive, and pervasive.

Prior terminology that specified levels of retardation is clearly consistent with the new approach and, in any case, will likely prevail for quite some time. For these reasons, I have chosen to blend the old approach (levels of retardation) with the new approach (intensities of needed support) in Table 5.6. The reader will notice zones of uncertainty between levels of retardation. The purpose of the uncertainty is to emphasize that clinical judgment about all sources of information is mandatory in diagnosis. Furthermore, the reader should remember that IQ is but one of three criteria for the diagnosis. Under no circumstances is low IQ a sufficient basis for diagnosing a particular level of mental retardation in a client. As discussed previously, the examinee also must show corresponding deficits in two or more areas of adaptive skill.

TABLE 5.6   Four Levels of Mental Retardation

Mild Mental Retardation: IQ of 50–55 to 70–75+, *Intermittent Support* required. Reasonable social and communication skills; with special education, attain 6th-grade level by late teens; achieve social and vocational adequacy with special training and supervision; partial independence in living arrangements.

Moderate Mental Retardation: IQ of 35–40 to 50–55, *Limited Support* required. Fair social and communication skills but little self-awareness; with extended special education, attain 4th-grade level; function in a sheltered workshop but need supervision in living arrangements.

Severe Mental Retardation: IQ of 20–25 to 35–40, *Extensive Support* required. Little or no communication skills; sensory and motor impairments; do not profit from academic training; trainable in basic health habits.

Profound Mental Retardation: IQ below 20–25, *Pervasive Support* required. Minimal functioning; incapable of self-maintenance; need constant nursing care and supervision.

Source: Reprinted with permission from R. J. Gregory, *Psychological Testing: History, Principles, and Applications* (2d ed.) (Boston: Allyn & Bacon, 1996).

The WAIS-R in the Assessment of Mental Retardation

Although the WAIS-R can play an important role in the diagnosis of mild mental retardation, its value in the assessment of moderate mental retardation is questionable, and for the severe and profound classifications the test is altogether useless. The essential weakness of the WAIS-R in this application is that Full Scale IQ "bottoms out" at too high a score. Consider the extreme, limit-testing case of an older examinee who fails every item on every subtest. This individual would still obtain a Full Scale IQ of 51!

The crucial shortcoming of the WAIS-R for this type of assessment is that too many of the subtests have inadequate "floors" for adults with mental retardation (Kaufman, 1983). For example, on Picture Arrangement the second item (FLIRT) is a five-card item that is difficult for retarded adults. There is no transition between the first item (easy, three cards), and the next several items (hard, five or six cards). By failing to add a few easy items at the beginning of most subtests, Wechsler foreclosed the possibility that the WAIS-R would be useful with adults functioning below the mild retardation level. Consequently, the WAIS-R is useful mainly in the assessment of mild mental retardation.

In some respects the apparent attempt to restrict application of the WAIS-R by failing to provide a lower floor for subtests is understandable. There is evidence that mental retardation is actually two distinctly different categories of disabilities, with the WAIS-R being an appropriate assessment tool for only the higher-functioning of these two categories. For example, Maloney and Ward (1979) place the mentally retarded into one of two groups: those with distinct neurological impairment, with IQs below 50; and those without overt organic pathology, whose IQs generally fall in the 50 to 70 range. In their scheme the individuals with IQs in the 50 to 70 range are considered "functionally" mentally retarded. "They are considered to be natural variants of the normal distribution of intelligence or those whose intellectual development was adversely affected by psychological or sociocultural factors" (Maloney & Ward, 1979, p. 135). This latter group is often described as "culturally deprived" or "cultural-familial." Insofar as theirs is a lower-functioning extension of the normal continuum of intelligence, the WAIS-R is an adequate instrument for their intellectual assessment.

In contrast, the 0 to 50 IQ group is best thought of in medical, disease, or pathological terms, as neurological impairment is usually obvious. Their low IQ is a pervasive influence on their behavior and social competence. Usually these persons reveal attendant physical problems, are likely to be wheel-chair bound, and exhibit multiple sensory and perceptual disabilities. "The social context is negligible in defining their mental retardation. They will be seen as mentally retarded in all social contexts and cultures" (Maloney & Ward, 1979, p. 135). For such persons the WAIS-R yields little information of value. A structured checklist of behavioral capacities (e.g., Can he use a spoon? Does he possess traffic safety skills?) is much more appropriate. This is the approach taken in the measures of adaptive skills listed above. These instruments not only provide a useful basis for diagnosis of moderate, severe, and profound mental retardation; they also translate more readily to specific goals for remediation.

The WAIS-III in the Assessment of Mental Retardation

In the assessment of mental retardation the WAIS-III represents a significant improvement over the WAIS-R. The primary improvement has been the addition of simple items for most subscales so that the test is able to make finer discriminations of ability at the lower end of intellectual functioning. The Full Scale IQ now extends downward to 45 for examinees of all ages (whereas on the WAIS-R the lowest possible score differed slightly by age group and was in the low 50s). Thus, the WAIS-III is useful in the assessment of mild and moderate mental retardation, whereas the WAIS-R was helpful only in the assessment of mild mental retardation.

The *Administration and Scoring Manual* (Wechsler, 1997) reminds the test user that the diagnosis of mental retardation involves more than a low IQ (below 70 to 75). An individual must also demonstrate significant adaptive impairment in two of ten areas (discussed above); onset before age 18 is also required. But even when these criteria appear to be met, there is reason for caution:

> Just as low intellectual functioning does not necessarily indicate a diagnosis of mental retardation, a low score on the WAIS-III does not necessarily reflect a low level of intellectual functioning. Low IQ scores may and most often do reflect a low level of intellectual functioning, but other factors such as the following may be implicated: cultural or linguistic discrepancy from the test's standardization sample, disabling distractibility or anxiety, severe psychopathology, deafness, poor motivation or inadequate persistence, and extremely oppositional behavior or very poor rapport with the examiner. Before diagnosing low intellectual functioning or mental retardation, the examiner must rule out these factors. (Wechsler, 1997, p. 8)

The Problem of Marginal Intelligence

Setting the cutoff for mental retardation at an IQ of 70 is, of course, an arbitrary designation. In fact, the early definitions of mental retardation (Heber, 1961) used a more liberal score of 85 as the demarcation. The newer and more conservative criterion reflects at least two factors, one pragmatic, the other humanistic.

The practical concern was to define mental retardation in such a way that society reasonably could be expected to provide appropriate programs and human services to the affected individuals. Setting the cutting point at an IQ of 85 resulted in a mammoth 16 percent of the population falling in the retarded classification. Clearly, this was too large a group for existing human resource programs to manage.

The humanistic concern was to avoid stigmatizing persons who were making an adequate social adjustment but whose IQs were in the 70 to 84 range. Many such individuals were holding down jobs, living independently, and making constructive contributions to society. Many were part of the normal distribution of IQ, albeit functioning at the lower end of that continuum. Applying a descriptive label of "mental retardation" to their intellectual functioning seemed both unfair and unnecessary. Hence, for humanistic as well as practical reasons, the modern diagnostic consensus emerged: Use the more conservative cutting point of IQ below 70 for the first of the three criteria of mental retardation.

On the whole, this new viewpoint is preferable to the old one, precisely because it is less stigmatizing and more optimistic in outlook. However, there is one danger associated with it. The danger is that we will minimize or overlook the very serious adjustment problems faced by those with low IQs who do not technically meet the criteria for mental retardation. Maloney and Ward (1979) use the term "marginal intelligence" to refer to those persons not retarded by AAMR criteria who, nonetheless, reveal significant problems related to low intelligence. The term is not used as a diagnostic category, but as a general concept to indicate a high-risk population. Included are persons in the IQ range of 70 to about 90 who are marginal in their ability to cope successfully with the demands of society.

A modern industrial society demands of its citizens a high degree of intellectual competence. Insurance contracts, tax returns, and job application forms are but a few examples of the many high-level intellectual demands made by today's modern technological societies. The adaptation problems encountered by marginally intelligent individuals will be even more severe in the future. Western society is becoming more complex and technological developments are eliminating the need for simple and repetitive jobs. Modern technology is eliminating the menial and repetitive tasks often handled by citizens with low IQ. Robots are replacing assembly line workers and more efficient farm machinery is eliminating the need for common labor. These societal trends have a much more serious impact on the marginally intelligent, who have less flexibility in occupational choice, than on those with normal to superior intelligence, who might retrain in a new field.

To clarify the extent to which a marginally low WAIS-III IQ might result in adaptive deficits, we will consider the capabilities on the verbal subtests of a hypothetical examinee whose IQ is in the low 80s. Such a person very likely would belong to Maloney and Ward's (1979) "marginally competent" category. Nonetheless, the official classification on the WAIS-III would be Low Average.

We begin with the assumption that our hypothetical examinee is 30 years old and has a Full Scale IQ of 85. From this information it is possible to "work backward" to the expected scaled scores on the subtests of the WAIS-III and, in turn, examine the individual scales and extrapolate the typical items passed and failed that would result in such a score. Specifically, such a subject would need a total of 86 scaled score points on the eleven subtests, that is, an average scaled score of about 8. To avoid releasing the actual content of the copyrighted WAIS-III questions, items of comparable difficulty are used for the following discussion.

On Information items our examinee would know that Argentina is located in South America and would understand that fiberglass insulates better than wood because of the trapped air spaces. However, he would not know that Athens is the capital of Greece, nor would he recognize that Jesse Jackson was an African American civil rights leader. In other words, his basic fund of information about the world would be constricted. Whether this would have serious adaptive consequences would depend on his occupational standing and aspirations. For example, assume that our examinee completed the academic demands required for a teaching certificate. We can well imagine the disrespect he might experience from colleagues and students if his deficiencies of basic information became evident. For many other occupations his low fund of information would not pose a problem.

For the immediate memory of orally presented digits (Digit Span), our examinee would be able to recall about five digits in normal (forward) order and four digits when required to repeat them in reverse. Therefore, it would be unlikely that he could retain a telephone number in short-term memory, as is needed when using pay phones with anchored phone books underneath them. If he had a pencil, he could take the intermediate step of writing the number down, then transacting the phone call from the written copy. However, without this adaptation he might find it difficult to use a public pay telephone.

His vocabulary would be sufficient for most everyday transactions and would likely include such words as "conclusion," "meditate," and peaceful." However, he would be a little fuzzy on the meaning of "aversion," "impede," and "asylum." Words such as "palpable" "servility," and "auspicious" would be completely foreign to him. With these limitations in vocabulary he might find it difficult to profit from the normal forms of adult education such as evening classes. This might lead to a serious constraining effect on his occupational attainment.

On Arithmetic, he could tell you that 29 cents change is due if you give a fifty-cent piece in payment for seven 3-cent stamps, and he would know that nineteen dollars minus eight dollars and fifty cents leaves ten dollars and fifty cents. However, when asked to give the average speed in miles per hour of a family that drove 330 miles in 6 hours, he would balk and likely fail. Dealing with fractions and algebraic expressions probably would be impossible.

Comprehension questions such as "Why do many nations have a draft for the army?" would be successfully managed, but more complex issues such as "Why do you need a license to buy a hand gun?" or "Why does land near a river usually cost more than land on a desert?" would be greeted with vague and incorrect responses. Sayings such as "Strike while the iron is hot" and "Shallow brooks are noisy" would be failed. Their abstract, metaphorical quality might not be appreciated, and concrete responses ("You can't forge iron when it's cold") could be given.

Our examinee would know what left and right share in common (Similarities) but would fail to identify the critical similarity between scissors and an iron rod, or between work and love. The ability to make conceptual judgments and to assimilate the similarities and differences in the facts, objects, and ideas around him would be minimal.

These specific examples of equivalent WAIS-III items have been presented so that the reader has a tangible example of the verbal and problem-solving abilities that would be typical of a young adult with a tested IQ of 85. The verbal subtests were chosen because they tap abilities that are most directly relevant to successful adaptation to the demands of our modern technological society. It should be clear, in spite of the nonpejorative description of this IQ score as "low average," that serious difficulties in coping skills might accompany this level of functioning.

In proposing the term "marginal intelligence," Maloney and Ward (1979) were not trying to expand the classification scheme in mental retardation. Rather, they were attempting to establish that persons who are not technically mentally retarded may still manifest coping problems related to low intelligence. Furthermore, these potential problems are directly related to accelerating social changes in which Western societies are becoming more technologically complex and making greater intellectual demands on their citizens. Most likely, the adaptive difficulties of the marginally intelligent will worsen in the years ahead.

The difficulties in societal adaptation encountered by persons with marginal intelligence are perhaps best illustrated by a case history. Before looking at a representative story, we need to realize that no single case history could possibly illustrate the incredible variety of adult outcomes that can occur for those with low IQ. No doubt there are other citizens with marginal intellectual ability who are self-fulfilled and functioning completely independently. However, most likely this would be the exception, and the majority of those with low IQ would experience problems similar to those described in the following case study. The case of Brian T. was mentioned briefly earlier in this chapter.

A Case Study in Marginal Intelligence

Brian T. was tested on behalf of a state agency for vocational rehabilitation. Coincidentally, the examiner had known Brian for about 5 years and had assessed him 4 years previous for the state agency on developmental disabilities. He was normal at birth and was on time for the usual developmental landmarks of crawling, standing, walking, and uttering one- and two-word sentences. He had no unusual diseases or accidents and seemed quite normal through kindergarten and the first grade, where his achievement levels were deemed slightly above average. In the second grade, Brian was hospitalized with a serious illness that was diagnosed as "encephalitis," a diffuse inflammation of the brain of unknown origin. He recovered after several weeks, but was more active and distractible than before. His parents described him as a "short sampler" after his illness; he would go from one activity or toy to the next, sampling each for a few seconds, never sticking to anything for any length of time. In addition, his language skills regressed somewhat, and his sentences were shorter and less rich in detail. And he seemed more prone to temper tantrums and outbursts of anger if thwarted by parental discipline or frustrated by a difficult task.

While in elementary and junior high school, Brian was a frequent referral to the school psychologist because of social problems and achievement difficulties.

The diagnostic terms "hyperactive" and "learning disabled" are encountered time and again in his school records. In spite of these difficulties, he was promoted into high school, where he attended regular classes most of the day, supplemented with a few hours in the "resource room." He took Ritalin periodically from the sixth grade through high school graduation. In spite of extensive remedial tutoring, his achievement levels were about 6 years behind his peers, and his graduation was "social," based mainly on good attendance.

Upon high school graduation, Brian worked briefly as a dishwasher at a local restaurant. He found the work too dull and quit to join the Army. His adjustment in the Army was clearly unsatisfactory, although precise details are unavailable. Whatever the reasons, his early discharge was a mutually desirable outcome for both him and the Army. At this point he returned home to live with his parents and just "kicked around" for several months, unable to find any jobs above the level of dishwasher. Such menial positions irritated him, because he felt he had the ability to handle something at a higher level. But he had no particular training and offended many prospective employers with his angry insistence that he was meant for better things than dishwashing.

At this point his parents accompanied him to a state agency for the developmentally disabled, and he was given an extensive social and psychological evaluation. This is where the examiner met and evaluated Brian T. the first time. When he came for testing, Brian impressed the examiner as a handsome, well-dressed 23-year-old who was reasonably articulate in spite of a basic, restricted vocabulary. He was cooperative, maintained good eye contact, and tried to do his best on the tests. The examiner occasionally had to interrupt him when he would start haranguing about the "raw deal" that life had handed him. His general attitude was that he was a bright, capable young man who was being discriminated against by employers for reasons that he couldn't understand. He was clearly very angry about his inability to find meaningful employment. And he wanted something done about it, right now.

His performance on the WAIS was punctuated by irritable exclamations when a task would become too difficult. He had a clear tendency to become frustrated and to give up easily. His scores were Verbal IQ 78, Performance IQ 98, and Full Scale IQ 86. This test was given just months prior to the release of the WAIS-R, and it is worth noting that subjects score about 8 points higher on the WAIS than on the WAIS-R (Wechsler, 1981). Hence, his WAIS-R Full Scale IQ could well have been somewhat below 80 at this time.

The examiner made the obvious recommendation that vocational training was appropriate and that it should concentrate on his relatively superior performance skills. Low frustration tolerance was noted as a major problem, and supervisors should help him deal with this. Brian was encouraged to enroll in a social skills training class. Attempts were made to train him in skills needed for the food service industry. Several months later he was employed at a fast food restaurant, but he was soon terminated shortly thereafter because he couldn't work fast enough in the food assembly line during the peak hours of business.

A couple of years passed before the examiner encountered Brian again. In the interim he had worked at below minimum wage in a sheltered workshop training site, making wooden survey stakes for contractors. He related numerous conflicts with supervisors, whom he accused of "leading me on." From his viewpoint, he was always being promised bigger and better training opportunities at higher pay, but these never materialized. Finally, he quit in disgust and sought help through another state agency involved with vocational rehabilitation. It was in this context that the examiner tested him again.

Brian T. still had a "chip on his shoulder" and continued to maintain that nobody in the helping agencies was really doing their job. He was hoping that the test results might warrant a recommendation that some form of applied 2-year college degree program would be feasible. In spite of his anger, he was fully cooperative, and the resulting WAIS-R scores are good representations of his functioning at age 24.

He obtained a WAIS-R Verbal IQ of 73, Performance IQ of 79, and Full Scale IQ of 75. In spite of an apparent decrement in Performance IQ for which no explanation is available (98 on the WAIS to 79 on the WAIS-R), the Full Scale IQ was consistent with the earlier testing (especially when we recall that the WAIS yields an IQ score up to 8 points higher than the WAIS-R). It was clear that he was educable. Nonetheless, it was also clear that he would continue to experience frustration at the disparity between his aspirations and his abilities.

Even though he was living in his own apartment and in many respects functioning independently, this was only because his parents were willing to support him financially and oversee legal matters such as apartment leases and automobile insurance. Whether he would ever achieve true social independence and gainful employment was questionable. Surely a realistic observer would have reason for doubts.

Amplifications of Case Study

The example provided in this case study is not necessarily typical of all adults with low IQs in the "marginally competent" 70 to 90 range. We should always avoid the human tendency to stereotype or to make self-fulfilling prophecies come true. Many individuals with low IQs, even as low as 75, will make successful adaptations, and they deserve our best efforts at remediation and social support. But we must be realistic, too. A low IQ is a significant handicap in modern Western societies, a handicap that will not disappear merely because we now describe the results with nonpejorative labels (e.g., Low Average, Well Below Average).

The WAIS-III in Neurological and Cognitive Disorders

The WAIS-III is an important diagnostic tool in the assessment of various neurological disorders (e.g., traumatic brain injury) and cognitive disorders (e.g., learning disability). However, no single test, including the WAIS-III, is a sufficient basis for adequate diagnosis in the assessment of brain-impairing conditions. Two problems arise when the examiner relies on an individual intelligence test for the assessment of problems as complex and multifaceted as neurological and cognitive disorders.

The first problem is test misses. A test miss occurs when the IQs, Index scores, and subtest scores in isolation look reasonably good and do not indicate the existence of neurological or cognitive disorder—yet the client later is found to manifest such a disorder. The problem is that performance on most of the WAIS-III subtests is reasonably resilient in the face of many forms of brain impairment (although there are exceptions, discussed below). Even in those conditions of brain impairment for which particular WAIS-III score patterns are common and for which specific subtests tend to indicate relative deficits, these findings are based on *group averages*. Confronted with an *individual* WAIS-III protocol, the examiner will find it difficult to discern whether the pattern of scores indicates impairment or is merely one of those variations so maddeningly common in the standardization sample (see previous discussion on discrepancy analysis).

The second problem with using a single intelligence test is that even when a brain-impairing condition is strongly suggested by the results, additional tests are needed to clarify the full nature and extent of the impairment. The WAIS-III is an excellent measure of intellectual functioning, but it is not intended to assess a full range of neuropsychological variables. In addition, conditions with very different prognoses and treatment implications may reveal similar patterns of scores on the WAIS-III. For example, an intelligence test alone may not distinguish the fair prognosis of a person with unilateral stroke from the poor prognosis of a patient with a degenerative condition such as Alzheimer's disease. Additional tests pertaining to motor skills, memory ability, sensory functioning, and mental status would be needed for a fuller understanding of these clients. In sum, the practitioner is cautioned not to use the WAIS-III in isolation when testing persons with presumed neurological or cognitive impairment.

Another cautionary note pertains to a subtle error of reasoning that can arise when practitioners analyze a profile of test scores. The fact that a certain condition (e.g., a neurological disease or a cognitive disorder) commonly produces a certain test profile does not necessarily mean that individuals with that test profile therefore manifest that condition. Stated in the language of propositional logic, if A implies B, it does *not* follow that B implies A. What this means with WAIS-III results is that a certain degree of tentativeness is usually appropriate in test interpretation. A specific profile of test scores may suggest as a *working hypothesis* that the client manifests an impairing condition, but additional information and test results will be needed to confirm the hypothesis.

In spite of these needs for caution, the WAIS-III is nonetheless a valuable assessment tool for referrals in whom a neurological condition or cognitive disorder is suspected. Certain profiles of test scores *do* tend to be associated with specific conditions, and this information will be helpful in the detective work of assessment. Fortunately, the developers of the WAIS-III included test data for common neurological and cognitive disorders in their validational work (Tulsky, Zhu, & Ledbetter,

1997). The development team limited the reporting of test data to IQs and Index scores, presumably because these variables possess a greater degree of reliability than results at the level of the fourteen subtest scores. The *WAIS-III Technical Manual* reports average test scores for several neurological groups. The sample sizes, average age, and level of education for some of these groups are summarized here:

- Alzheimer's Disease: 35 individuals, average age 72, half with college degrees
- Parkinson's Disease: 10 individuals, average age 71, mainly high school education
- Traumatic Brain Injury: 22 persons, average age 27, generally a few years of college
- Chronic Alcohol Abuse: 28 individuals, average age 53, mainly high school or less
- Korsakoff's Syndrome: 10 persons, average age 61, mainly high school or less

In Figure 5.2 we depict the average IQ and Index score profiles for these neurological conditions. What stands out in this figure is that *for every single condition* the PSI score is relatively the lowest of the IQ scores and Index scores. This is especially true for the group with traumatic brain injury, where the PSI score drops well below the other component and Index scores. Apparently, neurological conditions of many kinds cause a greater impairment in processing speed than in any other component of intelligence assessed by the WAIS-III.

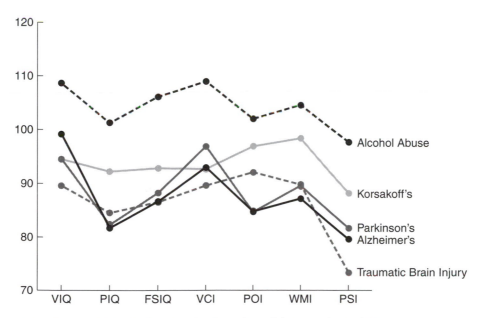

FIGURE 5.2 WAIS-III Results for Samples with Neurological Disorders

Several other comparisons and conclusions also are evident in these data. For example, the group with traumatic brain injury reveals a very large discrepancy between the POI score and the PSI score (18.7 points). The patients with Alzheimer's disease manifest a very large discrepancy between VIQ score and PIQ score (17.5 points). The patients with Parkinson's disease reveal a very large discrepancy between VCI score and PSI score (15.2 points). Most likely, these discrepancies signal cognitive impairments underlying the neurological disorders.

In addition to information for several neurological disorders, the *WAIS-III Technical Manual* also provides average test scores for three psychoeducational conditions in which cognitive impairment is a common result. In summary, the sample size, average age, and level of education are:

- Attention-Deficit/Hyperactivity Disorder (ADHD): 30 individuals, average age 20, most with high school or some college
- Learning Disability (Math): 22 students, average age 18, most still in high school
- Learning Disability (Reading): 24 students, average age 18, most still in high school

In Figure 5.3 the results for the three psychoeducational conditions are graphed. The students diagnosed with ADHD manifest a relatively flat profile with a slight high point on VCI and a slight low point on PSI. The discrepancy between these two index scores is 12 points, on average. Apparently, the distractibility

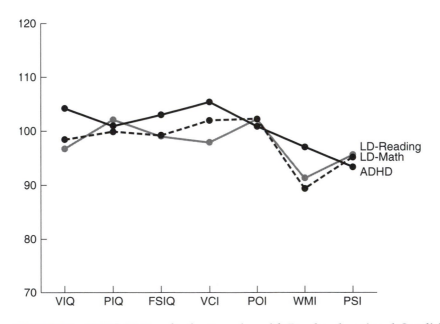

FIGURE 5.3   WAIS-III Results for Samples with Psychoeducational Conditions

observed in many young adults with ADHD shows itself as a moderate impairment in processing speed.

The average test results for the two groups of LD students indicate a departure from the patterns discussed previously (in which PSI was the prominent low score). In particular, what these groups share in common is relatively poor performance on the WMI score coupled with strength on the POI score. The POI-WMI discrepancy ranges from about 11 to 13 points. In sum, both groups show relative competence in the nonverbal types of intelligence captured by the POI score but also display a significant weakness in working memory as assessed by the WMI score. As might be expected, the LD-Reading group scored 4 points lower on VCI than did the LD-Math group.

It is hoped that the graphs of average profiles for these neurological and psychoeducational conditions will be helpful to practitioners who seek to understand the meaning of WAIS-III results. However, this section ends with a cautionary refrain. Even when a profile of test scores is highly similar to one of the clinical or psychoeducational groups described above, this does not prove that the client manifests the disorder in question. Additional information such as case history, results of screening tests, reports from friends and relatives, and medical consultation would be needed to strengthen a hypothesis of neurological or cognitive disorder.

Additional Measures of Intellectual and Adaptive Skills

There are many referral questions for which the WAIS-III is not the test of choice. For example, a mental health center may desire only a rough estimate of the intellectual level of its new referrals. Administration of the WAIS-III would be too time-consuming and expensive for this purpose. A brief test such as the Kaufman Brief Intelligence Test (K-BIT) would be a better choice. Another option would be a short, self-administered screening test such as the Shipley Institute of Living Scale (SILS; Zachary, Crumpton, & Spiegel, 1985; Shipley, 1983).

A different challenge is how to assess the intellectual ability of an examinee whose verbal skills are known to be deficient. The extreme case is the totally mute individual who otherwise seems to demonstrate a high degree of intellectual proficiency. The majority of subtests from the WAIS-III require a verbal response, so it is clear that other intellectual measures are needed. The performance subtests would be useful, but they do not tap verbal abilities. Thus, a nonverbal method for testing verbal concepts would be an ideal supplement to the WAIS-III performance subtests listed above. For this purpose the Peabody Picture Vocabulary Test—Revised (PPVT-R; Dunn & Dunn, 1981) would be a good choice.

Another area in which the WAIS-III is limited is the assessment of persons with mental retardation, particularly those with significant levels of disability. In addition to the weakness cited previously—that the WAIS-III does not extend downward in the lowest ranges of mental retardation—another problem is that the test provides no basis for identifying specific deficits in adaptive skills. A treatment-oriented measure such as the Scales of Independent Behavior-Revised (SIB-R; Bruininks et al., 1996) provides much more useful information than does the WAIS-III in this instance.

The final justification for alternatives to the WAIS-III is simply that there are other valid conceptions of intelligence embodied in meritorious tests. A well-trained examiner never should rely on one test of intelligence to the exclusion of other worthy measures better suited to specific referral questions. For example, the Stanford-Binet: Fourth Edition (Thorndike, Hagen, & Sattler, 1986) provides a more comprehensive assessment of memory skills than does the WAIS-III. If the referral question hinges on memory difficulties, the SB:IV would be the preferred intelligence test. Another example is when the examiner desires to test high-level abstract reasoning in a client. Raven's Progressive Matrices (Raven, 1956; Raven & Summers, 1986) would provide a better measure of this kind of reasoning skill than would the WAIS-III.

Kaufman Brief Intelligence Test (K-BIT)

Responding to the need for a brief, easily administered screening measure of intelligence, Kaufman and colleagues developed the K-BIT (Kaufman & Kaufman, 1990; Kaufman & Wang, 1992). The K-BIT consists of a Vocabulary subtest and a Matrices subtest. The Vocabulary test includes two parts: Expressive Vocabulary (naming pictures) and Definitions (providing a word based on a brief phrase and a partial spelling). The Matrices subtest requires the solution of 2×2 and 3×3 analogies using abstract stimuli.

The K-BIT is well normed on 2,022 subjects ages 4 to 90 years and can be administered with minimal training in 15 to 30 minutes. The test provides standard scores (mean of 100, SD of 15) for Vocabulary, Matrices, and the IQ Composite. These scores possess exceptional reliability (split-half and test-retest reliabilities mainly in the .90s) and substantial validity. For example, in a sample of 200 referrals for neuropsychological testing the IQ Composite correlated an amazing .88 with WAIS-R Full Scale IQ, although the K-BIT yielded scores that were about 5 points higher (Naugle, Chelune, & Tucker, 1993). The K-BIT is not intended as a substitute for more comprehensive tests, but it is an excellent screening test when a rough estimate of intelligence is sufficient.

The Shipley Institute of Living Scale (SILS)

Because it was developed in Hartford, Connecticut, the Shipley Institute of Living Scale (Shipley, 1983) also is known as the Shipley-Hartford. The test consists of forty multiple-choice vocabulary items and twenty abstractions items. The SILS is self-administered with a 10-minute limit for each of the two sections. Some clinicians favor an untimed use of the test; separate norms have been developed for this approach (Heinemann et al., 1985).

The vocabulary items start easy and increase in difficulty. Each stimulus word has four alternatives, including the correct choice that is similar in meaning. For the abstractions section the subject must discern a principle that explains the ordered progression within each item and then determine the next entry for that item. For example, What is the next entry in this series: A, B, D, G, K, _? Notice that going from A to B is one letter, from B to D is two letters, from D to G is three letters, and from G to K is four letters. The next entry will be five letters removed from K, that is, P. Thus, P is the correct answer. The vocabulary items are scored at 1 point each, whereas the abstractions items are awarded 2 points each. Thus, the maximum possible score for each half of the test is 40 points, while the entire test has an 80-point ceiling.

It is more than coincidence that each half of the test has the same maximum total of 40 points and a similar difficulty level. The original intention of the test (Shipley, 1940) was to detect organic deterioration by contrasting performance on the separate vocabulary and abstractions sections. Vocabulary was thought to be relatively unaffected by organic deterioration, whereas it was expected that abstraction ability would show significant decline. Thus, a large discrepancy favoring vocabulary over abstractions would signify the presence of brain impairment.

However, a nice theory is no guarantee that confirmatory facts will be found. Numerous studies and reviews have concluded that the SILS does poorly at detecting brain impairment. Few practitioners take seriously the hold/don't hold approach exemplified in the test; consequently, the SILS seldom is used in the assessment of brain impairment.

The SILS more typically is used to estimate Full Scale IQ in settings where precision is not important. For example, many mental health centers and Veterans Administration (VA) outpatient clinics have found the SILS useful as a screening device to determine if a client is a good candidate for individual psychotherapy. For this purpose it does not matter whether the true IQ is 103 or 123. Either score would provide the therapist with confidence that the client can manage psychological concepts and might profit from traditional talking psychotherapy.

Zachary, Crumpton, and Spiegel (1985) used linear regression techniques to develop a procedure for estimating WAIS-R IQ scores from SILS scores. The procedure was derived on a mixed psychiatric sample of 100 inpatients in a VA hospital and then replicated on a new sample of 50 psychiatric inpatients. Both samples used subjects with widely varying WAIS-R IQs that ranged from well below 85 to 115 and above. After the prediction formula was developed on the derivation sample of 100 inpatients, it was applied to the 50 subjects in the replication sample. The correlation between estimated WAIS-R IQ and actual WAIS-R IQ was an impressive .85. Their procedure also compared favorably to previous techniques for estimating WAIS and Wechsler-Bellevue IQs from SILS scores. In particular, the new method did not result in numerous overpredictions.

A potential drawback to their prediction method is that the examiner must use a four-step procedure and insert intermediate values into various prediction equations. The likelihood of clerical error is quite high. Fortunately, the authors have provided a table (Zachary, Crumpton, & Spiegel, 1985, pp. 537–539) that shows the predicted WAIS-R IQs for different age groups from 16–17 to 70–74. The authors are honest in citing the need for additional replication. They also point out that predicting very low WAIS-R IQs (below 60) is tenuous because of the lack of these individuals in their research. Nonetheless, their results are quite compelling and provide a satisfactory basis for a quick and economical estimate of a client's overall intellectual functioning.

Peabody Picture Vocabulary Test—Revised (PPVT-R)

The PPVT-R (Dunn & Dunn, 1981) is a specialized picture vocabulary test well suited to examinees with verbal disabilities. The test is one of the few intellectual tests that permits the examinee to respond merely by pointing. The PPVT-R is thus especially pertinent in the assessment of individuals with verbal impairment such as from recent stroke, cerebral palsy, hearing impairment, or deprived educational background.

The instrument consists of a series of 175 plates, each containing four pictures. The examiner presents a plate, states the stimulus word orally, and asks the client to point to the one picture that best illustrates the word. Of course, clients are administered only a portion of the 175 plates. The exact "run" of stimuli each person receives is determined by his or her successes with easy items and failures as the stimuli become more difficult. The test is untimed, but administration time seldom exceeds 20 minutes.

The PPVT-R is available in two parallel forms, each using different plates and stimulus words. Individuals of preschool to adult age can be tested. Raw scores can be converted to standard scores with the usual mean of 100 and standard deviation of 15. The test has been standardized on large samples of children and adolescents between the ages of 2 1/2 and 18 years with the usual concern for stratification on geographical region, parent occupation, community size, and ethnic group. Adult norms were obtained on 800 persons ages 19 through 40. This reflects a current limitation of the test: questionable applicability to subjects older than 40.

Test-retest and parallel forms reliability studies can be summarized with one representative value: $r = .80$. This is not a very healthy reliability statistic (compare to the high .90s for the WAIS-III), but it is sufficient for a short test that seeks to measure only one domain of intellect. Direct validity data for the revised version of the Peabody are somewhat limited, but promising. Vance, Kitson, and Singer (1985) correlated the PPVT-R with the Wide Range Achievement Test (WRAT) for thirty-seven children ages 6 to 15 years. The PPVT-R revealed a significant correlation ($r = .30$) with the reading subtest of the WRAT, but not with the spelling and arithmetic subtests, suggesting that it has appropriate discriminant validity. A factor analytic study by Altepeter and Handal (1985) on a sample of 208 children ages 6 to 12 also supported a "verbal comprehension" interpretation of PPVT-R performance. Their study used the WISC-R and WRAT in conjunction with the PPVT-R and found the latter to load substantially on the first factor of the Wechsler scales, namely, verbal comprehension. Prout and Schwartz (1984) investigated the validity of the PPVT-R with twenty-one mildly mentally retarded adults by comparing its results with the PPVT and WAIS-R. Even though the revised Peabody had a robust correlation of .85 with its predecessor, IQ equivalents on it were substantially lower (mean = 56) than for the original Peabody (mean = 73). The PPVT-R also scored a full 9 points lower than the WAIS-R IQ (mean = 65) even though it had a healthy correlation of .71 with the more comprehensive Wechsler scales. The authors suggest caution when using the PPVT-R within the adult mentally retarded population.

Dunn and Dunn (1981) surveyed over 300 studies of the PPVT and found generally high correlations with other vocabulary tests, and modest correlations with tests of verbal intelligence and scholastic aptitude. The current revised version is highly similar to its predecessor. By extension, then, it is a reasonable assumption that the PPVT-R will prove to be a useful test for quick, nonverbal assessment of verbal concepts. The verbal loading of the Peabody is well illustrated by a recent study of PPVT validity in adults (Maxwell & Wise, 1984). Using eighty-four inpatients from psychiatry and neurology wards, the study used partial correlation and multiple regression procedures to investigate the hypothesis that the PPVT assesses more than vocabulary in adults. The WAIS-R, Wechsler Memory Scale, preferred hand name writing speed, and years of education were assessed in addition to the PPVT. Even though all variables had significant correlations with PPVT IQ, WAIS-R Vocabulary had by far the strongest correlation ($r = .88$). More important, when the variance accounted for by Vocabulary was removed, none of the remaining variables had any predictive relationship with PPVT. I concur with the conclusion reached by Maxwell and Wise (1984) that the PPVT-R (as an extension of the PPVT) is a good measure of vocabulary but could be misleading if used as a global measure of intellect. The third edition of the Peabody, the PPVT-III, was released just as this book was published.

Scales of Independent Behavior—Revised (SIB-R)

As mentioned previously, the WAIS-III is a poor choice in the assessment of severe and profound levels of mental retardation. The reason is that the test contains too few easy items to test the more significant degrees of retardation. A related shortcoming is that the WAIS-III is heavily loaded on cognitive and academically related tasks and has only indirect bearing on the questions of personal responsibility and social independence. Yet a significant adaptive impairment that interferes with independent personal and social functioning is the cornerstone of diagnosis in mental retardation.

The purpose of the SIB-R (Bruininks et al., 1996) is to measure adaptive behavior in a way relevant to the diagnosis and treatment of mental retardation. The test consists of a series of fourteen subscales that are administered to a parent, caregiver, or teacher well acquainted with the examinee's daily behaviors. For each subscale the examiner reads a series of graded items and for each item records a score from 0 (never or rarely does task) to 3 (does task very well). For example, the subscale on Eating and Meal Preparation consists of sixteen graded items including: spearing food with a fork, eating soup with a spoon, taking appropriate-size portions, and preparing snacks that do not require cooking. A "ceiling" on this subscale is reached when three of five consecutive items are scored 0.

The fourteen subscales from the SIB-R are grouped into four clusters as follows:

- Motor Skills: Gross Motor, Fine Motor
- Social Interaction and Communication Skills: Social Interaction, Language Comprehension, Language Expression
- Personal Living Skills: Eating and Meal Preparation, Toileting, Dressing, Personal Self-Care, Domestic Skills
- Community Living Skills: Time and Punctuality, Money and Value, Work Skills, Home/Community Orientation

In addition to these four cluster scores, a Broad Independence Cluster (Full Scale) can be obtained by combining results from all fourteen subscales.

The SIB-R was nationally normed on 2,182 persons, sampled to reflect the 1990 census characteristics. Reliability data are generally respectable, but somewhat variable from subscale to subscale and from one age group to another. The individual subscales tend to show corrected split-half reliabilities in the vicinity of .80; the four clusters have median composite reliabilities of around .90; the Full Scale or Broad Independence Cluster has a very strong reliability in the high .90s.

The content validity of the SIB-R would appear to be very strong. It assesses a broad range of skills and traits that are commonly included in models of adaptive behavior. Norms are available for several age intervals, including five levels in early childhood, and ranging all the way through mature adult levels (age 40+ years). Practitioners in the field of mental retardation generally concur that it measures behaviors of central relevance in the understanding and treatment of their clientele.

Other forms of validity are also very promising. Mean scores of various samples of disabled and nondisabled persons show the appropriate relationships; namely, levels of performance are lowest in those persons known to be most severely impaired in learning and adjustment. The test is highly related to other measures of adaptive behavior and is strongly predictive of successful placements in different service settings (Bruininks et al., 1996).

Stanford-Binet: Fourth Edition (SB:IV)

The SB:IV has a longer history and tradition than any other test in the English language (Thorndike, Hagen, & Sattler, 1986). The roots of the test go back to the 1905 Binet-Simon scale, a crude instrument designed as a preliminary tool for identification of the mentally retarded in the French school system. Binet concluded that complex tasks requiring judgment, comprehension, and reasoning were best for this purpose. As obvious as this seems to us now, it was a major breakthrough in intelligence testing. Up to this point, psychology had been dominated by the "brass instruments" approach—so named because instruments made of brass were used to measure reaction time and sensory skills in the mistaken belief that these abilities were pivotal for intelligence.

A central feature of the 1905 Binet-Simon was the notion that certain intellectual tasks should be commonly passed by children at specific age levels. Thus, items were characterized as being at the 7-year-old level, 8-year-old level, and so on. Shortly thereafter the concept of ratio IQ was born: IQ = 100 × (mental age)/(chronological age). The test became known as the Stanford-Binet when Terman and his associates at Stanford undertook extensive revisions of the Binet-Simon in 1916, 1937, and 1960. These revisions ignored theoretical concepts of intelligence and built upon Binet's original, practical outlook. The earlier versions yielded a measure of overall intellectual functioning or "general intelligence."

By 1960 the ratio concept of IQ had been abandoned in favor of the deviation IQ concept. This approach used a mean of 100 and a standard deviation of 16 for each age group. In 1972 the Stanford-Binet was completely restandardized on 2,100 white, African American, and Hispanic children between the ages of 2 and 18.

The fourth edition of the Stanford-Binet incorporated major revisions in the theoretical rationale, content, and format of intelligence testing (Thorndike, Hagen, & Sattler, 1986). While many item types from the 1960 scale were retained and the general concept of basal-ceiling format is still used, the latest edition of the Stanford-Binet is really a new test that has little in common with its predecessors.

Foremost among the changes in the SB:IV is the use of fifteen subtests in a hierarchical model of intelligence. The model is outlined in Figure 5.4. Not all subtests are administered to every age group. Harder subtests such as Verbal Relations and Equation Building are reserved for older examinees, while easier subtests such as Absurdities and Copying are normally administered only to persons under 10

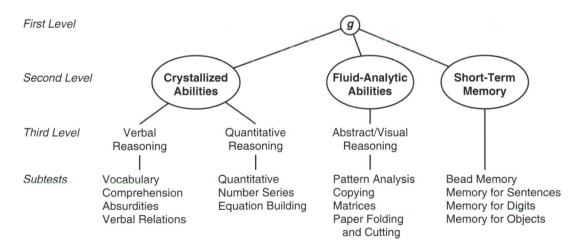

FIGURE 5.4   The Stanford-Binet: Fourth Edition Model of Intelligence

years of age. Six subtests span all age groups: Vocabulary, Comprehension, Quantitative, Pattern Analysis, Bead Memory, and Memory for Sentences.

At the highest level of the hierarchy is a general reasoning factor, g, that reflects overall test performance on all administered subtests. Nested below the g factor are three second-level factors that, in turn, have three third-level factors underneath them. The importance of these second- and third-level factors is that they allow the examiner to derive four content area scores:

- Verbal Reasoning
- Quantitative Reasoning
- Abstract/Visual Reasoning
- Short-Term Memory

Each content area score is based on two to four of the fifteen individual tests.

The addition of new nonverbal tests to the 1986 version answers the long-standing criticism that the Stanford-Binet was too heavily loaded on verbal abilities. Several new items that measure quantitative reasoning (as in Number Series, Equation Building) and fluid-analytic abilities (as in Pattern Analysis, Matrices) have been added to the new edition.

The partitioning of overall IQ into four content areas is both a strength and a weakness of the test. It is a strength because examiners may desire information on a subcomponent of intelligence such as short-term memory, which the test provides. But it is also a weakness in that other researchers do not find evidence for the reality of the four composites provided. Most researchers have concluded that the SB:IV is really a two-factor test for ages 2 through 6 (Verbal, Nonverbal) and a three-factor test for ages 7 and older (Verbal, Nonverbal, Memory). In any case, for older examinees the Memory component does emerge, which constitutes an important justification for selective use of the SB:IV.

The Stanford-Binet long has been considered a worthy alternative to the various Wechsler scales such as the WPPSI-R, WISC-III, and WAIS-III. In fact, there are some situations in which the SB:IV, with its wealth of very easy items, is clearly superior to the Wechsler scales. The SB:IV can be used with patients who are too impaired (such as from severe head injury) to give meaningful responses to the relatively more difficult Wechsler items. For the same reason, some examiners prefer the SB:IV in the assessment of mental retardation.

Raven's Progressive Matrices (RPM)

A prominent model of intelligence is Cattell's (1971) division of general intelligence into two categories. The two subtypes are called crystallized (G_c) and fluid (G_f), reflecting the formation over time and resulting stability of the former and the changeable nature of the latter. Oversimplifying somewhat, crystallized intelligence is acquired through educational and life experiences, whereas fluid intelligence consists of "innate" capabilities that are more physiologically based and less dependent on educational background. The two are conceptually separate but related in that G_c develops as a result of G_f being "invested" in cultural products and education.

Most intellectual measures are heavily loaded on G_c and are weak measures of G_f. An exception is the RPM (Raven, 1956; Raven & Summers, 1986), which is often considered the quintessential measure of G_f. RPM is a 60-item, multiple-choice paper and pencil test of abstract reasoning. The examinee must be able to induce or abstract the logical principle that is represented in a 3×3 grid of geometric designs. The lower right-hand design is missing, and eight choices are offered as possible completions of the grid. The problems range from very simple and concrete to very complex and abstract (see Figure 5.5). At the simplest level a form of visual pattern matching is needed. As the problems become more difficult, the subject must use abstract reasoning. For example, to solve Figure 5.5b, it is necessary to realize that each row has one, two, or three arcs, as does each column. Also, the arcs become smaller from left to right and top to bottom. By inference, the missing figure is choice number one. Needless to say, the later problems become more difficult.

The test is untimed and can be administered by a clerical worker. Few examinees require more than 40 minutes to complete the test. Answers are either right or wrong, so scoring is straightforward. Recent American age norms are provided by Burke (1985). These are based on 500 vocational counseling and 2,992 psychiatric patients newly admitted to a VA general medical and surgical hospital. It is likely that these norms have general applicability in that sex differences on the RPM are minimal and veterans roughly represent a cross-section of the population. Earlier norms from Peck (1970) are strikingly consistent with the recent Burke (1985) data.

Reliability of the RPM is excellent, with odd-even split-half corrected coefficients in the high .90s. However, reliability was much less impressive for those scoring in the lower ranges. Therefore, the RPM should be used cautiously, if at all, with low-IQ subjects (Burke, 1985). The RPM has a modest correlation with Shipley-Hartford vocabulary ($r = .48$) and a stronger correlation with SILS abstractions ($r = .68$) (Burke, 1985). This is suggestive evidence of appropriate discriminant validity; namely, the RPM is more strongly related to G_f measures than to G_c measures. Evidence that the RPM measures a physiologically based G_f type of intelligence is provided by Brooks and Aughton (1979). Among patients with blunt head injury, RPM scores decreased regularly as the duration of post-traumatic amnesia increased. In summary, RPM is a good choice for a nonspeeded group test to identify intellectual potential. The test is considered an outstanding measure of the fluid intelligence construct. However, its use with low-IQ individuals is questionable.

Final Comment

The choice of tests for an assessment should hinge upon the nature of the referral questions. For this reason, the competent practitioner will shun a limited battery and choose instruments suited to the needs of the client. These may include screening tests for cognitive impairment—which is the focus of the next chapter.

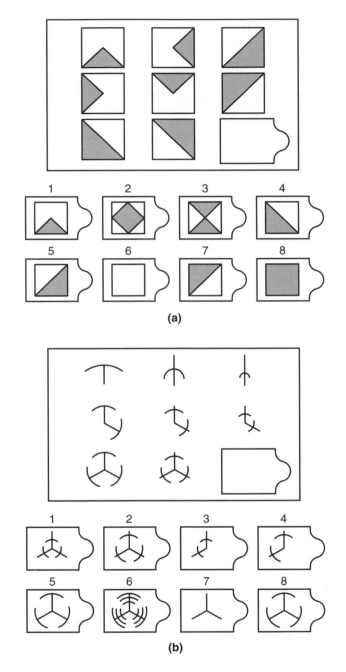

FIGURE 5.5   Examples of Raven Progressive Matrices–Type Items

6 Screening Tests for Cognitive Impairment

A common referral question for clinical psychologists is whether a client displays evidence of cognitive impairment. One example is the elderly gentleman complaining of memory problems who is referred by his physician for psychological evaluation. Implicitly or explicitly, the physician hopes that the consultation will serve to rule out dementia. Another example is the failing college student with a prior history of drug abuse who is referred by a psychiatrist for intellectual appraisal. The psychiatrist wants to know whether diminished attentional capacity might explain the student's puzzling academic problems. A final example is the rebellious teenager confined to a group home who is referred by a social worker for cognitive testing. The social worker suspects that the teenager's penchant for trouble stems from a constitutional inability to foresee the consequences of his behavior.

In each of these examples the underlying question is whether cognitive impairment plays a part in the problematic behavior of the referred individual. The primary task of the clinician is to *rule out* cognitive impairment—or to conclude that cognitive impairment is contributory. For many referrals it is possible to perform this function by administering a short battery of screening tests. This chapter explores the issues raised in screening for cognitive impairment and also introduces the reader to a selected compendium of simple screening tests.

Beyond a doubt, comprehensive batteries such as the Halstead-Reitan Neuropsychological Test Battery (Reitan & Wolfson, 1993) will generate more detailed information than will any short battery of screening tests. But for many referrals a comprehensive battery amounts to overkill—a selection of brief tests would suffice to address the referral issues. In other cases an extensive test battery might be desirable but is simply not feasible. After all, standardized test batteries possess a number of liabilities: They require many hours to administer (for the Halstead-Reitan, 6 hours is not unusual), significant professional training is needed to learn them (months of specialized supervision is not unusual), and they cost more than many clients or their insurance companies might be willing to pay (a thousand dollars is not unusual). Fortunately, in many circumstances a selection of screening tests will prove satisfactory for answering important referral questions.

Nature and Purpose of Screening Tests

Brief cognitive assessment is typically performed with one overriding goal in mind, namely, to rule out (or to rule in) cognitive impairment as a contributory factor in the problematic behavior of a referred client. Often this goal is tied to the question of whether the client should be referred for additional medical, neurological, or neuropsychological evaluation. Such referral should not be taken lightly, insofar as it may cost the client a lot of money. However, it would be a serious error not to make a referral if the individual reveals significant cognitive deficits with implications for diagnosis or treatment. How is the clinician to make the decision about advocating time-consuming and expensive referrals? Often a few screening tests for cognitive impairment will clarify the need (or lack thereof) for this recommendation.

Two examples will serve to illustrate the dual roles of screening tests in clinical assessment. In the first case, a graduate student consulted with a clinical psychologist, certain that he (the student) suffered from brain damage. His symptoms were vague and not seriously debilitating. He complained of difficulty concentrating and held the conviction that he could not solve statistics problems as well as the other students. Even though the student was willing to take an expensive and time-consuming neuropsychological battery, the psychologist opted instead to administer several short screening tests of cognitive impairment, including some advocated in this chapter. The student's performance was superlative on all tests. In subsequent interviews it became clear that depression, marital conflict, and fear of failure were the real problems. Once these issues were dealt with, his difficulties with concentration and his complaints of inferior problem-solving ability disappeared.

In the second example a client complained of subtle perceptual disturbances that interfered with his reading. This individual had been evaluated by his physician and also by an ophthalmologist. Both practitioners failed to find any physical disease and each suspected that psychological stress was the cause of his vague symptoms. This individual was an ideal candidate for screening tests of cognitive impairment. Unfortunately, the tests revealed a grave neurological problem warranting immediate referral to a neurologist. The evidence of cognitive impairment included a blatant inability to copy simple geometric shapes (discussed below). Later the patient was diagnosed with multiple sclerosis, a degenerative disease of the central nervous system that features demyelinization of neurons.

Characteristics of Good Screening Tests

It is self-evident that good screening tests should be short, simple to administer, and easy to interpret. Tests not having these characteristics require too much time to deal with and lose their appeal as *screening* tests. These points are so obvious that they will not be discussed further.

What is less obvious is that good screening tests should have a low false positive rate. In the context of screening tests for brain impairment, a *false positive* is a client whom the test identifies as cognitively impaired when, in fact, he or she is normal. In contrast, a *false negative* is a client whom the test identifies as normal when, in fact, he or she is cognitively impaired.

Curiously, in the context of screening for cognitive impairment, false negatives present less of a problem to the clinician than false positives. The reason has to do with the *low base rate* of impairment among persons who are candidates for a screening battery. Stated less pedantically, the characteristic we wish to detect (cognitive impairment) has a low rate of occurrence among persons typically referred for assessment; that is, examinees typically possess normal cognitive functions. Consequently, if the false positive rate is high, the clinician will end up referring a large proportion of patients for more extensive testing, the vast majority of whom will check out with a "no impairment" diagnosis. This will prove undesirable to the extent that it imposes serious demands on limited medical, neurological, and neuropsychological resources.

In contrast, a false negative on any one test (calling an impaired person normal) generally is a less serious error. The reason is that the client will be administered additional screening tests involving diverse cognitive functions. It is likely that one or more of these additional tests will "flag" the truly impaired individual and signal the need for additional referral or testing. Of course, no test or screening battery is perfect, and some false negatives will slip through no matter what. Yet, while desiring to minimize the false negative rate, the clinician must also seek to avoid the unmanageable chaos that a high rate of false positives would create.

These points can be summarized in two principles: First, normal persons generally should perform well on screening tests of cognitive impairment. Second, impaired persons such as those with brain damage or other cause of cognitive impairment should experience difficulty on at least a few tests in the battery, although not necessarily all of the tests. A screening battery for cognitive impairment that meets both these criteria will consist of *simple, diverse tasks*. Later in this chapter we consider a collection of tests meeting these criteria. But first we address a more fundamental question: When should the clinician administer these tests?

When to Administer Screening Tests

Many referral issues present a clear and compelling mandate for the examiner to administer screening tests of cognitive impairment. Some examples include: the client with a history of concussion and unconsciousness who is seeking counseling at a mental health center; the previously high-achieving college student who is experiencing serious academic difficulties; the highly successful researcher who now questions his capacity to present technical data at a professional conference; the reformed alcoholic who can't hold a job because he repeatedly shows up too early or too late or on the wrong day; the elderly mother who is suspected of "senility" by her children; and the young adult who fell off his bicycle, striking his head on the pavement.

In cases such as these in which the medical history or referral issues serve as "red flags," it is clear that testing for cognitive impairment is justified. The problem arises when clients do not have blatant problems with a probable neuropsychological basis. There are many "borderline" cases in which cognitive impairment might be suspected, but the evidence is not particularly compelling. For example, should a client who drinks regularly and gets into heated arguments with his wife be referred for an assessment of cognitive functions? What about the 63-year-old housewife who complains of depression but doesn't appear depressed on psychological tests or in interview? Or the low-achieving college student who has smoked marijuana on an irregular basis for the last 3 years?

It is not realistic for practicing psychologists routinely to give each client a series of screening tests that may take an hour or two. Tests should be given "with cause" and for good reasons. The initial question "When should these tests be administered?" can therefore be rephrased as "What are good reasons for administering a collection of screening tests for cognitive impairment?"

Good reasons tend to fall into one of two categories. The first category is where the neuropsychological history or referral issue raises a suspicion that the individual has experienced an impairment of cognitive functions. Examples include: episodes of unconsciousness, significant head injuries, complaints of memory disturbance, history of developmental disability, recent decrements in intellectual functioning, or "unexplained" poor academic achievement.

The second justification for screening tests is that the client's specific complaints are potentially "neuropsychological." A variety of symptoms fall in this category, including complaints such as "I forget what I'm saying" or "My mind works slowly" or "My speech gets mixed up" or "My brain gets stuck" or "I get confused" or "I drop things" or "I fall apart under pressure" or "I have trouble with the right side of my body."

The clinical literature is replete with indications of potential cognitive impairment. Textbooks in neuropsychology, neurology, and psychiatry as well as clinical experience provide a useful list of these signs, symptoms, and complaints. The diverse literature and clinical wisdom are summarized in Table 6.1. Individuals who display one or more of these indicators of cognitive impairment would be appropriate candidates for a short battery of screening tests. However, the reader is reminded that any of these symptoms could have a more benign explanation than brain damage.

A Compendium of Screening Tests

We turn now to consideration of several useful screening tests and procedures. Literally hundreds of tests are available for cognitive screening. The ones discussed here are representative and useful instruments that are simple, well researched, and easy to obtain. The instruments and procedures discussed fit into several categories of cognitive functioning, as follows:

TABLE 6.1   Signs, Symptoms, and Complaints That May Signify Cognitive Impairment

Developmental delay for standing, walking, or talking
Clumsiness, dizziness, or coordination problems
Loss, change, or peculiarities of smell or taste
Visual disturbances such as blank spots, double vision, blurring, or flashing lights
Auditory losses or ringing in the ears or strange sounds
Muscle weakness, trembling, twitching, or paralysis
Numbness, tingling skin, or loss of feeling
Blackouts, fainting spells, or periods when time is unaccounted for
Seizures or lapses of consciousness
Severe headaches, especially if not explained by life stresses
Head injury, especially if it resulted in unconsciousness
Trouble following conversations
Memory problems, especially if not explainable by depression
Difficulty thinking clearly or concentrating
Loss of own thoughts in conversation or inability to find simple words
Decline in reading, writing, or arithmetic skills
Hyperactivity, restlessness, or distractibility
Anger outbursts or problems with temper control, especially if no apparent cause
Perceptual distortions in size, shape, or color of objects
Feelings of unrealness that are difficult to verbalize
Disturbances of body image such as feeling that head or limbs are changing in size

Attention/Concentration:	Subtracting serial 7s, *Paced Auditory Serial Addition Task, Trail Making Test*
Sensory/Perceptual	*Finger Localization Test*
Psychomotor Speed	*Symbol Digit Modalities Test*
Memory	*Rey Auditory Verbal Learning Test, Serial Digit Learning Test*
Language Tests	Clinical examination for aphasia, *Word Fluency Test*
Drawing/Constructional Tests	*Bender Gestalt, Greek Cross*
Higher Cognitive Functions	Clinical assessment of executive functions, *Short Category Test, Booklet Form*

Brevity is crucial in a screening test, and each of these procedures (except one) takes only a few minutes for administration. The single exception is the last test in the list—Short Category Test, Booklet Form—an untimed test that usually requires about a half hour for completion.

Of course, practitioners need not administer all these tests and clinical procedures but might instead choose an appropriate subset based on the nature of the referral issues. Additionally, the reader should remember that these tests are *representative and illustrative* only; dozens of other viable screening instruments are available. This survey of selected screening tests is intended to convey the essential idea that screening for cognitive impairment is a relatively straightforward procedure available to the generalist practitioner, and not a course of action accessible only to the neuropsychologist or other specialist.

Subtracting Serial 7s

Although not a formal, structured test, subtracting serial 7s is a well-known task usually included in the MSE (Strub & Black, 1985). The procedure is considered sensitive to attentional impairments, although poor performance may have other causes as well. The examinee is told to "subtract 7 from 100." When this is completed, the examinee is told, "Now subtract 7 from 93 and keep on subtracting 7s until you can't go any further." The examiner records the responses and then determines the number of individually incorrect subtractions. The examiner may also record the time taken and make note of pauses longer than 5 seconds.

Normative results for this procedure are scant, although Smith (1967) has reported useful data for 132 employed adults, most with college or professional degrees. Only 2 percent of his sample was unable to complete the test, while another 5 percent made more than five errors. Sex, age, and education were important moderator variables. Specifically, women were more error-prone than men, particular women over age 45 with no college education. I once employed serial 7s with a group of seven college professors—and was surprised to find that two of them made two errors each (the other five performed perfectly). In sum, examiners should not overinterpret minor problems with the task. On the other hand, grossly defective performance—an inability to proceed, very high error rate, or very slow subtractions—may characterize persons with significant attentional impairment.

Paced Auditory Serial Addition Task

The Paced Auditory Serial Addition Task (PASAT) is a simple measure of mental tracking that is highly sensitive to impairments in attention (Gronwall & Wrightson, 1974; Gronwall & Sampson, 1974). In this test the examinee is instructed to add together a series of digits (1 through 9) that are presented on audiotape. The challenge is that each successive pair must be added together such that the last digit of the preceding pair becomes the first digit of the current pair. For example, if the initial three digits are "4-1-8," the subject should first respond "5" [4 + 1] after the first two digits are presented and then respond "9" [1 + 8] after the third digit is presented, and so on. Thus, if the initial numbers presented are "4-1-8-5-4" the examinee should respond "5, 9, 13, 9." Of course, the task is explained in detail before the examinee begins so that the test is truly an index of mental tracking, and not just a measure of the ability to understand an unusual request.

The PASAT was originally devised for the assessment of patients who had experienced a concussion. A concussion is a transient alteration of consciousness caused by a blow to the head. According to clinical lore, persons who experience a concussion have a strong tendency to recover spontaneously and there is usually no evidence of brain damage (McMordie, 1988). A concussion often is followed by temporary amnesia, dizziness, nausea, weak pulse, and slow respiration, but these effects pass quickly in most cases. What tends to linger for longer and highly variable periods of time in concussion patients is a loss of mental efficiency.

A case example illustrates the illusory, fluctuating nature of symptoms following a concussion. An accountant sustained a concussion when she lost control of her car and ran into a telephone pole, causing her head to strike the top of the steering wheel. She recalled a very brief period of unconsciousness followed by a "dazed feeling" in which things seemed unreal. Within minutes a passing motorist called the police, who summoned an ambulance. The paramedics took her to the emergency room, where she was found to be fully alert and oriented. The attending physician judged her condition to be good. Although she felt weak and dizzy, she had suffered no apparent injuries and was told to return home under the watchful eye of a close friend. She took 3 days off and then returned to work on the following Monday. However, she continued to feel a vague malaise and complained of slight fatigue and distractibility. Work that was previously easy for her was now a challenge, especially when background noise (phones ringing or colleagues talking) interfered with her concentration. Her work performance deteriorated for several weeks before she was advised by a physician to take 2 weeks of sick leave and then return to work. Two months later she was back to peak efficiency in her employment, free of the malaise and distractibility that had plagued her for several months.

Although it has many other uses, the PASAT was originally devised for serial testing of concussion patients so that physicians could determine when a patient was ready to return to work (Gronwall, 1977; Gronwall & Wrightson, 1981). As indicated in the preceding case vignette, a critical issue in concussion is how long the patient should recuperate. One way to approach this question is through serial testing with the PASAT. When the scores finally return to the normal range—which can take hours, days, or many weeks—the practitioner has a benchmark by which to recommend that the patient is ready to return to work. Of course, as a general measure of attentional efficiency the PASAT has many applications in addition to the serial testing of concussion patients.

The PASAT comes in two versions that differ mainly in the number of trials per series. The original PASAT consists of a brief ten-digit practice series followed by four test series of sixty-one digits (sixty additions) each (Gronwall & Wrightson, 1974). The four subtests become increasingly difficult as the presentation speed increases: 2.4, 2.0, 1.6, and 1.2 seconds between digits. PASAT results consist of four scores, the number correct at each of the four presentation rates. These results can be compared to findings for various normative samples to determine whether performance is normal or possibly impaired. Some typical normative data obtained from a sample of healthy, relatively well-educated adults ages 16–69 years are reported in Table 6.2. Results that fall more than 2 standard deviations below the mean on any trial should be considered suspect.

What is more typical and diagnostic of impaired patients, however, is that the task quickly becomes overwhelming such that they offer only an occasional answer rather than trying to track and respond to each successive pair of digits. For this reason, the two faster rates (1.6 and 1.2 seconds) are given only if the examinee has performed adequately at the slower rates (e.g., above 20 correct on the second trial at the pacing rate of 2.0). Spreen and Strauss (1991) discuss the subtleties of PASAT administration and scoring. The test can be ordered from the Neuropsychology Laboratory, University of Victoria, P.O. Box 170, Victoria, British Columbia, V8W 3P5, Canada.

Levin (1983) constructed a revised PASAT that consists of fifty digits (forty-nine additions) per series instead of the sixty-one stimuli (sixty additions) used in the original test. This version has been well received because the auditory tape was produced by a computer-controlled, synthesized speech program so that the stimulus characteristics and the rate of presentation are tightly controlled. Brittain and colleagues (1991) have published extensive norms for the revised PASAT based on 526 normal, healthy adults and stratified by age and IQ. The coverage here is restricted to the original PASAT developed by Gronwall and associates (sixty additions).

The PASAT is well validated as a measure of attention, and it is especially sensitive to the effects of concussion (O'Donnell et al., 1994; Stuss et al., 1989). As might be expected, the test is susceptible to age effects with younger subjects outperforming older examinees. Age makes little difference at the slowest rate (2.4 seconds), but makes a larger difference at faster rates. Fortunately, the available normative data for both versions of the PASAT provide age-graded norms (Brittain et al., 1991; Roman et al., 1991; Stuss et al., 1988). Clinicians who use the PASAT should consider age as a significant moderator variable in test interpretation.

TABLE 6.2   Mean Number of Correct Responses by Age Group on the Original Sixty-Item PASAT

Presentation Rate	Ages 16–29		Ages 30–49		Ages 50–69	
	Mean	*SD*	*Mean*	*SD*	*Mean*	*SD*
2.4 sec	47.4	10.1	43.4	10.2	43.5	13.6
2.0 sec	42.0	12.5	41.9	10.2	35.6	14.6
1.6 sec	36.0	13.0	33.1	12.2	30.8	15.9
1.2 sec	27.4	9.9	24.6	10.6	21.2	14.4

Source: Based on data from D. T. Stuss, L. L. Stethem, and G. Pelchat (1988), "Three Tests of Attention and Rapid Information Processing: An Extension," *The Clinical Neuropsychologist, 2,* 246–250.

Practice effects on the PASAT are substantial in healthy adult samples retested after 1 week and also in patients with HIV infection (Stuss et al., 1988; McCaffrey et al., 1995). However, it is unclear whether patients with concussion also show practice effects in addition to the improvement that can be expected from spontaneous recovery over time. Nonetheless, the data for healthy adults serve as a reminder that clinicians might expect scores to improve gradually when the PASAT is used for serial testing of impaired patients—even when the underlying condition has not changed.

Trail Making Test

The Trail Making Test includes two parts, A and B. Part A consists of twenty-five circles printed randomly on a white sheet of paper. Each circle contains a number from 1 to 25. The task assigned to the examinee is to draw a pencil line connecting the circles in their correct order as quickly as possible. Part B consists of twenty-five circles numbered from 1 to 13 and lettered from A to L. The task assigned to the examinee is to draw a pencil line connecting the circles in their correct order, alternating between numbers and letters, that is, 1-A-2-B-3-C and so on. The score for each part is the number of seconds required to connect all the circles.

The Trail Making Test has an obvious motor component but is best thought of as a screening test of general brain functions:

> The Trail Making Test requires immediate recognition of the symbolic significance of numbers and letters, ability to scan the page continuously to identify the next number or letter in sequence, flexibility in integrating the numerical and alphabetical series, and completion of these requirements under the pressure of time. It seems likely that the ability to deal with the numerical and language symbols (numbers and letters) is sustained by the left cerebral hemisphere, the visual scanning task necessary to perceive the spatial distribution of the stimulus material is represented by the right cerebral hemisphere, and speed and efficiency of performance may be a general characteristic of adequate brain functions. (Reitan & Wolfson, 1993, p. 74)

Especially in light of its brevity (5 minutes or so to administer both portions), the Trail Making Test is an outstanding choice as a screening measure of general cognitive functions. The test can be ordered from Reitan Neuropsychology Laboratories, 2920 S. Fourth Avenue, South Tucson, AZ 85713.

Although both parts of the test are useful in screening for cognitive impairment, Part B is somewhat more sensitive to the effects of brain lesions and other neurological conditions. Reitan and Wolfson (1993) recommend a four-fold classification of scores in which outcomes are categorized as perfectly normal (0), normal (1), mild to moderate impairment (2), and severe impairment (3), as follows:

	0	*1*	*2*	*3*
Trail Making Test, Part A	0–26 sec	27–39 sec	40–51 sec	52+ sec
Trail Making Test, Part B	0–65 sec	66–85 sec	86–120 sec	121+ sec

Because performance on the Trail Making Test is significantly influenced by age in samples of normal adults, other researchers recommend the use of age-graded normative data in the interpretation of results. The effect of age is particularly pronounced on Part B with elderly individuals, for whom a total time of several minutes is not unusual. Spreen and Strauss (1991) collated data from several sources to produce an extensive table of normative data for 861 healthy adults 15 through 79 years of age (Table 6.3). Results that fall well below the 10th percentile should be considered suggestive of cognitive impairment. Another source of normative data for young adults has been provided by Yeudall and colleagues (1987). These researchers tested 225 normal adults 15–40 years of age. Their sample was well educated, with most subjects (except those 15–20 years of age) having completed several years of college (Table 6.4). These normative data are appropriate for well-educated clients, and scores more than 2 standard deviations below the mean should be considered suggestive of cognitive impairment. Heaton, Grant, and Matthews (1991) provide additional comprehensive norms for the Trails test and many other instruments. These norms are especially important because they incorporate demographic corrections for age, sex, education, and other variables.

Finger Localization Test

A useful screening test for sensory impairment is the Finger Localization Test presented in Benton et al. (1994). This sixty-item test consists of three parts:

1. With the hand visible, the examinee identifies single fingers touched by the examiner with the pointed end of a pencil (ten trials on each hand).
2. With the hand hidden from view, the examinee identifies single fingers touched by the examiner with the pointed end of a pencil (ten trials on each hand).
3. With the hand hidden from view, the examinee identifies pairs of fingers touched simultaneously by the examiner with the pointed end of pencils (ten trials on each hand).

The maximum possible score is 60. The average score for normal individuals is approximately 58 correct, so this test functions well as a screening test in that low scores are strongly indicative of impaired functioning. Persons who score poorly on this test often show evidence of significant brain disease.

In addition to providing extensive normative data for adults and children, Benton and colleagues (1994) define a number of performance patterns that go beyond the usual designation of normal versus defective. For example, a bilateral asymmetric (right-hand) defect is defined as single-hand scores of less than 26 (30 per hand is maximum), and right-hand score 4 or more points lower than left-hand score. The relevance of such performance patterns is that they provide an objective basis for inferences about laterality of brain impairment, with an excess of right-hand errors indicative of left cerebral hemisphere impairment, and vice versa.

TABLE 6.3 **Normative Data for the Trail Making Test for Normal Control Subjects at Different Ages**

Percentile	15–20 Years (N = 108)		20–39 Years (N = 275)		40–49 Years (N = 138)		50–59 Years (N = 130)		60–69 Years (N = 120)		70–79 Years (N = 90)	
	A	*B*	*A*	*B*	*A*	*B*	*A*	*B*	*A*	*B*	*A*	*B*
90	15	26	21	45	18	30	23	55	26	62	33	79
75	19	37	24	55	23	52	29	71	30	83	54	122
50	23	47	26	65	30	78	35	80	35	95	70	180
25	30	59	34	85	38	102	57	128	63	142	98	210
10	38	70	45	98	59	126	77	162	85	174	161	350

Source: Reprinted with permission from O. Spreen and E. Strauss, *A Compendium of Neuropsychological Tests: Administration, Norms, and Commentary.* New York: Oxford University Press. Copyright © 1991 by Oxford University Press, Inc. Used by permission of Oxford University Press, Inc.

TABLE 6.4 **Normative Data on the Trail Making Test for a Younger, Well-Educated Sample**

	15–20 Years (N = 62)		21–25 Years (N = 73)		26–30 Years (N = 48)		31–40 Years (N = 42)	
	Mean	*SD*	*Mean*	*SD*	*Mean*	*SD*	*Mean*	*SD*
Part A	25	8.2	25	7.9	24	7.2	26	7.5
Part B	49	15.2	50	13.0	52	15.8	59	17.1

Source: Based on data from L. Yeudall, J. Reddon, D. Gill, and W. Stefanyk (1987), "Normative Data for the Halstead-Reitan Neuropsychological Tests Stratified by Age and Sex," *Journal of Clinical Psychology, 43,* 346–367.

Symbol Digit Modalities Test

As mentioned in Chapter 5 on intelligence testing, the digit symbol task is generally recognized as one of the best indicators of possible cognitive impairment on the adult versions of the Wechsler intelligence tests (WAIS-R/III). Persons with neurological involvement often show diminished performance on this subtest, which tends to be sensitive to impaired brain functions of almost any type or degree. It is not surprising, then, that researchers have embraced the digit symbol approach in the design of screening tests for cognitive impairment.

The most successful extension of Wechsler's digit symbol approach is the Symbol Digit Modalities Test (SDMT; Smith, 1968, 1982). In the SDMT the symbols are printed on the page and the examinee writes corresponding numbers underneath—that is, the transcription task is the reverse of that encountered on the original Digit Symbol subtest. A brief portion of the test is depicted in Figure 6.1. The advantage of the SDMT over the traditional approach is that the examiner can administer both a written and an oral trial, which helps isolate the source of difficulty with the substitution task. For each trial the examinee has 90 seconds to provide as many substitutions as possible. Score for each trial is the total number of correct substitutions. The SDMT is normed for subjects from 8 through 78 years of age. The entire test can be administered in less than 5 minutes.

Comparison of relative performance under the two modalities (written and oral) allows the examiner to determine whether the client has a problem with motor control (oral trial relatively better than written trial) or a more pervasive difficulty with on-the-spot learning (both trials impaired). Cutoff scores suggestive of impaired brain functions (2 standard deviations below the mean) are provided in Table 6.5.

The SDMT reveals a very strong correlation ($r = .91$) with Digit Symbol scores, which speaks well to the validity of this screening test (Morgan & Wheelock, 1992). Because the SDMT involves only geometric figures and numbers, it is relatively culture free and can be administered to persons who do not speak English. The test is particularly valuable as a screening test in psychiatric settings because psychiatric patients do relatively well whereas patients with cognitive impairment from brain damage perform poorly. For example, in one sample of seventy-five patients admitted to the psychiatric unit of a general hospital, the SDMT was 87 percent correct in identifying the fifteen patients whose ultimate diagnosis revealed a brain-based pathology. On the written portion the average number correct for the sixty psychiatric patients was 43.5, whereas the fifteen patients in whom brain damage was later confirmed scored only 25.9 (Riley, Mabe, & Schear, 1987). In a study by Ponsford and Kinsella (1992) the SDMT fared better than several other cognitive measures in the statistical discrimination of forty-seven head-injured patients from thirty control subjects.

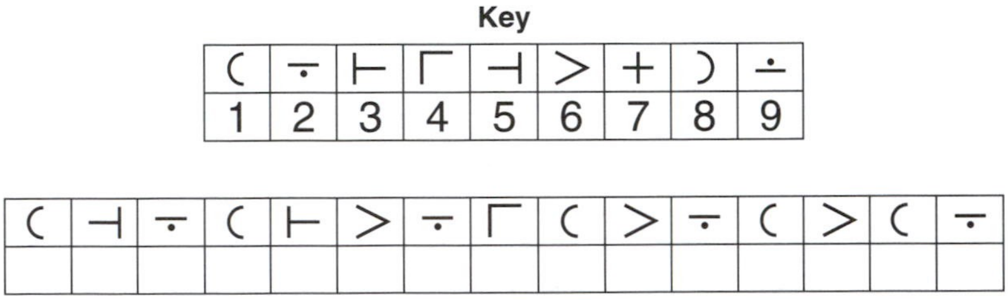

FIGURE 6.1   The Symbol Digit Modalities Test (SDMT)

Source: Material from the Symbol Digit Modalities Test copyright © 1973 by Western Psychological Services. Reprinted by permission of the publisher, Western Psychological Services, 12031 Wilshire Boulevard, Los Angeles, CA 90025, U.S.A. Not to be reprinted in whole or in part for any additional purpose without the expressed, written permission of the publisher. All rights reserved.

TABLE 6.5   Cutoff Scores by Age and Education Suggestive of Brain Impairment on the SDMT

	Age Range										
	18–24		**25–34**		**35–44**		**45–54**		**55–64**		**65 +**
	Wr	*Or*	*Wr*	*Or*	*Wr*	*Or*	*Wr*	*Or*	*Wr*	*Or*	*Wr*	*Or*
12 Years or Less of Education	38	39	37	42	35	39	28	33	27	31	15	20
13 Years or More of Education	42	45	40	42	32	38	35	41	31	37	21	26

Note: Wr = Written, Or = Oral. The scores listed in this table are 2.0 standard deviations below the mean of the standardization sample of 1,300 normal subjects.

Source: Based on data from A. Smith, *Symbol Digit Modalities Test Manual* (Los Angeles: Western Psychological Services, 1982).

Rey Auditory Verbal Learning Test

The Rey Auditory Verbal Learning Test (AVLT) is a simple measure of verbal learning and verbal memory that first appeared in France (Rey, 1964). This useful test was quickly translated into English by several authors and then popularized by Lezak (1983, 1995). Apparently, there is no official publisher for the AVLT. The most widely used approach to this test is summarized in Lezak (1995).

In administering the AVLT, the examiner reads a list of fifteen concrete nouns at the rate of one per second. The subject then immediately recalls as many words as possible in any order. The examiner then reads the same list a second time and requests the subject to recall all the words. A third, fourth, and fifth reading of the list and immediate recall by the examinee also are completed. These five learning trials are followed by an interference trial in which a new list of fifteen words is read (only once) and recalled. Finally, a delayed recall of the original list is requested—but the examiner does *not* read the list for this trial. Finally, a recognition trial is included in which the examinee must underline the administered words found within a written paragraph that contains many distractor words in addition to the fifteen stimulus words. The AVLT provides the following scores: the number recalled (of 15) for each of the five learning trials, the total for all five trials (75 possible), the immediate recall after the distractor list (of 15), and the recognition score. Some practitioners also compute a learning score by subtracting the Trial I score from the Trial V score.

A sample protocol for a 19-year-old head-injured client is depicted in Figure 6.2. What stands out in these results is that the young man displayed absolutely no learning curve for the first four trials, then improved substantially on the fifth trial.

FIGURE 6.2   **Rey AVLT Protocol of a 19-Year-Old Head-Injured Person**

Original List A	I	II	III	IV	V	Interference List B		VI	VII
Drum	x	x	x	x	x	Desk	x		x
Curtain	x	x		x	x	Ranger			x
Bell	x	x	x	x	x	Bird			
Coffee		x	x		x	Shoe			x
School	x		x	x	x	Stove			x
Parent	x	x	x	x	x	Mountain			x
Moon	x	x	x	x	x	Glasses			x
Garden						Towel			
Hat						Cloud			x
Farmer					x	Boat			x
Nose					x	Lamb			x
Turkey					x	Gun			x
Color					x	Pencil			
House						Church	x		x
River						Fish	x		x
Total:	6	6	6	6	11		3	0	12*
Norm:	8	9	10	12	14		6	13	14

*But 13 false recognitions

Note: Normative performance is based on norms provided by Wiens, McMinn, and Crossen (1988).

However, after contending with the interference list in which he recalled only three words, his recall of the original list was completely impaired—he was unable to recall even a single word. His recognition score was a respectable 12 of 15, but this was artificially inflated by his tendency to underline practically every concrete noun in the written paragraph, including thirteen words not found on the original list! These results indicate a substantial impairment of both immediate and (especially) delayed memory.

The most sensitive measure of impaired memory functions is probably the total recall for trials I through V, as this index will reflect the cumulative impact of slight impairments on the individual trials. However, interpretation of the total recall score is not straightforward because AVLT achievement is influenced by several factors. Performance is a function of age (younger persons do better than older persons), sex (females outperform males slightly on recall but not recognition), and intelligence (recall is substantially better at higher IQ levels). As a consequence of these relationships, the interpretation of AVLT scores needs to be moderated by knowledge of age, sex, and intellectual level of the examinee.

As a starting point for interpretation, based on a subjective collation of several normative studies, it would appear that young adults (ages 16–40) of average intelligence recall a mean total of about 55 words across the five trials, with a standard deviation of about 7.5. This would suggest that for young adults of approximately average intelligence, scores below 45 for total recall (sum of trials I through V) raise the suspicion of impaired cognitive functioning whereas scores below 40 (2 standard deviations below the mean) are strongly indicative of impairment. Normative expectations will be somewhat lower than this for older subjects but somewhat higher for subjects of above average intelligence. For further details on normative data, the reader should consult D'Elia, Boone, and Mitrushina (1995), Geffen, Moar, O'Hanlon, and others (1990), Ivnik, Malec, Tangalos, and others (1990), and Wiens, McMinn, and Crossen (1988).

The AVLT has been shown to be highly effective in the identification of persons with cognitive impairment in a study by Powell, Cripe, and Dodrill (1991). These researchers contrasted two groups: fifty patients with medically confirmed neuropathologies and fifty controls with no evidence of neurological history. The two groups were equated for age (mean of 26 years), education (mean of 12.6 years), and sex (54 percent female, 46 percent male). In addition to the AVLT the researchers administered a comprehensive battery of neuropsychological tests including the Halstead-Reitan battery. Median performances on the AVLT are shown in Table 6.6. Score on the Trial V performed better than *any other single test* with a correct "hit rate" of 74 percent. The optimal cutoff score for Trial V was 12/13 (12 or below impaired, 13 or above normal). The total score (trials I through V) performed almost as well, with a correct classification rate of 71 percent. The optimal cutoff score for this index was 50/51 (50 or below impaired, 51 and above normal).

TABLE 6.6 Median AVLT Scores for Matched Neurologic and Control Subjects

	I	II	III	IV	V	Total I–V	Recall	Recog
Control Subjects (N = 50)	7	11	12	13	14	56.5	12	14
Neurologic Subjects (N = 50)	5	8.5	9	10.5	11	46	9	13

Source: Based on data from J. Powell, L. Cripe, and C. Dodrill (1991), "Assessment of Brain Impairment with the Rey Auditory Verbal Learning Test: A Comparison with Other Neuropsychological Measures," *Archives of Clinical Neuropsychology, 6,* 241–249.

Serial Digit Learning Test

In the Serial Digit Learning Test, examinees receive repeated opportunities to learn a single series of eight or nine digits presented orally in the usual format for digit span (Benton et al., 1994). An eight-digit series is used when the examinee is over the age of 65 or has less than 12 years of education; the nine-digit series is used in all other cases.

The instructions for the Serial Digit Learning Test inform the examinee that an eight- or nine-digit number will be presented orally, following which the examinee should try to report as many of the digits as possible. The subject is warned that it is a hard task and that up to twelve trials will be allowed. The examiner then chooses one series from the manual, reads it out loud at one digit per second, and records the examinee's response. Two points are awarded for a perfect reply, whereas 1 point is awarded for near perfect responses (only one digit omitted, substituted, or transposed). After two perfect responses in a row, the examinee is given full credit for any remaining trials. Thus, a perfect score would be 24 points.

The origin of serial digit learning as a memory test was a clinical observation by Zangwill (1943) that some persons with brain injury had a normal digit span of six or seven digits but could not learn an eight- or nine-digit series even with repeated trials. Zangwill argued that rote *learning* tasks were more successful than short-term *memory* tasks, such as digit span, in discriminating between organic and functional disorders of memory. Of course, the distinction between learning and memory tests is somewhat artificial: Learning a series of digits requires the repeated use of memory.

Subsequent empirical research confirmed Zangwill's assertion. Drachman and Arbit (1966) studied persons with known or presumed hippocampal dysfunction by contrasting their performance on digit span and serial digit learning. Compared to normal control subjects, the hippocampal dysfunction group showed no deficits in digit span. However, there was a substantial difference between these groups on the serial digit learning task. Drachman and Hughes (1971) found similar results when comparing older normal subjects versus older amnesic patients.

Hamsher, Benton, and Digre (1980) and Schinka (1974) demonstrated that serial digit learning was far superior to digit span in the detection of brain disease. Schinka used large samples of brain-damaged and normal control patients 20–64 years of age to investigate optimal hit rates for the Serial Digit Learning Test and Digit Span separately. The Serial Digit Learning Test correctly classified 76 percent of the patients, as compared to only 58 percent for Digit Span. Hamsher, Benton, and Digre (1980) reported comparative hit rates of 46 percent versus 31 percent, again favoring serial digit learning.

Benton et al. (1994) report extensive normative data for the Serial Digit Learning Test. The test was standardized with 500 hospitalized patients who exhibited no evidence or history of brain disease, psychiatric impairment, or other mental disorder since childhood. Percentile score distributions are reported separately for the eight- and nine-digit versions and for different age ranges and educational levels. When subjects with some college education were administered the nine-digit version, only 3 percent failed completely, receiving a score of zero. This kind of dramatically poor performance is not unusual among brain-impaired persons, many of whom never learn the list.

The Assessment of Aphasia

In Chapter 3 the physiological substrates of left cerebral hemisphere language function were outlined and the major syndromes of fluent and nonfluent aphasia were introduced. This section builds upon those concepts and introduces clinical procedures for the detection of aphasia. However, before discussing specific tests and procedures, it is necessary to introduce a definition of aphasia and to discuss the varied symptoms and syndromes that might be encountered in clinical practice. Only then can the reader appreciate the design, scope, purpose, and limitations of aphasia screening.

A Definition of Aphasia.   Aphasia is any disturbance in the comprehension or expression of language caused by damage to areas of the brain that subserve language functions. In most cases the symptoms of aphasia occur in conjunction with a more global impairment such as observed in head injury or dementia. But aphasia can be the primary presenting complaint, especially in selected cases of left hemisphere stroke. However, from a practical standpoint, the symptoms of aphasia usually signify that incapacities with other intellectual skills will be found.

Specialists in speech and language pathology often make tight distinctions between three kinds of language-based disorders: aphasia, apraxia of speech, and dysarthria (Dworkin & Hartman, 1994). Within this framework, aphasia refers to impaired comprehension, formulation, or functional use of language. The disorder is *central* in the sense that it is caused by damage to the brain sites needed for language production and/or comprehension. In contrast, apraxia of speech is caused by faulty programming of the musculature that controls the sequential movements needed for ongoing speech production. Primary language deficits are not observed in pure cases of apraxia of speech; that is, the disorder is primarily one of *articulation*. Affected individuals show difficulty in planning nonspeech acts such as pursing of the lips and wiggling of the tongue. Pure cases are rare; apraxia of speech typically co-occurs with symptoms of aphasia. Finally, dysarthria refers to a group of speech disorders characterized by poor control of speech secondary to neural-based weakness or partial paralysis of the respiratory and articulatory musculature.

All three categories of language disorder are secondary to brain damage, although the likely sites may differ. The classic aphasias result from damage to Broca's area, Wernicke's area, or associated brain sites, whereas the dysarthrias typically signify damage to one or more cranial nerves. The disorders often occur together. An individual with a classic aphasia might also exhibit an apraxia of speech. Because our interest here is in screening for cognitive impairment that may signify brain damage, we do not make precise distinctions between the aphasias, apraxias of speech, and dysarthrias. For example, we can follow the conventional view in which dysarthia is considered a sign of aphasia even though, technically speaking, it is a separate symptom.

Aphasia with onset in adulthood is always the result of disease or brain injury. In particular, aphasia typically has a sudden onset stemming from lesions in the left hemisphere of the brain. Lesions to Broca's or Wernicke's area or the nearby pathways are usually involved. Of course, degenerative brain diseases eventually will lead to symptoms of aphasia as well. However, the diagnosis of dementia usually is suspected long before the language disturbance is noticeable. As a result, the psychological practitioner is more likely to encounter these common causes of aphasia: disruption of blood supply to the brain (stroke), cancerous growth of brain tissue (tumor), and trauma to the brain (head injury). Davis and Holland (1981) have noted that 80 percent of the adult aphasia caseload in clinics and hospitals is the result of stroke, and that the average age of the clinical population with aphasia is around 55 to 57 years.

Among patients who have definite brain disease or injury, symptoms of aphasia are quite common. Reitan (1984) compiled the aphasic and related disorders among 174 persons with independently established neurological evidence of cerebral disease or damage. The prevalent aphasic symptoms and their rates of occurrence were as follows:

- Dyscalculia—inability to perform simple arithmetical computations, 45%
- Central dysarthria—difficulty articulating words smoothly, 39%
- Dysgraphia—difficulty writing a simple sentence, 39%
- Right-left confusion—problems in identifying the left and right sides of the body, 35%
- Spelling dyspraxia—difficulty spelling simple words, 33%
- Dysnomia—inability to name common objects, 32%
- Dyslexia—difficulty in reading simple words or phrases, 28%

It should be stressed that all of these symptoms were acquired; that is, they were not attributable to preexisting low intelligence or lack of education.

Whether it is the primary disorder or just one symptom of a more diffuse disease, *aphasia* as a diagnosis means that the patient has brain impairment. For this reason, the term should not be bandied about lightly. It should not be applied to inarticulate individuals with merely mediocre language skills.

Symptoms of Aphasia.   Summarizing briefly, for the purposes of the nonspecialist interested in screening for cognitive impairment, aphasia is any deviation in language performance caused by brain damage. In some cases the symptoms are dramatic, as when the patient unintentionally "invents" a new word (saying "husbelt" instead of "book"). In other cases the symptoms are subtle, as when the patient uses roundabout speech as a substitute for a simple word (saying, "the thing you tell time with" instead of "watch").

As has been stressed, aphasia has been traditionally divided into the broad categories of nonfluent (expressive) aphasia, signified by serious difficulties with language output; and fluent (receptive) aphasia, involving fluent but meaningless output alongside serious difficulties with comprehension. While this division is useful at the theoretical level, in practice the distinction is often difficult, a point stressed by Reitan (1984):

> An individual subject may not be able to name an object because of an expressive naming difficulty (dysnomia) or, alternatively, because of a deficit such as visual form dysgnosia [a receptive symptom]. There is no absolute manner in which to resolve a question of whether the deficit is expressive or receptive. Even the most simple type of response requires input, central processing, and output in order for the cycle to be completed.

Many symptoms of aphasia can be revealed in the course of a simple clinical interview, while others require special tests for detection. Although specific aphasic symptoms can be quite varied, they do tend to fall into one of four categories: spoken language, written language, auditory comprehension, and reading. In the sections that follow, various symptoms of aphasia are defined, and examples of each are given. The full catalogue of aphasic errors constitutes a veritable introduction to the Greek language. Nonetheless, it is a valuable starting point in studying screening procedures for aphasia. An attempt has been made to give commonly accepted definitions for terms and concepts; the reader should recall that theorists differ as to the use of specific terms and the identification of categories or classifications of aphasia.

Spoken Language Aphasia. Aphasic errors of spoken language include omissions in which words cannot be retrieved and commissions in which incorrect words are selected unintentionally. Such errors are the easiest for the clinician to detect, and for this reason they have been thoroughly classified and researched.

Significant difficulty in finding a common word may signal the aphasic symptom of *anomia*. Mere hesitation in finding a word in conversation, a symptom that most persons have experienced, does not constitute true anomia. Anomia refers to prolonged delays in the search for a simple word, or the use of inefficient verbal expressions when describing a stimulus. For example, all normal persons can quickly state that a drawing of a baby is a "baby," while an anomic subject might require many seconds or never find the correct word. Often the examinee will resort to circumlocution, that is, "talking around" the correct word. When asked about a pencil, "What is this?" the subject might say, "It is a thing that you use for writing or drawing."

The *paraphasias* are another varied group of aphasic errors of spoken language. In a paraphasia, an incorrect word is substituted for the intended word. Paraphasic errors are usually unintentional and are typically observed in a person with fluent speech. There are many different subtypes of paraphasia, and some of them are subtle mistakes that are occasionally observed in normal individuals. For example, a semantic verbal paraphasia is a word substitution that bears a meaningful relationship to the intended word. Example: A patient says, "I can *see* you talking that way…" instead of "…*hear* you talking that way" (Davis, 1983). A more easily diagnosed type of paraphasia is the *neologism*, the invention of an entirely new word that bears no phonemic or semantic similarity to the target word:

> In his hospital room, the patient might ask someone to turn on the "pinwad" or request a "ferbish" to quench his thirst. A patient might even call a comb a "planker" and then insist, "p-l-a-n-k-e-r!" (Davis, 1983, p. 12)

Even though neologisms can be described as "invented" words, it is important to note that they appear to be produced fluently and unintentionally.

A patient whose speech sounds like a telegram may be demonstrating the aphasic symptom of *agrammatism*. In agrammatism the main content words such as nouns and verbs are present, but the small connecting words that give speech its richness are lacking. Articles, prepositions, and adverbs tend to be omitted. Speech is slow and labored. It is as if the person is trying to reduce conversation to the barest minimum needed to get the point across. When asked to describe a picture of three people waiting in the rain at a bus stop, the patient might reply, "Three people...rain...bus...that's all." Because patients who display agrammatism have such trouble with the small connecting words, a useful interview tool is to ask them to say, "No ifs, ands, or buts."

The opposite of agrammatism is *jargon*, the uttering of lengthy, verbally fluent statements that make no sense to the listener (gibberish or nonsensical speech). Typically, jargon contains many neologisms, and the speaker may show a press for speech, the tendency to start talking before the current speaker has finished.

Written Language Aphasia.   Aphasic patients often show the same symptom pattern in writing that they show in speaking. When this is observed, the writing component of aphasia is called *agraphia*. No doubt this reflects the fact that writing, like speaking, must begin as an internal phonemic code. The difference is that the code is translated into motor output at the hands instead of motor output through the mouth, tongue, and larynx. A reasonable assumption is that both speaking and writing must use the same brain systems for the initial processing that occurs prior to the actual motor output, which explains the commonality for some aphasic symptoms in speaking and writing.

Keenan (1971) has argued that writing tends to be more impaired by brain damage than is speech. Consequently, the examination of writing skills is crucial in the investigation of possible mild aphasia. Occasionally, clinicians observe patients who are not noticeably impaired in everyday conversation but who are incapable of writing a simple sentence dictated to them. An example is an elderly woman who could not write "I would like to come for my appointment," instead producing "I would t come for my appoint."

Auditory Comprehension Aphasia.   Comprehension of spoken words is a private event and therefore relatively easy for an impaired individual to fake. For this reason, the detection of auditory incomprehension represents a challenge to the practitioner. Nonetheless, a skilled examiner usually can reveal deficits in auditory comprehension that may accompany aphasia.

One approach is to ask the client to repeat a brief sentence such as "He jumped out of the roadway." The inability to repeat a simple phrase like this may indicate an auditory perceptual deficit form of aphasia. The client also may be asked to explain the meaning of the phrase. Individuals who can repeat the phrase but who cannot offer a reasonable explanation of its meaning may have a semantic deficit. That is, they may fail to understand the meanings of words or phrases. When told that "The lion was killed by the lamb" affected individuals cannot reliably report which animal was killed. Likewise, from the sentence "My mother's brother had an operation" they fail to understand whether it was a mother or a brother who needed surgery.

Especially when the deficit is mild, auditory comprehension aphasia is difficult to detect. Therefore, a wise examiner always will ask the patient and the family if they can give any examples of failures in auditory comprehension. When the patient responds, "Yes, when I listen to a lecture, it seems like my mind is stuck in glue," as did one referral, there is good reason to suspect a deficit in auditory comprehension.

Reading Aphasia. The reading deficit that accompanies some aphasias is called *alexia* or *dyslexia*. Typically, these symptoms are tested through silent reading for comprehension or through reading out loud. For example, a printed word is shown and the patient is asked to point to an appropriate picture. Or the patient might be asked to read a sentence or short paragraph and then answer several yes-no questions. A simple office procedure is merely to ask the patient to read out loud from a book that is at an appropriate level considering his or her education. Errors made during this procedure can be quite revealing. In one instance a college-educated examinee with high IQ read "on" as "for" and "spouse" as "house" and had to pause on the word "age" because he had seen it as "wage" but knew from the context that this couldn't be correct. Ensuing medical tests indicated that he had a serious neurological disease with diffuse effects.

Brief Clinical Exam for Aphasia

The brief clinical exam is probably used more frequently than any standardized test in the assessment of aphasia. It has the advantages of being brief and flexible. Flexibility is particularly important when dealing with severely impaired patients, who may require bedside testing. While every practitioner has a slightly different version of the brief clinical exam, certain elements are commonly assessed (Spreen & Risser, 1981; Lezak, 1995; Reitan & Wolfson, 1993). A representative exam is as follows:

1. Spontaneous Speech. The examiner looks for distinctive symptoms of aphasia such as agrammatism or jargon, referred to previously.
2. Repetition of sentences, phrases, and multisyllabic words. Typical stimuli are:
   - "He jumped out of the roadway."
   - "No ifs, ands, or buts."
   - "Methodist Episcopal."

3. Comprehension of Spoken Language. A variety of tasks may be employed here. The patient may be asked to obey simple commands such as:
   ■ "Stick out your tongue."
   ■ "Touch your left cheek with your right hand."
   ■ "Take this paper, fold it in half, and put it on the floor."
   In addition, yes-no questions may be asked, for example: "Does a car have handlebars?" or "Is a ball square?" The client may be asked to point to specific objects.
4. Word Finding. The examiner points to common objects easily recognized by normal persons and says, "What is this?" Typical choices include shoes, pen, pencil, watch, glasses, and ring. Additionally, the patient may be asked to name numbers, letters, or basic colors.
5. Reading. Intactness of reading skills is first tested by having the patient read a paragraph suited to his or her prior level of education and intelligence. To test for comprehension, have the patient follow *written* instructions such as:
   ■ Close your eyes.
   ■ Clap your hands three times.
   ■ If you are a man [woman], stand up.
6. Writing. Three variations are frequently employed in writing tests. Spontaneous writing is assessed by asking the patient to write a sentence about some innocuous topic such as the current weather. Copying printed matter such as an address in script may reveal aphasic and perceptual impairments. Taking a sentence from dictation also is commonly employed. Typical sentences are: "The quick brown fox jumped over the lazy dog" or "After lunch he went to the ball game."

The comprehensive assessment of aphasia can take several hours and should be completed by a specialist in speech or language disorders. Diagnosis is further complicated by the dynamic nature of aphasia. Patients can change diagnostic categories as their underlying brain disease progresses or heals. In fact, a patient may display striking inconsistencies within the space of a few hours. Reitan (1984) relates a case in which a patient was able to write words upon request but, at a later point in time, had no idea what his own legible writing represented. These points should make it clear that extensive training is needed for the comprehensive assessment of aphasia. The clinical procedures discussed above and the word fluency test described below serve only to identify the need for additional assessment.

FAS Word Fluency Test

Several researchers have devised a family of procedures that assess word fluency as an indicator of cognitive impairment. In a typical word fluency test the examinee is asked to produce *quickly* in spoken form as many words as possible beginning with a designated letter. The instructions specify that proper names are not allowed. Using the same word with a different ending (e.g., "fast" and "fasting") also is prohibited. Score for the test is the number of words produced within a specified time limit. Usually there is more than one trial so as to enhance the psychometric properties of this procedure.

Word fluency is known to be a sensitive index of brain impairment, especially when the dysfunction involves the frontal lobes. Fluency scores are substantially lower in patients with frontal lesions, and left-sided impairment produces the greatest deficit (Lezak, 1995). Patients with Alzheimer's disease often reveal a striking deficit in word fluency, as do most individuals with degenerative forms of dementia. For obvious reasons, patients with left hemisphere stroke typically reveal drastic impairments in word fluency.

Probably the most widely used word fluency test is the FAS test, which is one small part of the Neurosensory Center Comprehensive Examination for Aphasia (NCCEA; Spreen & Benton, 1977). In this test the patient is seated comfortably and given instructions like these:

> I'm going to say a letter of the alphabet. I want you to tell me as many words that begin with that letter as you can as *quickly* as possible. For example, if I say "D" you might say "dog," "door," "dance," and so on. Do not use words that are proper names such as "Donald" or "Disneyland." Also, do not use the same word with a different ending such as "dance" and "dancing." Any questions? [pause] The first letter is "F." Go ahead.

The examiner begins timing immediately, allowing 1 minute for each of the three trials (F, A, and S). A brief rest period occurs between trials. If the examinee is silent for 15 seconds, the trial is ended. The examiner writes down the actual words for purposes of scoring at a later time. The score is the sum of all acceptable words for the three trials. Proper nouns, variations, repetitions, and words beginning with a nondesignated letter are not counted.

The typical performance of healthy young adults is summarized in Table 6.7. The reader will notice that average performance actually improves slightly from young adulthood into middle age. These data are from subjects with relatively high levels of education (some college education). Performance of individuals with high school education or less is four to five words lower, on average. The impact of education is revealed in Table 6.8, which shows typical performance for older subjects with and without college education. A useful guideline is that performance more than 2 standard deviations below the mean should be considered highly suggestive of cognitive impairment. These tentative cutoffs are indicated in Tables 6.7 and 6.8. However, an important caveat is that performance on the FAS test is substantially affected by major depression (Hart et al., 1988). Clinicians should remember that significant depression might be a contributing factor to low scores on a word fluency test.

Bender Gestalt

The Bender Gestalt is one of the top four or five most widely used tests in all of clinical psychology. No treatise on intellectual assessment would be complete if it overlooked this valuable screening instrument. The Bender Gestalt is a design-copying test. The examinee has as much time as needed to copy nine geometric designs, one

TABLE 6.7   FAS Word Fluency Test: Normative Data for Males and Females Stratified by Age

Males	15–20 Years (N = 32)	21–25 Years (N = 37)	26–30 Years (N = 32)	31–40 Years (N = 26)
Mean	42	45	45	49
SD	7	6	5	6

Females	15–20 Years (N = 30)	21–25 Years (N = 36)	26–30 Years (N = 16)	31–40 Years (N = 16)
Mean	41	45	43	50
SD	7	7	6	6

Note: Subjects had relatively high education levels. Subjects with education less than grade 12 usually score 4–5 words fewer.

Source: Based on data from L. T Yeudall, D. Fromm, J. Reddon, and W. Stefanyk, (1986), "Normative Data Stratified by Age and Sex for 12 Neuropsychological Tests," *Journal of Clinical Psychology, 42,* 918–945.

TABLE 6.8   FAS Word Fluency Test: Normative Data for an Elderly Sample Stratified by Age and Education

Years	50–54 (N = 42)	55–59 (N = 67)	60–64 (N = 70)	65–69 (N = 56)	70–74 (N = 55)	75+ (N = 55)
Education						
≤ 12 years Mean	42	37	38	39	36	35
SD	12	10	11	12	13	12

Years	50–54 (N = 56)	55–59 (N = 78)	60–64 (N = 87)	65–69 (N = 90)	70–74 (N = 60)	75+ (N = 59)
Education						
≥ 13 years Mean	42	46	41	44	41	39
SD	11	11	10	11	10	14

Source: Based on data in O. Spreen, and E. Strauss. *A Compendium of Neuropsychological Tests: Administration, Norms, and Commentary* (New York: Oxford University Press, 1991).

at a time. The deceptive simplicity of this procedure masks the fact that it assesses the integrity of a complex series of psychological functions. The client must first perceive each design, interpret the spatial relationships of the components, and then integrate this interpretation with the appropriate motor output. Hence, "visual-perceptual-motor integration test" would be a more accurate label.

Design-copying tests such as the Bender Gestalt are clearly multifactorial measures; that is, the client must have normal functioning for many different abilities (psychomotor, perceptual, visual-motor, memory) in order to perform well. As such, drawing tests are useful for the screening of cognitive impairment but seldom indicate the precise source or degree of impairment. As with any screening test, drawing tests such as the Bender Gestalt yield a significant proportion of false negatives or "test misses." Whereas poor performance on the Bender Gestalt is highly suspicious of cognitive impairment, good performance does not mean that the examinee is necessarily free of such impairment.

The Bender Gestalt is named after Lauretta Bender (1938), who devised this simple test as a means of studying the relationship of perception to various types of psychopathology. The full title is Bender Visual Motor Gestalt Test, but almost everyone refers to it as the Bender Gestalt. The nine stimulus figures (see Figure 6.3) were adapted from a larger number of designs devised by Max Wertheimer (1923), one of the founders of the gestalt school of psychology. Wertheimer had used the designs to study the gestalt principles of visual perception, for example, the tendency to organize dots into a perceived line.

Early research with the Bender Gestalt was mainly descriptive, and there was considerable emphasis on its use as a projective personality instrument (Hutt & Briskin, 1960). However, most users were more interested in practical questions such as the quick and reliable diagnosis of cognitive impairment, and this became the focus of subsequent research. The importance of scoring systems as a means of improving accuracy and validity became evident, and several innovative approaches have been pursued (Pascal & Suttell, 1951; Hutt & Briskin, 1960; Hain, 1964; Pauker, 1976; Lacks, 1984).

Administering the Bender Gestalt.   The Bender Gestalt is deceptively simple to administer. Instructions for administration vary slightly from one authority to another. In general, we follow the recommendations of Hutt (1977) here. The examiner places a small pile of blank, unlined paper in front of the client, with three number 2 pencils to the side. The short side of the paper faces the client. The following instructions are then read or paraphrased:

> I am going to show you these cards, one at a time. Each card has a simple drawing on it. I would like you to copy the drawing on the paper, as well as you can. Work in any way that is best for you. This is not a test of artistic ability, but try to copy the drawing as accurately as possible. Work as fast or as slowly as you wish. (Hutt, 1977, p. 64)

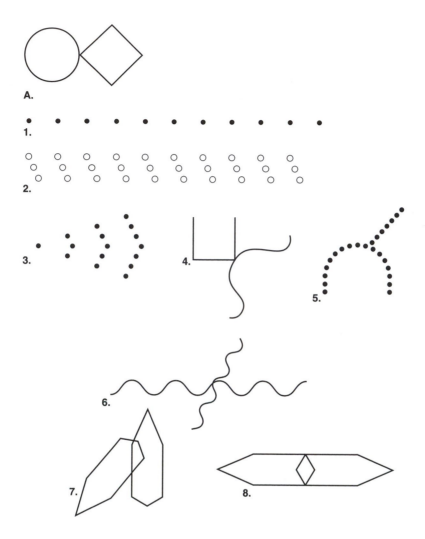

FIGURE 6.3   Nine Stimulus Figures from the Bender Gestalt Test

Source: Reprinted with permission from L. Bender, *A Visual Motor Gestalt Test and Its Clinical Use* (New York: American Orthopsychiatric Association, 1938). Bender® Visual Motor Gestalt Test published by the American Orthopsychiatric Association, © 1938, renewed 1965, by Lauretta Bender and the American Orthopsychiatric Association, Inc.

Subsequent questions from the client (e.g., "Do I have to count the dots?" or "Can I turn the card?" or "Can I use more than one sheet of paper?") are responded to with a non-committal "It's up to you" or similar indirect response. The answer to "May I use a ruler?" is "No." The client is encouraged to finish all the drawings on a single piece of paper. Any rotations of the paper for specific designs are mentally noted. Once the client begins drawing the designs, the average time required to complete all nine designs is about 6 minutes.

Bender Gestalt Scoring Systems.   Practitioners typically use the Bender Gestalt as an aid in the differential diagnosis of psychiatric patients, particularly the diagnosis of suspected brain impairment versus psychiatric disorder. Psychiatric patients tend to do more poorly on virtually any psychological test than do normal individuals, so a clinically useful screening test for cognitive impairment must demonstrate its ability to detect persons with cerebral impairment when they are intermixed with patients who have serious emotional disturbance but no cerebral impairment.

The Bender Gestalt meets this criterion to a reasonable degree. In a review of hit rates in studies conducted from 1960 through 1975, Heaton, Baade, and Johnson (1978) noted a median result for correct classification of 76 percent. Lacks and Newport (1980) reported hit rates of 82–86 percent in a mixed sample of admissions to the acute psychiatric treatment unit of an urban community mental health center. This hit rate is particularly impressive in that the patients were selected to match hospital diagnostic base rates (34% neurological disorder, 30% psychosis, 16% personality disorder, 20% chronic alcoholism); that is, the diagnostic task for the Bender Gestalt was both realistic and challenging.

The Bender Gestalt works well in a psychiatric setting because it is especially sensitive to diffuse, slowly progressive types of brain damage such as multi-infarct dementia, Alzheimer's disease, alcoholism, or cardiovascular insufficiency. These are precisely the types of cerebrally impaired individuals likely to be seen in a typical psychiatric setting. In this type of referral setting the Bender Gestalt can serve as a brief, inexpensive, low-risk screening test for cognitive impairment (Russell, 1976).

Although clinicians commonly interpret Bender Gestalt results subjectively ("These drawings contain signs indicative of cognitive impairment"), it is also important for examiners to become familiar with one or more scoring systems. The problem with clinical judgment is simple—it may reduce validity! Robiner (1978) asked five professional clinical psychologists and five clinical graduate students to evaluate the same Bender Gestalt protocols used by Lacks and Newport (1980), omitting results from ten chronic alcoholics. When they used subjective clinical judgment, the psychologists obtained 71 percent hit rates, significantly below the 82–86 percent reported in the original study.

In general, clinical judgment is inferior to a good scoring system, although there may be exceptions. Lezak (1995) discusses several instances in which clearly impaired patients obtained normal-range scores on the Bender Gestalt. Yet in each case the drawings contained one or more clinical signs of cognitive impairment. Responsible clinicians would be well advised to learn a good scoring system, but should keep in mind that no system is perfect. Clinicians need to "look beyond the scores" and consider that a "normal" score for a Bender Gestalt may signify a false negative.

The Quick-Scoring system (Pauker, 1976) is a good first choice for scoring systems because it takes only minutes to learn and reveals respectably high hit rates, for example, 79 percent in the Lacks and Newport (1980) study. The inter-rater reliability of .95 is outstanding. The aim of the Pauker system is to arrive quickly, easily, and reliably at a measure of "difficulty in drawing" the nine Bender Gestalt figures. "Difficulty" is defined in terms of deviations from the original drawings in spatial orientation, directional orientation, or form.

Each figure is scored on a 0 to 4 basis. A score of 0 indicates a reproduction close to the original figure, a 2 indicates a significant deviation from the original, and a score of 4 is reserved for severely distorted drawings. Scoring should be done quickly, without agonizing, but conservatively. If there is doubt as to whether the figure is a 0 or a 2 (or a 2 or a 4), it is best to score at one of the in-between points (1 or 3) without wasting time.

Pauker (1976) discusses a number of specific criteria, which are summarized here:

0: Reproduction is close to the original with respect to number of components, shape, spatial orientation, relative size of the components.

2: The figure can be identified readily as a copy of the original figure but deviates significantly from the original. Includes distorted shape, variation in relative size of components, missing angles, addition of parts, and rotations of 45 degrees or 180 degrees.

4: Drawing is severely distorted; for example, drawing is almost unrecognizable, a major component is missing or grossly misplaced, or rotation of about 90 degrees is present.

The Pauker system has no standard cutoff. However, Lacks and Newport (1980) used a breaking point of 8 and below for normal, 9 and above for impaired, to obtain an optimal hit rate of 79 percent. Figure 6.4 shows a Bender Gestalt test protocol scored according to the Pauker system.

A more complex scoring system that produces slightly higher hit rates (82–86 percent) has been proposed by Lacks (1984). Her system is a refinement of the approach advocated by Hutt (1977, 1985). This approach is summarized here, mainly because it embodies a "sign" approach that is useful in learning about the qualitative indications that may occur in a protocol when cognitive impairment is present. The Lacks system takes several hours to learn and requires the use of a self-tutored scoring manual (Lacks, 1980) for best results. Highly useful software for learning the Lacks system is available (see below).

Lacks (1984) uses the twelve organic signs developed by Hutt and Briskin (1960). The presence of any five of these errors or signs is taken to indicate cognitive impairment. In addition, it can be counted as an extra error if the examinee takes more than 15 minutes to complete the task. The examiner also must evaluate such examinee characteristics as impulsivity, carelessness, hostility toward the examiner, and lack of interest in the task. Scoring is conservative, and only errors caused by true perceptual-motor difficulties are included. If a sign appears more than once, it is still scored as only 1 error. The maximum score is 13.

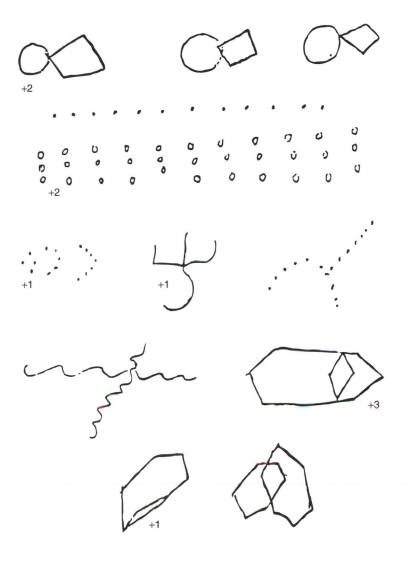

FIGURE 6.4   Sample Bender Gestalt Test Protocol Scored by the Pauker System

The twelve qualitative signs (plus a thirteenth quantitative sign) are as follows:

1. Rotation: Figure is rotated 80 to 180 degrees. Not scored if subject shifts the position of the card and then copies it accurately.
2. Overlapping Difficulty: Difficulty in drawing the portions of the figures that should overlap.
3. Simplification: Figure is oversimplified.

4. Fragmentation: The figure is broken up into parts and the overall gestalt is destroyed or incomplete.
5. Retrogression: Substitution of a more primitive gestalt form than the stimulus.
6. Perseveration: Features of a previous stimulus carry over into the current stimulus, or intradesign perseveration wherein the figure is continued beyond needed limits.
7. Collision: Two separate figures overlap or are drawn within 1/4 inch of one another.
8. Impotence: Inability to draw a figure correctly. Often demonstrated by statements such as "I just can't make this drawing right" or by repetitious drawings or numerous erasures.
9. Closure Difficulty: Difficulty in getting adjacent parts of a figure to touch or in getting the joining parts of figures together. More than 1/8-inch gap is scored as Simplification, not Closure Difficulty.
10. Motor Incoordination: Tremor when drawing.
11. Angulation Difficulty: Severe difficulty in reproducing the angulation of figures. Scored for figures 2 and 3, particularly for Figure 2.
12. Cohesion: Isolated decrease or increase in size of subportion of one design. Example: On design A the circle is too small by one-third or more. Scored very conservatively.
13. More than 15 minutes to complete the test.

In addition to scoring items 1–13 on a present versus absent basis, it is important for the examiner to note any behavioral peculiarities that might influence the interpretation of the test protocol. Figure 6.5 is a composite Bender Gestalt protocol that illustrates the twelve possible errors.

The book *Bender Gestalt Screening for Brain Dysfunction*, by Patricia Lacks (1984), should be a required reference for practitioners who use this test. The Bender Gestalt stimulus cards can be ordered from Western Psychological Services, 12031 Wilshire Boulevard, Los Angeles, CA 90025. A computerized scoring and reporting system for the Bender Gestalt based on the Lacks (1984) approach is available from Psychological Assessment Resources, P. O. Box 998, Odessa, FL 33556.

We have only touched on the essentials of the Bender Gestalt here. Many variations in administration, scoring, and other factors are available. For example, Canter (1996) devised what is known as the background interference procedure for the test. In this approach the examinee first completes the test in the normal way. Then on a second administration, the test is carried out on specially prepared interference paper. This is paper that contains randomly placed, intersecting, curved black lines that the examinee must ignore in copying the test designs. The interference procedure poses a relatively greater challenge for persons with cognitive impairment and is therefore believed to increase the sensitivity of the test. Canter (1996) provides an excellent review of his approach and other variations of the Bender Gestalt.

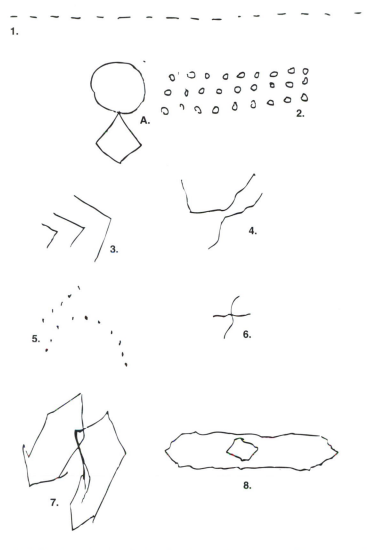

FIGURE 6.5 Composite Bender Gestalt Test Protocol Illustrating the Twelve Errors
Source: Based on Lacks (1980).

Greek Cross Test

The Greek Cross Test is another effective drawing test for the identification of possible cognitive impairment. The test is normally administered as part of an aphasia screening test (Wheeler & Reitan, 1962), but its content is clearly visual-motor and not linguistic. The examinee is asked to copy a single figure, a simple line drawing of a Greek cross. However, to make the task somewhat more challenging, the client

FIGURE 6.6   Greek Cross Stimulus Figure

is told to trace the perimeter of the object such that the pencil line starts and ends at the same point. This extremely simple and short screening device has a long history of successful use in more extensive neuropsychological test batteries (Russell, Neuringer, & Goldstein, 1970; Reitan & Davison, 1974; Swiercinsky, 1978).

The Greek Cross Test has proven satisfactory as a short and simple screening device for visual-motor impairment. The examinee is asked merely to copy carefully the design shown in Figure 6.6, as described above. It is essential that the examinee trace the perimeter, as interpretive norms are based on this particular method of execution. These norms become meaningless if the client is allowed to pursue the easier method of drawing horizontal lines or vertical lines separately, lifting the pencil, checking position, correcting minor deviations, and so on.

Clients with significant brain impairment almost always will reveal difficulty when drawing the Greek cross. For example, omission of one arm of the cross may indicate a serious lesion on the opposite side of the brain because of the contralateral control of the visual fields. Significant distortions of the shape may result from impairment to either cerebral hemisphere. However, the right cerebral hemisphere is more likely to give rise to these errors. Simplification of the overall design may signal a diffuse dementia. Rather than inferring specific pathologies from defective drawings, the examiner should consider poor performance on drawing the Greek cross as a signal that additional testing or referral is warranted. Examples of various errors are shown in Figure 6.7.

Assessment of Executive Functions

The executive functions include those capacities that allow an individual to engage successfully in independent, goal-directed, self-serving behavior (Lezak, 1995). In the assessment of executive functions the crucial issue is not *what or how much* a person knows, but *how or whether* a person will do something. Thus, executive functions involve the ability to identify a relevant goal, form a plan to pursue the goal,

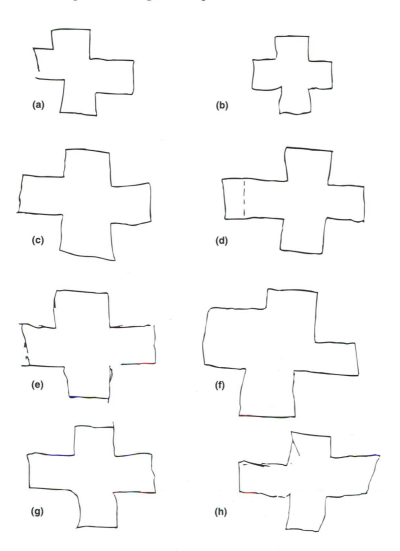

FIGURE 6.7 Examples of Defective Performance on the Greek Cross Test

(a) Clerical worker whose test battery showed generalized right hemisphere dysfunction of unknown etiology, leading to motor slowing and perceptual processing deficits in the left hand. Stimulus was drawn with the dominant right hand; distortion of the shape reveals the *construction dyspraxia* commonly observed in right hemisphere impairment. **(b)** College student referred for learning disability who had various subtle deficits on a larger test battery. **(c)** College student with a severe drinking problem. Note the fine line and motor tremor. **(d)** Sixty-two year-old college professor 2 years after an extensive right hemisphere stroke. He added the dotted lines to indicate that he knew the drawing was deficient. **(e)** The extensive reworking of the lines is sometimes observed in generalized, diffuse dementia. **(f)** This patient had a tumor removed from the cerebellar region on the right side of his brain stem 2 years prior to testing. **(g)** A patient with alcoholic Korsakoff's syndrome. Note again the fine line and tremor. **(h)** An older person with generalized dementia of unknown etiology.

monitor progress, and modify the plan as needed. Executive functions include qualities such as logical analysis, reasoning, planning, and flexibility of thinking. In addition, executive functions extend beyond these cognitive abilities and include the capacities to initiate activity, inhibit inappropriate behavior, monitor ongoing progress, change tactics, and incorporate new strategies, as needed. Lezak (1995) notes that executive functions are not easily tested by traditional psychometric instruments. Almost by definition, psychometric instruments are structured—yet, paradoxically, the goal is to see whether patients can provide their own structure.

One approach followed by Lezak (1982) is to provide fifty Tinkertoy® pieces and tell the patient: "Make whatever you want with these. You will have at least 5 minutes and as much more time as you wish to make something." Scoring of this Tinkertoy® Test is from −1 to +12 based on several variables including the number of pieces used, symmetry and mobility of the structure, and whether the construction is given a name. Head-injured patients and others who have sustained impairments of executive functions produce impoverished designs that use only a small number of pieces. Their constructions often are immobile and unnamed (Bayless, Varney, & Roberts, 1989). Unfortunately, the Tinkertoy® Test has not received wide acceptance. In part, this is because the company producing this toy periodically changes the size and structure of the component elements, which makes it nearly impossible to specify a "standard" set of pieces for the test.

Typically, the assessment of executive functions proceeds clinically by means of interview and checklist. For example, Pollens, McBratnie, and Burton (1988) have developed a structured checklist that is helpful in the assessment of executive functions. Based on observation and interview with the client and family members, the clinician fills out the structured checklist depicted in Figure 6.8. The items on this checklist define important aspects of global cognitive functions: awareness, goal setting, planning, self-initiation, self-inhibition, self-monitoring, ability to change set, and strategic behavior. Difficulties with these elements of executive functioning are common in cases of diffuse brain impairment such as found in head-injured persons.

Short Category Test, Booklet Form

The original Category Test dates back to the 1940s when Ward Halstead (1947) devised a measure of the capacity to deduce general principles from experience with specific stimuli. Halstead noticed that brain-injured persons were deficient at precisely this intellectual capacity. In designing the Category Test, he sought to capture the consequences of brain damage in a simple assessment tool. The test was refined and validated by Ralph Reitan shortly thereafter, and it quickly became one of the premiere instruments for the assessment of brain-impaired individuals (Reitan & Wolfson, 1993).

In the original Category Test the examinee views a series of 208 individual slides of geometric shapes (e.g., three small squares and one large square all in a single row) and must pull one of four toggle switches, numbered 1 through 4. The goal

Awareness						
denies deficits	1	2	3	4	5	insight about deficits
Goal Setting						
structure-dependent	1	2	3	4	5	sets long-term goals
Planning						
haphazard approach	1	2	3	4	5	careful planning with new tasks
Self-Initiating						
prompts to start	1	2	3	4	5	completely independent
Self-Inhibiting						
socially inappropriate behavior	1	2	3	4	5	behavior is appropriate to situation
Self-Monitoring						
unable to detect errors	1	2	3	4	5	corrects, makes changes as needed
Ability to Change Set						
perseverates, no benefit from cues	1	2	3	4	5	tries variety of solutions
Strategic Behavior						
cannot incorporate new strategies	1	2	3	4	5	creates new strategies

1 = profoundly impaired
2 = severely impaired
3 = moderately impaired
4 = mildly impaired
5 = normal

FIGURE 6.8 Structured Checklist for the Clinical Assessment of Executive Functions
Source: Reprinted with permission from R. Pollens, B. McBratnie, and P. Burton (1988), "Beyond Cognition: Executive Functions," *Cognitive Rehabilitation, 5,* 26–33.

is to identify an underlying principle or concept (e.g., the ordinal position of the odd stimulus) that will allow for correct answers, which are signaled by a bell. The examinee is allowed only one response per slide; incorrect answers result in an unpleasant buzzer sound. There are seven different subtests, the first six of which have their own underlying principle. The seventh subtest is announced as a review of the previous six and does not embody a single principle for the examinee to deduce.

The Category Test is one of the best single measures of cognitive impairment available for assessment. Unfortunately, in its original version the instrument has a number of significant drawbacks. One problem is its sheer size. The apparatus for the test consists of a large plywood box with interior mirrors and projection screen.

A carousel projector sits at the back and delivers the stimuli. The instrument is heavy and cannot be moved easily. This means that the examinee must come to the test, which is not always practical. A second problem is the time required to administer the test. With 208 untimed trials, the test can take a prohibitive amount of time to administer. Finally, a third problem has to do with the buzzer sound given for incorrect responses. This can be demoralizing, especially for highly impaired persons who encounter one buzzer after another.

Several variant tests patterned on the original Category Test have appeared over the years. Most have far fewer stimuli, and several use a different format in which the client is merely told "right" or "wrong" by the examinee instead of receiving bells and buzzers for feedback. One simple, 100-item booklet form of this test is the Short Category Test, Booklet Form (Wetzel & Boll, 1987). This test consists of five small ring binders, each containing 20 stimuli, for a total of 100 items. Suitable for persons 15 years of age and older, the test can be administered in just 15 to 30 minutes.

The examinee is told for each set of stimuli that a single idea or principle underlies all of the items. The single idea or principle will suggest a correct answer from the alternatives 1-2-3-4 that are printed underneath the stimulus cards. The task of the examinee is to figure out the correct idea or principle from ongoing feedback ("right" or "wrong"). The score on the test is the total number of errors for the 100 stimuli. Wetzel and Boll (1987) report that using an error score of 41 as a cutoff score for persons age 45 and under and an error score of 46 for those over the age of 45 correctly classified 83 percent of all subjects, including normal volunteers and patients. The test is available from Western Psychological Services, 12031 Wilshire Boulevard, Los Angeles, CA 90025.

Final Comment

Whether the goal is basic intellectual assessment or screening for suspected cognitive impairment, the administration and interpretation of tests are just the beginning of the assessment process. In addition, the practitioner needs to synthesize the results usefully. The final chapter introduces the reader to professional standards and principles of effective report writing.

7 Report Writing and Professional Standards

This final chapter provides guidelines for writing assessment reports and also summarizes professional standards that influence the crafting of these documents. The chapter closes with a sampling of representative reports written for diverse audiences. The character of a report is shaped by issues of informed consent, cautious provision of feedback to clients, sensitivity in the assessment of minorities, and a host of other ethical and professional concerns. Thus, we begin the chapter with a review of these crucial foundations of clinical assessment.

Professional and Ethical Standards in Assessment

Clinical psychology and other helping professions have evolved a number of guidelines relevant to assessment. These standards acknowledge that assessment is more than a contract between the examiner and examinee. In addition, the evaluation of an individual potentially impacts his or her family, employers, and the wider network of social institutions involved in the referral (Matarazzo, 1986, 1990). The examiner must approach the assignment with tact, sensitivity, and an eye to the societal impact of the endeavor. Over the years, professional organizations and alliances have put forth ethical principles and standards of practice that circumscribe the practice of assessment. Three sources are of particular significance:

- *Ethical Principles of Psychologists and Code of Conduct* (APA, 1992)
- *Responsible Test Use* (Eyde et al., 1993)
- *Standards for Educational and Psychological Testing* (AERA, APA, & NCME, 1985, 1997)

Many of the principles and guidelines emphasized in these sources pertain to therapeutic relationships, and it is beyond the scope of this book to review them. For example, practitioners from any background and in any specialty are required to preserve the *confidentiality* of their client interactions, except when clearly demarcated boundaries are crossed (e.g., the client abuses a child or reveals a potential for imminent self-harm). Practitioners also are advised to avoid *dual relationships* (e.g., a psychologist tests her physician for memory loss). Further, practitioners are expected to use techniques that have been carefully validated and to possess *expertise* concerning these techniques. Regarding assessment, it is nearly a self-evident guideline that the practitioner should be well versed in the psychometric properties of the instruments chosen for assessment. These and other general guidelines are not mentioned further. Instead, what follows is a summary of principles that possess particular relevance to the ethical and responsible practice of psychological assessment.

Informed Consent

Before beginning an assessment, the examiner must obtain informed consent from the client or a legal guardian. The principle of informed consent is so important that it is spelled out in detail by the *Standards for Educational and Psychological Testing:*

> Informed consent implies that the test takers or representatives are made aware, in language that they can understand, of the reasons for testing, the type of tests to be used, the intended use and the range of material consequences of the intended use, and what testing information will be released and to whom. (AERA, APA, & NCME, 1985)

The principle of informed consent arose in the field of psychiatry in the 1960s as a means of humanizing the practitioner–patient relationship. The intention was to promote individual autonomy and to encourage rational decision making. In today's litigious climate, the doctrine now serves to protect the interests of both patient and practitioner.

From a legal standpoint, there are three elements to a valid informed consent: disclosure, competency, and voluntariness (Melton et al., 1997). Disclosure refers to whether the client is given sufficient information to make a reasonable decision. In the context of assessment, adequate disclosure would include a description of the intended testing; a discussion of the purposes of the testing; an analysis of possible risks of the endeavor; and an explicit statement as to when, where, and how the test results will be released. Competency refers to the mental capacity of the examinee to provide consent. Competency is usually assumed with adults unless the examinee is very elderly or mentally disabled (especially if mentally retarded). When testing persons with significant mental incapacity, a guardian, spouse, or other caregiver may possess the legal authority to provide consent. Of course, when testing children, examiners must obtain the informed consent of parents or other legal guardians. Finally, the criterion of voluntariness implies that the choice to undergo an assessment battery is given freely. This is rarely a concern in most consultation settings but could prove relevant in selected institutional environments. For example, voluntariness may not exist for an inmate who is promised release time if he participates in an assessment-based research study.

In most cases, informed consent is accomplished by means of a written informed consent form. The practitioner explains the form, responds to questions, and then asks the client or guardian to affirm, by signature, that he or she agrees to the nature and purpose of the assessment. An example of an *abbreviated* informed consent form is shown in Figure 7.1. Most informed consent forms are much longer—six to ten pages, single-spaced, is not unusual. Because informed consent forms may contain legal and contractual implications, practitioners are advised to consult with local counsel when devising a form for personal use.

Sensitivity to Individual Differences

The American Psychological Association lists respect for individual differences as one of its six guiding principles:

> Principle D: Respect for People's Rights and Dignity...Psychologists are aware of cultural, individual, and role differences, including those due to age, gender, race, ethnicity, national origin, religion, sexual orientation, disability, language, and socioeconomic status. Psychologists try to eliminate the effect on their work of biases based on those factors, and they do not knowingly participate in or condone unfair discriminatory practices. (APA, 1992, p. 1599)

Sensitivity to individual differences is important in any field of psychology, but it is especially crucial in assessment because the meaning of test results often is moderated by the age, sex, race, language, social status, and other characteristics of the examinee.

In *Responsible Test Use*, Eyde et al. (1993) document several assessment cases in which psychologists failed to respect individual differences. In each instance the aftermath was potentially destructive for the examinee:

- A 31-year-old service station manager suffered a head injury from a tire explosion and was unconscious for 3 months. Upon receiving the referral for assessment, the examiner administered a test of intelligence and a test of immediate memory. Based on good scores on these two tests, the examiner's conclusions were that the patient was ready to return to work. Fortunately, the patient's wife appealed the conclusion, and a more comprehensive evaluation by a neuropsychologist revealed severe deficits from frontal lobe brain damage verified by a CT scan. The patient never returned to normal employment.
- The Luria-Nebraska Neuropsychological Battery (LNNB) was administered to a foreign national who had been struck over the head with a bottle in a bar fight. The examinee did not speak English, so the examiner deviated from standard instructions and also eliminated difficult items. The consequence was an apparent misdiagnosis of brain injury that confused litigation issues.
- A 75-year-old man received an evaluation at the request of his wife, who suspected memory problems. A large discrepancy between certain subtest scores on the WAIS-R was interpreted as indicating a deterioration of intellectual functioning in the husband. However, this interpretation was based on faulty use of non–age-corrected subtest scores. The large discrepancy disappeared

FIGURE 7.1 **Informed Consent for Psychological Assessment**

This is an agreement between [Client's name] and [Practitioner's Name], Ph.D. I am a licensed psychologist in the state of Illinois. You are encouraged to ask questions about my experience or professional credentials at any time.

1. General Information: The purpose of this assessment is to provide your [physician, counselor, therapist] with information about your intellectual functioning that may prove helpful in his/her work with you. The assessment will involve a brief interview; some paper-and-pencil tests; and person-to-person tests of attention, memory, learning, intelligence, and other cognitive functions. The assessment will take several hours of your time.

2. Test Report: The relevant information from the interview and the test results will be summarized in a written report. Two copies of the report will be produced: one for the referral source [name], and one that I will keep securely filed for a minimum of 15 years. I will review the test results and the report with you in approximately 1 week.

Confidentiality: The report will not be released to any other source unless you request this formally in writing. Exceptions to this rule of confidentiality include these situations: your life or another person's life is in danger, child or elder abuse is reported, or a court orders the disclosure of the report.

3. Cost: The cost of psychological assessment varies depending on the tests used, and includes the time required for interviewing, test administration, scoring, interpretation, and report writing. An hourly rate of $XXX is used in arriving at the total fee. Some or all of this cost may be covered by your health insurance policy. The estimated total cost for your assessment is $XXX.

4. Side Effects: Although most individuals enjoy the process of taking psychological tests, some persons find it uncomfortable, especially if the tests indicate that they have cognitive impairments. It is also possible during interview that you may recall painful memories from the past. It is appropriate for you to discuss these feelings with me. You are free to withdraw your consent for ongoing testing at any time.

5. Alternative Procedures: You are not required to complete this assessment in order to receive ongoing treatment. Many of the questions that will be answered with this assessment might be answered over the course of continued consultations with your [physician, counselor, therapist]. However, the questions may be answered more quickly and accurately by participating in this evaluation, and your treatment may be more effective.

6. Refusal of Assessment: You have the right to refuse this assessment. You are not required to complete this evaluation in order to continue working with your [physician, counselor, therapist]. By not participating in this assessment, you may hinder an accurate assessment of your current problems and thereby decrease the likelihood of effective treatment. Upon request, I will discuss referral options with you.

_____   _____

Client's Name   Date

Note: This form is for illustrative purposes only. Practitioners should consult local counsel when writing an informed consent form.

when age-corrected scores were compared. This costly oversight caused the man and his wife weeks of unnecessary worry.

What all of these examples have in common is the examiner's insensitivity to the reality that *individual differences moderate the interpretation of test results*. In the first case the examiner should have known that "normal" test results do not necessarily indicate normal functioning in an individual with a preexisting disability. The error in the second case was a failure to acknowledge the effect of language differences upon test interpretation. In the third case the examiner was unaware of the major impact of normal age differences upon test results and interpretation. These potentially costly oversights could have been avoided if the examiners had been sensitive to individual differences.

Feedback about Assessment Results

In most cases, feedback about assessment results is provided not only in writing but also in a person-to-person conference. Pope (1992) has compiled several useful guidelines for providing written and verbal feedback to clients. Of course, the examiner should use language and concepts that can be understood by the client and referral sources. In addition, an essential component in feedback is that of *acknowledging fallibility*:

> The feedback process best focuses on hypotheses for which there are varying degrees of evidence in the test findings rather than on any sort of infallible, unchallengeable pronouncements. The clinician has the responsibility to ensure that the client not only understands this general lack of infallibility but also is aware of any specific reservations the clinician has about the validity, reliability, meaning, and implications of specific tests, findings, and so forth. (Pope, 1992, p. 270)

We have noted in a previous chapter that clients typically harbor serious misconceptions about the meaning of assessment results, especially when intelligence tests are used. It is the responsibility of the examiner to challenge these misconceptions by making statements of probabilities rather than pronouncements of certainties. For example, in describing the implications of an IQ score of 85 for a prospective college student, the examiner might indicate that the client will likely experience difficulty in pursuing an undergraduate degree rather than stating flatly that college is out of the question. This is not only tactful; it is also an accurate indication of the fallibility of test data.

Report Writing in Assessment

Report writing is an undervalued skill. The main reason for this is the common assumption among practitioners that reports are mainly for record keeping. From this perspective, there is no need to take report writing seriously. To meet administrative requirements, it will suffice to "dash off" a quick summary of the data for the sake of posterity. The unconscious assumption of the report writer is that the document will disappear into some large metal filing cabinet, never to see the light of day again. No point, then, in selecting words carefully or rewriting a lackluster report.

This all too common orientation to report writing is dangerous and misguided. The basic thesis of this chapter is that report writing is potentially serious business. Psychological reports can make a difference. They should be written with care. We will consider the importance of psychological reports and then look at general guidelines for report writing.

Importance of Psychological Reports

Once the interview and testing have been completed, it is the *feedback* that determines the degree to which an assessment proves helpful. Of course, the most essential element of feedback is the psychological report. A useful report contains clear findings and provides specific recommendations based on the referral issues. When implemented, the recommendations may change the life of the examinee. The responsibility of the practitioner is to fashion the report carefully, so as to maximize the likelihood of a positive impact on the examinee.

In Chapter 4 we noted the case of Daniel Hoffman versus the New York City Board of Education (Sattler, 1988). The case is worth repeating briefly in this chapter because it illustrates, in a profound and melancholy way, the importance of psychological reports. Daniel Hoffman was a 26-year-old man who brought suit against the board of education for being inappropriately placed in mentally retarded classes. The complaint alleged that the plaintiff was never retarded and only had a speech impediment, and that placing him in an educational environment for mentally retarded children deprived him of adequate speech therapy.

On the basis of a Stanford-Binet IQ of 74, the plaintiff was placed in a class for the mentally retarded and kept there for his remaining school years. The psychological report played a critical role in the lawsuit. One crucial point was that the psychologist failed to note in his report the potentially detrimental effects of a speech impediment on intellectual test results. As a consequence, Daniel Hoffman was inappropriately placed and experienced 10 years of educational deprivation.

A different type of problem was encountered by a graduate trainee who evaluated a seriously head-injured young adult. The graduate student wrote a very optimistic report that ignored and downplayed the many deficiencies revealed by a comprehensive test battery. The report was accurate in the sense that it correctly reported error scores and the like; however, the examiner found numerous extenuating circumstances that might explain the poor performance of the referral and generally interpreted all findings in the most positive light possible. At the time, the supervisor saw no harm in this "upbeat" approach, insofar as it seemed to be what the client and his parents wanted to hear. The client left the feedback session with high motivation to regain the many cognitive skills he had lost from the head injury.

Two years later the report was subpoenaed in a lawsuit filed by the head-injured client. Although he won a substantial settlement, it seems likely that the overly optimistic report only muddled the compensation issues raised in the lawsuit. Perhaps his interests would have been better served by a more realistic summary of his test results.

Another form of carelessness is the report that is full of spelling and grammatical errors. Many readers will immediately dismiss such a report as worthless, even though this might be a case of "throwing out the baby with the bath water." Whether poorly written reports deserve to be discredited is irrelevant. What is true is that most readers give them little credence.

In sum, carelessly written reports can harm the client, and carelessly written reports have a way of coming back to haunt the practitioner. In the sections that follow, specific guidelines are presented for writing constructive reports that minimize the likelihood of the unpleasantries illustrated in the previous paragraphs. A first step in that direction is to follow a logical and sensible outline.

Outline for Assessment Reports

No single approach to the assessment report will suffice for every occasion. I cannot overemphasize that the examiner should feel free to improvise and adapt reports so as to best serve the interests of the examinee. The precise nature of the report will depend not only on the referral issues, tests administered, and scores obtained, but also on who will read the report. One type of report will do when a state welfare agency has requested the WAIS-III IQs and subtest scores of a client with probable borderline intelligence. That same report would be inappropriate when it is the parents who have requested testing on their adult child with a history of special school placements. In the first case a simple statement of IQ scores and level of functioning is all that is desired. In the second case the goal is to explain the functional implications of the test results, and an entirely different kind of report is mandated.

In summary, the best approach is to individualize each report with these two questions in mind: First, who will be responding to the results or implementing the recommendations in the report? Second, what style of report will have the best chance of an ultimately beneficial impact on the examinee? As the answers to these questions vary, so will the outline, length, and writing style of the report. Every report needs to be tailored to the circumstances at hand. Examples of such individualized reports are provided at the end of this chapter.

Even though examiners should not blindly follow the same outline in all cases, there is a useful suggested format for reports. This outline will suffice in most cases, and is a good starting point from which to improvise an individualized report. A traditional outline contains the following sections:

- Title and Identifying Information
- Referral and Background Information

- Appearance and Behavior in Testing
- Test Results and Interpretation
- Summary and Recommendations

Guidelines for these sections of a report are discussed below.

Title and Identifying Information.   Avoid bland titles such as "Psychological Report." Instead, let the title reflect the specific emphasis of the report. For example, if the assessment mainly involved memory functions, an appropriate title might be "Assessment of Memory Functions." If the assessment relied heavily on interview impressions but also used a wide variety of screening tests, a helpful title might be "Report on Neuropsychological Test Results and Interview." If the main assessment instrument was the WAIS-R, "Intellectual Assessment" might be an appropriate title.

It is also possible to include identifying information in the title as well. For example:

"Intellectual Assessment Report on John MARX, age 25-7 on 1/17/1998"

Here the title, name, age, and date of testing are all displayed on one line, thereby reducing the clutter so often seen on the first page of psychological documents.

The more traditional approach is to include the identifying information just below the title. The following entries are typical:

Name:
Date of Birth:
Age:
Date of Testing:
Date of Report:

It is important to include the date of birth because this makes it easier for future readers to discern the examinee's current age. The date of the report is required by many agencies, even though it should differ little (if at all) from the date of testing.

Referral and Background Information.   It is important for the examiner to possess a clear idea of the referral question. In one psychiatric hospital a physician from the medical ward requested testing on a difficult patient by forwarding a note to the psychology service that said only "Psychometrics, please." This was clearly unacceptable, so the psychologist consulted with the physician to obtain a more problem-oriented referral question. The physician informed the psychologist that some of the patient's vague physical symptoms suggested a neurological problem. A brief screening battery revealed that this might well be the case, and the patient was referred for further medical evaluations.

Whenever possible, then, the practitioner should request that referral sources clarify the specific question or questions for which the assessment is requested. This will often mean that the rationale for using certain tests has to be explained to the referring individual. Although the process of educating referral sources can be arduous and time-consuming, it is well worth the effort because misconceptions and inappropriate referrals are thereby reduced to a minimum.

Specific referral questions might include the following:

- Is this individual mentally retarded?
- Does cognitive impairment help explain this individual's academic difficulties?
- Is there any evidence of impaired memory in this individual?
- Are the assessment results consistent with dementia?
- Do the test results have any implications for vocational counseling?
- Why is this student failing in college?
- From an intellectual standpoint, is this person a good candidate for psychotherapy?
- Has this person's drug abuse caused any impairment of cognitive functions?
- Which domains of cognitive functioning have been impaired by this person's head injury?
- Is this person a good candidate for a group home for the developmentally disabled?

Once the referral question has been clarified, the report writer should mention this explicitly in this section of the report. Avoid vagueness or ambiguity about the purpose of the testing. Declarative sentences are preferred, for example: "Mr. Jansen was referred for testing to determine if his apparent memory deficits indicate that he is experiencing cognitive impairment" or: "The counselors are mystified why Ms. Levine is unable to obtain passing grades in her freshman level classes, and the purpose of the testing is to provide information pertinent to this apparent puzzle." Readers appreciate directness and honesty in reports, and report writers should strive for such qualities from beginning to end.

This section of the report also reviews the specific problems noted by the referral source, such as suspected dementia, mental retardation, head injury, memory complaints, and so on. When relevant, neurological and medical history are reviewed here, particularly if the referral has experienced any diseases or conditions that would affect cognitive functioning. As reviewed in Chapter 1 (Introduction to Intellectual Assessment), the examiner should investigate and report whether the examinee has ever experienced unconsciousness, meningitis, head injury, convulsions or seizures, high fevers, sunstroke, oxygen deprivation, learning disorders, strange perceptual experiences, blurred or double vision, poisoning, paralysis, memory disturbance, difficulties in spatial orientation, and so on. In most cases this kind of medically relevant history will be a matter of record, but there is no harm in asking. For example, it might be that no one has ever bothered to inquire if the examinee has been exposed to toxic substances. This particular question was very important in one referral. It turned out that he had lived near a lead smelter years before and had probably ingested excessive amounts of lead. As a result, he manifested a very short attention span and various other vague and mysterious symptoms. Knowledge of this prior medical history proved important in the diagnostic understanding of this individual.

Previous test results are also listed in this report section. In most cases a brief summary of the prior results is preferable to an extended discussion.

Appearance and Behavior in Testing.   All reports should include a brief description of the examinee. It is particularly important to note any physical or behavioral characteristics that might affect the interpretation or validity of the test results. For example, did the examinee "strain" to hear instructions, raising the possibility that a hearing problem has contaminated the test results? Did the examinee squint when viewing stimuli, indicating a possible restriction of vision? Was the client overly anxious? Did he or she "fall apart" when tests were timed? Was the examinee so nonchalant that the results apparently underestimate true potential?

It is particularly important for the examiner to take note of the following behavioral dimensions:

- Reaction to failure: Did the examinee become discouraged and give up after a few failures? Or did the client press onward in spite of the inability to answer difficult questions?
- Degree of cooperation: Cooperation from referrals is usually good, but in those few instances where the examinee is passive-aggressive or outright hostile, it is obvious that the test scores might be affected. Even if optimal results are obtained from a cantankerous client, it may be of great clinical significance to note his or her interpersonal style.
- Reaction to praise: Is praise accepted gracefully, or is it scorned by the examinee? Reactions to praise can give clues to the individual's self-concept.
- Spontaneous conversation: Does the examinee speak only when spoken to, or does he or she converse freely and spontaneously? It is also important to note the style of language used when answers are given. Are the answers direct, or are they vague and circumlocutory?
- Concern for correctness: Some persons are careless in their answers and carefree in their problem-solving behavior on performance items. Others are meticulously thorough and greatly concerned about their perceptual-motor problem solving. Temperamental differences are of obvious relevance when determining whether test results are valid. Furthermore, these behavioral variations are potentially of diagnostic interest in their own right.
- Motor behavior: Does the examinee show any evidence of tremor? Are hand and body movements clumsy or skilled? Is reaction time fast or slow? Are problems approached impulsively or deliberately?

In the assessment report the examiner should mention only those testing behaviors that are pertinent to the interpretation of the overall assessment.

Test Results and Interpretation.   A useful practice is to begin the results section with a tabular listing of scores on all the tests administered. Readers who are knowledgeable about the tests will appreciate finding the raw data in one location, rather than having to search the whole report to locate the test scores. However, to avoid confusing the less sophisticated report reader, it is important to spell out the meaning of the various scaled scores, error scores, and so forth. Several of the reports at the end of this chapter indicate how test results can be summarized. The summary of scores is followed by a narrative discussion of the examinee's test performances. The strengths and weaknesses found on each test might be reviewed here.

Summary and Recommendations. This final section begins with a narrative summary of the overall pattern of findings. The examiner should *synthesize* results across tests, rather than merely reviewing the results of each test in isolation. Finally, any diagnostic implications are then stated.

The recommendations are the most important part of the report. The quality of the recommendations determines whether the assessment will prove helpful, superfluous, or damaging (a rare occurrence). It is important to be as specific as possible in suggesting treatment approaches or remedial exercises. For example, if a client needs practice in identifying perceptual similarities, the examiner might recommend, by name, a specific set of microcomputer rehabilitation exercises.

The recommendations usually tie in with the referral issues. For a student referred because of poor academic performance, the recommendations might emphasize steps that can be taken to improve academic achievement. If the referral issue involved testing for cognitive impairment, a positive finding might be accompanied by a recommendation for medical referral.

Finally, the need for additional testing or retesting at a later date would be mentioned in the recommendations section. A recommendation for further testing should be quite specific, noting particular tests and target dates for readministration. A recommendation might be made, for example, to readminister the WAIS-III and Wechsler Memory Scale–III in 1 year to determine whether a head-injured patient has made cognitive gains.

Common Pitfalls in Report Writing

Inappropriate Detail. Every sentence in the report should be important. Report writers should avoid sentences or paragraphs that have a "so what?" quality to them. For example, in a report on a high-functioning college student there is no point in providing long lists of the presumed abilities measured by each subtest on which the student excelled. It will suffice merely to state that the student is performing in the superior range of intelligence with no identifiable areas of cognitive weakness. Likewise, extensive description of the examinee's behavior in the testing situation should be avoided. Provide important details that will help the reader understand the individual, but do not give meaningless details. For example, the sentence "The subject wore a long-sleeved shirt, jeans, and well-worn sneakers" has a "so what?" ring to it.

Excessive Raw Data.   Closely related to the problem of inappropriate detail is that of excessive raw data. Tallent (1993) has written about the penchant for listing, in excruciating detail, scale names and scores that have little or no meaning to most readers. Some Rorschach scoring programs will provide an entire page of arcane data, with summary scores on ratios and obscure indices. It does not help that the examiner "clarifies" the tabular data with statements such as "The F+ % of 40 indicates that the client has a poor grasp of reality." Although it is acceptable to provide a summary of scales and scores in a psychological report, it is generally unwise to list scores and indices that have no meaning to those reading the assessment.

Unnecessary Jargon.   When a simple phrase means the same thing as professional jargon, substitute the former for the latter. For example, use "eye-hand coordination" instead of "visuo-motor coordination." Moore (1969) provides an extreme parody of an example that illustrates this point. The technical jargon might read:

> The patient exhibited apparent partial paralysis of motor units of the superior sinistral fibres of the genioglossus resulting in insufficient lingual approximation of the palatoalveolar regions. A condition of insufficient frenulum development was noted, producing not only sigmatic distortion, but also obvious ankyloglossia.

The examiner could have better communicated the nature of the problem by writing: "The patient was tongue-tied."

Unnecessary Abstraction.   Avoid high-level inferences about personality and intellectual constructs. Instead of writing abstractions such as "The client was hostile," provide the specific behavioral instances that substantiate the point. For example, the statement "The client was hostile" could be replaced by "The client was a half hour late and stated in an angry voice that he saw no point in being tested."

Vague Language.   Don't require the reader to be a detective who must decipher the meaning of vague language. When phrases or sentences are vague or ambiguous, the meaning may be misinterpreted. Don't write, "It is recommended that he be tested again after a year to determine whether or not maturation will outstrip environmental inputs." This is a poor way of saying "Retesting in a year is recommended in order to assess developmental changes."

Inappropriate Generalization.   Generalization should not be based on isolated pieces of information or data. A common statement in intellectual reports is "The client is distractible, as evidenced by poor performance on Digit Span." The problem with this kind of overgeneralization is that there are other hypotheses that might explain a low score on Digit Span. For example, a temporary level of high anxiety can disrupt short-term memory function. Before making generalizations like this, the examiner should perceive a pattern of behaviors to support the inference.

Careless Use of Technical Terms. Not all readers of psychological reports will be knowledgeable about subtest scores or other technical aspects of the tests. Consequently, it is potentially confusing to make statements such as "Class instruction should focus on John's vocabulary, as his scaled score of 12 on Vocabulary reveals this is a relatively weak area for him." Many readers won't know whether 12 is above or below the national average. Even those readers who know that 10 is the average subtest score may not have the slightest idea whether 12 is only slightly, or quite substantially, higher than 10. Writing that the standard deviation of subtests is 3 might make matters worse for readers untrained in statistics. Although it is acceptable to use technical terms, their meanings must be explained in sufficient detail that a naive reader won't be misled or confused.

Recommendations That Exceed Expertise. Particularly offensive to other professions is the tendency of some report writers to exceed their expertise. This is most commonly a problem when clinicians render medical recommendations. For example, it is never appropriate for a psychologist to recommend that a client undergo a specific medical procedure (such as a CT scan for an apparent brain tumor) or receive a particular drug (such as Prozac for depression). Even when the need for a special procedure seems obvious (e.g., the symptoms strongly attest to the rapid onset of a brain disease), the best way to meet the needs of the client is to recommend immediate consultation with the appropriate medical profession (e.g., neurology or psychiatry).

Exhibitionism. The clinician's goal should be to offer helpful perspectives on the client, not to impress the reader with erudition. When Tallent (1993) surveyed mental health practitioners about psychological reports, one respondent expressed disdain toward psychologists who "reflect their needs to shine as a psychoanalytic beacon in revealing the dark, deep secrets they have observed."

Poor Writing. Poor writing includes a hodge podge of offensive practices that should be avoided in any written document. A pet peeve is the use of nouns or adjectives as verbs: to parent, to impact, to interface, to optimize, to finalize, to target. As one writer exclaimed, tongue in cheek, there has already been too much verbing of nouns! Report writers should strive to avoid this stilted and incorrect practice.

Another problem with many reports is failure to use the precise word or phrase. The most common error here is confusing "affect" and "effect," words that have multiple meanings. "Effect" is both noun and verb. As noun it means result, but as a verb, it means to bring about or accomplish. "Affect" is usually a verb, and means to influence, or act upon, or alter. In psychological parlance, "affect" also can be a noun, and means, roughly, feelings. Some *incorrect* uses of these words are shown below:

"The timed tests had a negative affect on John." [should be "effect"]
"He was effected positively by the change in schools." [should be "affected"]

Another pair of words that causes confusion is "alternate" and "alternative." "Alternate" means every other, while an "alternative" is a choice. Here is a sentence that illustrates the *correct* use of both words:

> "One alternative would be to alternate spelling drill with arithmetic problems."

Report writers are reminded that "datum" is singular, "data" is plural (although there is a clear trend toward the acceptance of "data" as singular). "The data is consistent with…" is therefore less preferred and should read, "The data are consistent with…." Along similar lines, "criterion" is singular and "criteria" is plural.

Another poor practice is the use of affected and imprecise words. Be on the lookout for these stilted words currently in vogue: "viable," "input," "interface," "orient," "parameter," and "finalize." Finally, keep sentences short, on the order of twenty words or less. Readers may lose the meaning of a long sentence before they reach the end. Worse yet, long sentences are usually the result of vague, fuzzy, ill-defined thoughts. They may have little meaning in the first place. The following monster should be cut into two or three separate sentences, then revised: "Ian enjoyed the drawing tasks and had no difficulty with the Bender Gestalt, a test of copying several simple geometric designs, indicating that there is no evidence of deficiency in visual-perceptual organization."

Implications of Client Access for Psychological Report Writing

A trend in recent years is increased legal rights for clients to see reports written about them. Even though a report might be marked "Confidential" and written with the explicit understanding that it is for the eyes of other professionals only, legal precedents increasingly make it easier for clients to see reports written about them.

Perhaps this is as it should be. Some clinical professionals reveal an almost condescending attitude that their reports somehow might be misunderstood or otherwise harmful to the client and therefore should be kept confidential. For example, many clinicians show an ingrained bias that laypersons cannot possibly understand the limitations of IQ and are consequently reluctant to give other than general feedback about IQ scores. In effect, this amounts to trying to protect people from the truth by withholding important information.

The argument that clients might misunderstand test results is often a "smokescreen" that obscures the actual reason for refusing to let them see reports. When practitioners balk at releasing test results, the real explanation might be that the reports have been constructed carelessly, use obscure and jargonistic concepts, or contain pejorative and unwarranted conclusions. For a variety of reasons, then, including the legal trends toward client access and, in addition, a desire to ensure that examiners write honest, accurate, and understandable reports, it is best to assume that someday the client will read the report. Examiners should write reports with such care that they would be proud to have clients read them, rather than fearful that the reports might incite anger or disappointment. I urge all practitioners to adopt this frame of mind when writing reports.

Samples of Assessment Reports

The purpose of this section is to provide several intellectual assessment reports written for a variety of audiences. The reader should pay special attention to how the context and referral issues shape the style, length, and content of each report. The circumstances of the reports were as follows:

1. Harold D. was a 26-year-old college student with learning difficulties. This report was used, in part, for counseling purposes and therefore embodied a high degree of detail.
2. Adrianna W. was a 31-year-old woman at the center of a court case. The essential purpose of the assessment was to determine whether she met the criteria for mental retardation. The report is sparsely focused toward this goal.
3. Sarah D. was a 23-year-old college graduate with a possible mild head injury. The purpose of the assessment was to screen for cognitive impairment. When suspicion of impairment was confirmed, additional specialist assessment was recommended.
4. Mildred S. was a 46-year-old woman with a longstanding history of psychiatric difficulties. The assessment was requested by her therapist, who desired insight regarding realistic goals for vocational training.

1. Psychoeducational Assessment Report

Name: Harold D.   Date of Testing: 2/7/98
Age: 26   Date of Report: 2/9/98

Referral and Background Information:

Harold D. is a 26-year-old college sophomore referred for testing by his academic adviser. Harold is described by the adviser as a highly motivated student who received excellent preparation for college from a private high school. Nonetheless, he is earning mediocre grades in his business major. There is a danger he may not be allowed to finish his curriculum (which mandates a grade point average of 2.5 or higher). The reason for the assessment is to clarify the sources of difficulty with his studies and to offer suggestions for remediation.

Harold concurs that college seems harder for him than it should be. He reports that in high school his grades were all As and a few Bs. Background and developmental history appear unremarkable. He recounts a normal developmental history and the absence of any serious illness, injury, or disease (based on a lengthy questionnaire). Although he received treatment for mild depression 3 years ago, Harold is not taking any medication at the present time. He says that currently his mood and outlook are good—especially considering the circumstances—and he denies that depression is a factor in his academic difficulties.

His choice of business as a major is largely happenstance and not based on firm conviction. A friend decided to major in business, so Harold opted for that course of study, too. He is willing to consider other options.

Appearance and Behavior in Testing:

Harold was on time for each of two testing appointments. He is a well-dressed, socially appropriate, friendly young man who answers questions tersely. He speaks mainly when spoken to and offers little on his own. Harold appeared to have difficulty sitting still for more than 5 or 10 minutes. He fidgeted constantly during the two testing sessions. Nonetheless, he was clearly motivated to do his best. The test results are considered a valid representation of his intellectual functioning.

During testing, Harold revealed the same restricted verbal output observed in the initial interview. When asked to define words, he offered very short definitions and refused to elaborate. When asked to explain common social conventions, some answers were too brief to receive full credit. Even when encouraged to explain further, he declined the opportunity. In contrast, his perseverance with performance tasks was admirable. Confronted with a challenging (untimed) reasoning task, he simply refused to quit until the underlying logic of each item was apparent.

Test Results and Interpretation:

Harold was administered the Wechsler Adult Intelligence Scale-III (WAIS-III), a well-validated test of individual intelligence, and the Mini-Battery of

Achievement (MBA), a short test of school achievement skills in the areas of reading, writing, mathematics, and factual knowledge. A summary of test results is appended to this report.

On the WAIS-III, Harold earned a Verbal IQ of 108, a Performance IQ of 124, and a Full Scale IQ of 116 ±4. His true Full Scale IQ has about a 95% likelihood of falling in the 112–120 range. The overall score places him in the High Average classification of intelligence and ranks him at about the 85th percentile for people his age.

The test results for Harold reveal a significant degree of variability in the specific components of general intelligence. He performs at a very superior level on tasks that require fluid reasoning, visual-spatial problem solving, and attentiveness to detail (POI score of 138). He is relatively somewhat weaker but still above average on tasks that require verbal reasoning and verbal knowledge (VCI score of 116). In contrast to these areas of strength, Harold reveals a distinct weakness with working memory, which is attending to verbally presented information, processing the information in memory, and formulating a response (WMI score of 90). He is also relatively weak in the ability to process visual information quickly (PSI score of 93).

Fluctuations of this magnitude in the component scores of intelligence are rare. For example, compared to his strength in perceptual organization (POI score of 138), the relative weakness in working memory (WMI score of 90) is both statistically significant (well below $p < .05$) and extremely infrequent (the POI-WMI difference of 48 points occurs in less than 0.2 percent of the normative sample). The same general trend is true regarding the comparison of verbal comprehension (strong) and working memory (weak). In like manner, it is fair to characterize the test results as indicating a relative deficit in processing speed (PSI score of 93).

Summarizing the analysis of Index scores, Harold displays an outstanding capacity with regard to perceptual organization and is above average with regard to verbal comprehension. Compared to these areas of strength, however, he reveals distinct weaknesses in working memory and processing speed. A reasonable hypothesis is that Harold is experiencing deficits in working memory and processing speed. These findings indicate that he will function at a disadvantage in situations that demand the quick processing of verbal information. The same is true with regard to situations that demand the rapid processing of visual information.

The most important implication of these results is that Harold will experience great difficulty in learning from traditional lectures. With his relatively slow processing speed, it will be difficult for him to take extensive notes, especially when the professor presents material visually (e.g., overhead projector). His weakness in working memory will compound the difficulty, as he will experience problems in the quick processing of the verbal information provided by the professor.

Yet he clearly has a keen mind, especially when working with abstract, nonverbal problems (POI score of 138). His strength with nonverbal materials will shine forth especially when the tasks are untimed and do not require a rapid response. Furthermore, Harold is competent in verbal reasoning and verbal knowledge (VCI score of 116), although his above average score in this area is probably the norm for college students.

In order to assess Harold's aptitude and achievement with school-related skills, he was administered the Mini-Battery of Achievement (MBA). The MBA assesses four broad achievement areas: reading, writing, mathematics, and factual knowledge. The scores on the MBA are generally consistent with findings on the WAIS-III. His strongest area was Mathematics (128), with a secondary strength in Factual Knowledge (122). However, he was relatively weak, especially for a college student, in Reading (101) and Writing (108). These results dovetail with the WAIS-III findings: They indicate a relative weakness with verbal materials (lower Reading and Writing scores) combined with a strong point in a nonverbal area (Mathematics score of 128). General knowledge is also a strong area (Factual Knowledge score of 122).

Summary and Recommendations:

Harold D. is a 26-year-old business major who is struggling academically even though he appears to show strong motivation to succeed in college. Although Harold was treated for mild depression 3 years ago, both his self-report and interview impressions suggest this is not a current factor in his academic problems. On the WAIS-III the overall score of 116 indicates that his general intellectual functioning is at the 85th percentile and approximately normative for college students. However, these results are potentially misleading in that they hide areas of strength and weakness. An examination of component scores indicates an exceptional strength in perceptual organization (POI score of 138), which consists of fluid reasoning, visual-spatial problem solving, and attentiveness to detail. However, Harold also displays *relative* weaknesses in several areas: working memory (the capacity to process verbally presented information), processing speed (the capacity to respond quickly to visual stimuli), basic reading skills, and basic writing skills.

Combined with interview impressions, these test results convey the notion that Harold is very gifted in areas of nonverbal reasoning (especially mathematics), but that he is perhaps distractible and finds it difficult to sit still and process verbally presented concepts. Compared to classmates, he is also at a disadvantage when it comes to his comprehension of reading materials and somewhat weak with regard to essential writing skills. Interview impressions indicate that his verbal output tends to be sparse. A number of recommendations flow from these collective impressions:

1. A business major may not be the best fit for Harold. Certainly he has the nonverbal reasoning capacity and the mathematical prowess required, but he may experience difficulty because of weaknesses in essential reading and writing skills and also because of his restricted verbal style. It may be helpful for Harold to take a vocational interest test battery and to explore additional vocational options. He may perform best in academic and career settings that capitalize on high-level, abstract reasoning.

2. Harold should tape record lectures and play them back later so as to compensate for his relative weakness in working memory. Certainly he is capable

of understanding high-level concepts, but he probably needs additional time to process and internalize them.

3. He should consider cutting back on his courseload slightly. Harold has been taking a full load of 16 credits, which would be a challenge for any student. In his case, mastering lecture material and lengthy reading assignments may take extra time. A reduced course load would free up the time needed to do well in his remaining courses.

Overall, there is reason for optimism in Harold's situation. He possesses the gift of very strong nonverbal reasoning skills and he is strongly motivated. With a few adjustments as noted above, Harold will improve substantially the odds of completing a college degree.

Summary of Test Results for Harold D.

Wechsler Adult Intelligence Scale-III

116	Full Scale IQ
108	Verbal IQ
124	Performance IQ

15	Vocabulary	Verbal intelligence, educational background
12	Similarities	Verbal concept formation, abstract reasoning
8	Arithmetic	Concentration, numerical reasoning, schooling
8	Digit Span	Concentration, immediate auditory memory
12	Information	Remote memory, experience, and education
14	Comprehension	Practical knowledge, social judgment
9	Letter-Number	Working memory, complex memory span

11	Picture Completion	Visual concentration and differentiation
8	Digit Symbol-Coding	Visual-motor speed, quick learning of rote
18	Block Design	Spatial problem solving, perceptual organization
18	Matrix Reasoning	Nonverbal abstract reasoning, fluid intelligence
12	Picture Arrangement	Assessing nonverbal social situations, planning
10	Symbol Search	Visual scanning, processing speed

116	Verbal Comp. Index [Vocabulary, Similarities, Information]	Verbal reasoning, verbal acquired knowledge
138	Perceptual Org. Index [Pic. Completion, Bl. Design, Matrix Reasoning]	Fluid reasoning, visual-spatial problem solving, attentiveness to detail

90   Working Memory Index   Attention, memory, and processing of
      [Arithmetic, Digit Span,   verbal materials
      Letter-Number Seq.]

93   Processing Speed Index   Quick processing of visual information
      [Digit Symbol-Coding,
      Symbol Search]

Mini-Battery of Achievement

101   Reading
108   Writing
128   Mathematics
122   Factual Knowledge

2. Intellectual and Adaptive Behavior Assessment

Name: Adrianna W.
Date of Birth: 1/7/67

Date of Assessment: 2/22/98
Age: 31 years, 1 month

Referral and Background Information:

This assessment of Adrianna W. was completed at the request of the county prosecutor. Ms. W. is the alleged victim in a court case involving rape charges against a young man. Although overt force was not used, the prosecutor maintains that the young man engaged in psychological coercion with the victim. Furthermore, she is viewed as incapable of giving meaningful consent because of her intellectual limitations. The purpose of the assessment is to determine her current level of intellectual and adaptive functioning.

Ms. W. attended school until the age of 20 in a small rural town. She states that she quit school because "I got fed up with everybody." Specifically, she relates that "A bunch of kids they was talking behind my back and telling me how dumb I was." The client claims that she has never held a job. She receives monthly income from SSI (Supplemental Security Income), but was unsure if the amount was $200.85 or $285.00. When asked which amount would be greater, she did not respond for nearly a minute. Finally, she said "$285?" but seemed unsure if this was correct.

Ms. W. says that she has had seizures since she was a baby, "the shaky kind." She takes Dilantin and Tegretol for seizure control but still has seizures "every month or two." She denies the use of illegal drugs or alcohol. Married for about 2 months, the client says she has one child. She was uncertain of his age, but thought he might be 2 or 3 years old. The child lives with the parents of her husband. When asked why the boy is not at home with her, Ms. W. was vague and evasive. According to the office of the prosecutor, the child was removed from the home by court order because of a long pattern of neglect and suspected abuse.

Ms. W. has had a longstanding connection with the local mental health office and with state welfare agencies as well. Carol L., a licensed social worker, has known her for 5 years and has had direct contact with her, including home visits, on at least fifty occasions. Ms. L. served as the informant for some of the procedures discussed below.

Appearance and Behavior in Testing:

The client was brought to the testing session by her social worker. Ms. W. was neatly groomed, but her apparel did not seem appropriate for the occasion. She wore a soiled T-shirt, cut-off jeans, and battered rubber thongs.

The client is of about average height but appears somewhat underweight. She has attractive facial features. For most of the session she slouched in a chair, never making direct eye contact. Her expression remained impassive throughout. Ms. W.

was fully cooperative during testing and interview, but was completely passive from beginning to end. She did exactly what the examiner asked of her and attempted to answer every question. She appeared engrossed in the performance items of the WAIS-III and worked earnestly (well beyond the time limit on some items). However, she did not volunteer any information, offer any comments, or request even a single clarification. The test results are considered typical of her current intellectual and adaptive functioning.

Test Results and Interpretation:

On the WAIS-III, Ms. W. earned Verbal IQ 69, Performance IQ 76, and Full Scale IQ 70. The Full Scale IQ is considered accurate to ±5 points; that is, her true IQ is in the range of 65-75 (with 95% likelihood). The overall score places her at the 2nd percentile and corresponds to the lowest score in the Borderline classification.

Her verbal intelligence (VIQ of 69) is slightly below the 2nd percentile and is just within the Extremely Low classification. This suggests that Ms. W. has a significant deficit in understanding verbal concepts and in expressing herself verbally. Her performance intelligence (PIQ of 76) places her at approximately the 6th percentile and is in the middle of the Borderline designation. Comparatively speaking, she functions better with intellectual tasks that require perceptual organization and eye-hand coordination.

Ms. W. states that she has taken the WAIS-III recently, although she was not sure when or where this occurred. This may have been part of an assessment arranged by defense counsel. Prior exposure to the WAIS-III usually causes scores to increase, especially for Performance IQ. It is possible (perhaps likely) that her current scores are a slight overestimate of her true intellectual functioning. It would be important to confirm whether she has taken the WAIS-III recently.

The client was also assessed with the Scales of Independent Behavior--Revised (SIB-R), a measure of adaptive behavior. With this instrument the examiner displays a number of specific behavioral items to a knowledgeable informant who then offers a rating from 0 (never or rarely does task) to 3 (does task very well). Ms. W.'s social worker, Carol L., responded to the items from the SIB-R. The instrument is normed to the familiar mean of 100 and standard deviation of 15 in the general population.

Overall on the SIB-R, Ms. W. received a Broad Independence score of 66, which is in the range of mild mental retardation. The four subscales that compose Broad Independence revealed some variation. Moderate strength was indicated in Motor Skills, but lower scores were found in areas that assess functional independence and personal responsibility:

Motor Skills:	82
Social Interaction and Communication Skills:	61
Personal Living Skills:	60
Community Living Skills:	60

Summary and Conclusions:

Adrianna W. is a 31-year-old female evaluated at the request of the county prosecutor to determine her current level of intellectual and adaptive behavior. On the WAIS-III, she earned a Full Scale IQ of 70, which places her at about the 2nd percentile, with slightly lower functioning in verbal areas (VIQ of 69) and somewhat higher functioning in performance areas (PIQ of 76). These scores may be inflated (especially the PIQ) by prior exposure to the WAIS-III. Whether she has taken this test recently needs to be determined.

On the SIB-R, a measure of adaptive behavior filled out by her social worker, Ms. W. is characterized by adaptive deficits in several broad areas, including social interaction and communication skills, personal living skills (which includes self-care and activities of daily living), and community living skills (which includes essential work skills). Overall, her functioning is at the 1st percentile for adaptive behaviors.

Based upon interview impressions, WAIS-III results, information from her social worker, as well as SIB-R results, Ms. W. would be described as a person with mental retardation who needs limited supports in communication, self-care, and work skills (using terminology preferred by the American Association on Mental Retardation). The assessment findings point strongly to a descriptive label of mild mental retardation.

Summary of Test Results for Adrianna W.

WAIS-III Full Scale IQ: 70

Verbal IQ	69	Performance IQ	76
Vocabulary	5	Picture Completion	7
Similarities	6	Digit Symbol-Coding	5
Arithmetic	4	Block Design	6
Digit Span	4	Matrix Reasoning	6
Information	6	Picture Arrangement	7
Comprehension	4	Symbol Search	(4)
Letter-Number	(5)	Object Assembly	(5)

Scales of Independent Behavior--Revised

Broad Independence	66
Motor Skills:	82
Social Interaction and Communication Skills:	61
Personal Living Skills:	60
Community Living Skills:	60

3. Intellectual Assessment and Screening for Cognitive Impairment

Name: Sarah D.
Age: 23
Date of Testing: 2/20/98
Date of Report: 2/22/98

Referral and Background Information:

Sarah is a recent college graduate who is self-referred for testing. She was involved in an unfortunate accident when riding her bicycle 5 weeks ago. She was peddling down the sidewalk when a young man driving a car abruptly turned into a driveway just in front of her. Sarah was unable to stop and collided with the side of the car. The force of the impact catapulted her over the handlebars, causing her face to smash into the side window. Sarah relates being dazed and disoriented for several minutes. She was taken to an emergency room where she underwent minor cosmetic surgery. Fortunately, her facial wounds were not serious and have healed completely. She denies losing consciousness. However, she describes the accident as "traumatic." A vague sense of malaise and occasional periods of irritability have plagued her ever since. Her parents have urged her to undergo an assessment. The purpose of the testing is to determine whether her cognitive capacities might have been affected by the accident.

Sarah completed a bachelor's degree in English last June. Her cumulative grade point average was a superlative 3.6 (on a 4.0 scale). She has been employed as a copy editor for a large publishing firm and expects to do developmental editing as soon as a position opens up. Based on results of a lengthy background questionnaire, her developmental and medical history appear to be unremarkable.

Appearance and Behavior in Testing:

Sarah is a poised young woman who comes across as articulate and candid. She noted that her family has retained a lawyer and that they may sue the young man who caused the accident. Sarah went straight to the heart of one concern by saying "I want you to know that I'm going to do my very best on these tests. I'm more interested in getting a clean bill of health than I am in muddling the litigation issues. Besides, I don't think I'm brain-impaired and I don't want to be identified as such."

Her approach to testing can be described as determined. On verbal questions she elaborated extensively. On performance items she worked with frenetic energy. Her response to failure was to redouble her efforts. The test results are considered a valid indication of her current intellectual and cognitive functioning.

Test Results and Interpretation:

Sarah was administered the WAIS-III, an individual test of general intelligence, and also a battery of screening tests for cognitive impairment. These tests included the Trail Making Test, Rey Auditory Verbal Learning Test, Benton Visual Retention Test--Revised, Bender Gestalt, and Short Category Test (Booklet Form).

On the WAIS-III, Sarah earned a Verbal IQ of 115, a Performance IQ of 107, and a Full Scale IQ of 112 ±4. Her true Full Scale IQ has about a 95% likelihood of falling in the 108–116 range. The overall score places her in the High Average classification of intelligence and ranks her at about the 85th percentile for people her age.

The WAIS-III test results for Sarah reveal a significant degree of variability in the specific components of general intelligence. She performs in the high average range on tasks that require verbal reasoning and verbal knowledge (VCI score of 114) and also on tasks that require fluid reasoning, visual-spatial problem solving, and attentiveness to detail (POI score of 111). Sarah performs in the average rank on working memory, which is attending to verbally presented information, processing the information in memory, and formulating a response (WMI score of 102). But when it comes to tasks that need the quick processing of visual information, her performance is substantially lower, in the low average range (PSI score of 88).

The VCI-PSI discrepancy of 26 points is statistically significant (well below $p <$ .05) and also uncommon in the normative sample (found in only 8% of the standardization sample). These results suggest the hypothesis that Sarah is exhibiting a deficit in cognitive processing speed. Results from the screening tests of cognitive impairment (discussed below) can be used to examine this hypothesis in more detail.

On the Trail Making Test the examinee connects numbers (Part A) or numbers and letters in alternating order (Part B) with a pencil line under pressure of time. This test is a measure of scanning ability, mental flexibility, and processing speed. Sarah's performance on both parts was relatively slow, consistent with a hypothesis of mild to moderate impairment.

The Rey Auditory Verbal Learning Test is a measure of verbal memory. The examinee hears the same list of 15 words on five separate occasions and must recall as many as possible. Sarah was able to recall a total of only 43 words, which is well below the normative expectation of about 55 words. This test result also raises a suspicion of cognitive impairment.

In the case of the Benton Visual Retention Test--Revised (copying designs from memory after a short delay) and the Bender Gestalt (copying designs directly from a model), Sarah's performance was errorless. Positive performance on these tests is a good sign, but does not rule out cognitive impairments in other domains.

The Short Category Test, Booklet Form, is a 100-item test of abstract reasoning and concept formation. The examinee must figure out a rule for categorizing pictures of geometric shapes. Sarah made 38 errors on this test, which is a mediocre performance for a college student but not technically into the range of cognitive impairment (41 errors and above).

Interpretive Summary and Recommendations:

Sarah D. is a 23-year-old college graduate self-referred after a bicycle accident 5 weeks ago in which she struck her head. Although she states that she did not lose consciousness, she still experiences occasional periods of irritability and malaise.

Apparently there is some likelihood of litigation over the accident. Nonetheless, Sarah appeared to exert full effort in the testing and the results are considered a valid representation of her current functioning.

On the WAIS-III, Sarah earned a Full Scale IQ of 112, which is in the High Average classification. Although this is not inconsistent with her prior level of accomplishment, it is somewhat lower than what might be expected of an individual who recently completed college with superlative grades. Even more suspicious of cognitive impairment is the very large discrepancy between the Verbal Comprehension Index (score of 114) and the Processing Speed Index (score of 88). Of all the component scores on the WAIS-III, the PSI score is the most sensitive to cognitive impairment. A discrepancy of 26 points is statistically significant and also uncommon. These findings are suggestive of cognitive impairment, but not definitive.

A hypothesis of cognitive impairment receives further support from a battery of screening tests. Sarah's performance on the Trail Making Test (a test of scanning ability, mental flexibility, and processing speed) was in the range typical of individuals with mild to moderate impairment. Likewise, her performance on a test of verbal memory (Rey AVLT) was well below expectations for an individual at her general level of intelligence. She also revealed significant difficulty with the Short Category Test, Booklet Form, a cognitive screening test of abstract reasoning and concept formation. Performance on two drawing and copying tests was adequate (Bender Gestalt, Benton Visual Retention Test--Revised).

Overall, the test results are indicative of cognitive impairment but insufficient as proof of such disability. It is recommended that Sarah receive additional consultation from specialists in neurology and clinical neuropsychology. It is further recommended that Sarah complete this same test battery in 6 months to determine whether improvements in functioning can be documented.

Summary of Test Results for Sarah D.

Wechsler Adult Intelligence Scale--III Results

WAIS-III Full Scale IQ: 112

Verbal IQ	115	Performance IQ	107
Vocabulary	15	Picture Completion	13
Similarities	12	Digit Symbol-Coding	8
Arithmetic	9	Block Design	10
Digit Span	12	Matrix Reasoning	13
Information	11	Picture Arrangement	12
Comprehension	16	Symbol Search	(8)
Letter-Number	(10)		

Verbal Comprehension Index	114
Perceptual Organization Index	111
Working Memory Index	102
Processing Speed Index	88

Screening Test	Result	Interpretation
Trail Making Test, Part A	45 seconds	mild to moderate impairment
Trail Making Test, Part B	100 seconds	mild to moderate impairment
Rey AVLT Sum of Trials I-V	43 words	suspect cognitive impairment
Benton VRT-R	10 correct	normal
Bender Gestalt [Lacks scoring]	0 errors	normal
Short Category Test, Booklet Form	38 errors	borderline

4. Intellectual Assessment for Vocational Training

Client: Mildred S., Age 46   June 11, 1998

Referral and Background Information:

Ms. S. is referred by the county mental health center for intellectual evaluation centering around the question of vocational goals. Her social worker, John C., wants to know what kinds of vocational aspirations are realistic for her. Ms. S. has been hospitalized approximately seven times in the last 30 years for psychiatric problems variously diagnosed as major depression, schizoaffective disorder, and cyclothymic disorder. According to her therapist, a recurrent problem has been medication resistance/mismanagement. Most recently, she has been stabilized without need of medication for 2 years and 3 months. Prior to that she was taking Prolixin and Cogentin. Ms. S. attends supportive group therapy weekly and sees Mr. C. every other week.

The client finished high school at the usual age but has never obtained any additional education. She lived with her parents until age 33. Since then she has lived in a rooming house, supported in part by her parents. This income is supplemented by disability payments and an occasional paycheck for part-time work as a clerk in a local fabric store. When asked what occupations she might like to pursue, Ms. S. mentioned that she would enjoy secretarial work because of the emphasis on "working with words and ideas."

Ms. S. attends church sporadically but has never felt involved in her congregation. She enjoys watching situation comedies on television and attends movies about twice a week. An avid seamstress, she makes many of her own clothes. She has a boyfriend but describes their relationship as "not serious." They go on picnics and other outings every week or two.

Appearance and Behavior in Testing:

The client was well groomed and neatly but plainly dressed. A pleasant individual, Ms. S. seemed completely at ease during interview and testing. She maintained good eye contact. Her affect was generally cheerful, and she displayed a good sense of humor. She was very curious about the testing and asked many thoughtful questions about specific test items.

Ms. S. manifests a number of motor symptoms that appear to be neurologic in origin. When yawning, she reveals a prominent and unusual tongue thrust. She is aware of this odd behavior and explains it as tardive dyskinesia caused by heavy doses of antipsychotic medication many years ago. She also has a very noticeable tremor in her right hand that disappears when she engages the hand in purposeful activity. Her left hand and lower lip also show slight indications of tremor. An instance of right arm weakness 5 years ago also sounds "stroke-like," but this is not confirmed.

Ms. S. approached the testing with great enthusiasm. She responded to failure on test items with a slight frown, but would then smile and say something to the effect of "Wow, these really are getting hard." The results are considered indicative of her optimal functioning.

Test Results and Interpretation:

On the WAIS-III, Ms. S. earned a Verbal IQ of 110, a Performance IQ of 97, and a Full Scale IQ of 103. The overall score places her in the Average classification of intelligence and ranks her at about the 58th percentile for people her age. Her Verbal IQ of 110 (High Average) is significantly higher than her Performance IQ of 97 (Average), which indicates that she has stronger abilities in verbal reasoning/knowledge than in visual-spatial problem solving. In fact, her Vocabulary score of 15 (where 10 is average) represents an area of considerable strength. Ms. S. is able to provide word meanings with good facility.

An analysis of the WAIS-III Index scores is consistent with the above findings; namely, Ms. S. shows relative strength in verbal areas and relative weakness in areas of visual-spatial organization. However, one additional conclusion is suggested as well. Her lowest Index score of 93 was observed on the Processing Speed Index, which is a measure of the capacity quickly to process visual information and to provide a motor response. This suggests that Ms. S. may experience mild difficulty with speeded clerical tasks, for example, checking a list of names and addresses for errors.

The Mini-Battery of Achievement is a brief test of academic skills in four areas. For each area a score of 100 is average for the general population. Ms. S. earned scores of 122 for Reading, 115 for Writing, 107 for Mathematics, and 133 for Factual Knowledge. Except for the slight weakness (relatively speaking) in basic mathematics, these scores are typical of individuals with college-level academic skills.

Ms. S. also performed exceptionally on a variety of screening tests for cognitive impairment. These tests included measures of visual scanning, mental flexibility, and processing speed (Trails A and B), verbal memory (Rey Auditory Verbal Learning Test), visual-spatial design copying (Bender Gestalt and Benton Visual Retention Test-Revised), and abstract reasoning/concept formation (Short Category Test, Booklet Form). Not only were all test results within the normal range; some were completed in exceptional manner. This was especially true of the Short Category Test, Booklet Form, where she made only 17 errors (33 errors would be more typical for normal individuals her age).

Summary and Recommendations:

Ms. S. was referred for intellectual testing as a basis for determining realistic vocational goals. She has a recurrent history of psychiatric hospitalization, although recently she has functioned independently for more than 2 years and is not receiving psychotropic medications. However, prior medication apparently has led to mild tremor and occasional odd mannerisms (tongue thrust when yawning) attributed to mild tardive dyskinesia.

Overall, the test results provide a basis for optimism with regard to vocational retraining. General intelligence is in the average range (IQ of 103) with above average performance in verbal areas (VIQ of 110, Vocabulary subtest score of 15). Essential academic skills of reading, writing, and factual knowledge are well above average, in the range typical of college students. Several screening tests of cognitive impairment were completed in normal to superior manner. Areas of slight weakness include processing speed (below average) and mathematics (above average but not as strong as the typical college student). In sum, the results indicate that essential intellectual and academic skills such as verbal reasoning, verbal memory, abstract reasoning, reading, and writing are intact.

Although intellectual, academic, and cognitive skills appear sufficient for Ms. S. to succeed in college or technical school, the more significant issues concern her motivation to pursue educational/vocational goals, and her resilience in the face of stress. These are matters not easily evaluated by formal tests, and it is difficult to obtain reliable clinical impressions from a single interview. However, one recommendation does seem warranted, given her history. That would be to approach any changes in a gradual, incremental manner so that she is not overwhelmed by the stress of college-level courses, perhaps taking a course or two in the evening before jumping in with a full-time curriculum.

With regard to particular courses of study, three thoughts are offered. First, Ms. S. should prefer courses and curricula that emphasize verbal skills, as this is her strong suit. Second, she will probably encounter difficulty in areas that require strong math skills and so should approach these cautiously. Third, because of her prominent symptoms of tardive dyskinesia, she may experience disappointment in pursuits that focus on person-to-person interactions. Her stated interest in secretarial work might need to be redirected. For example, working as a copy editor might allow her to exercise her interest in words and ideas.

Summary of Test Results for Mildred S.

Wechsler Adult Intelligence Scale-III

| 103 | Full Scale IQ | |

| 110 | Verbal IQ | |
| 97 | Performance IQ | |

15	Vocabulary	Verbal intelligence, educational background
9	Similarities	Verbal concept formation, abstract reasoning
10	Arithmetic	Concentration, numerical reasoning, schooling
13	Digit Span	Concentration, immediate auditory memory
12	Information	Remote memory, experience, and education
11	Comprehension	Practical knowledge, social judgment
9	Letter-Number	Working memory, complex memory span

9	Picture Completion	Visual concentration and differentiation
9	Digit Symbol-Coding	Visual-motor speed, quick learning of rote
10	Block Design	Spatial problem solving, perceptual organization
11	Matrix Reasoning	Nonverbal abstract reasoning, fluid intelligence
9	Picture Arrangement	Assessing nonverbal social situations, planning
9	Symbol Search	Visual scanning, processing speed

110	Verbal Comprehension Index [Vocabulary, Similarities, Information]	Verbal reasoning, verbal acquired knowledge
99	Perceptual Org. Index [Pic. Completion, Bl. Design, Matrix Reasoning]	Fluid reasoning, visual-spatial problem solving, attentiveness to detail
102	Working Memory Index [Arithmetic, Digit Span, Letter-Number Seq.]	Attention, memory, and processing of verbal materials
93	Processing Speed Index [Digit Symbol-Coding, Symbol Search]	Quick processing of visual information

Mini-Battery of Achievement

122	Reading
115	Writing
107	Mathematics
133	Factual Knowledge

Screening Test	Result	Interpretation
Trail Making Test, Part A	19 seconds	completely normal
Trail Making Test, Part B	55 seconds	completely normal
Rey AVLT Sum of Trials I-V	61 words	above average
Benton VRT-R	10/10 correct	normal
Bender Gestalt [Lacks scoring]	0 errors	normal
Short Category Test Booklet Form	17 errors	normal range

REFERENCES

Abraham, I., Manning, C., Snustad, D., et al. (1994). Cognitive screening of nursing home residents: Factor structures of the Mini-Mental State Examination. *Journal of the American Geriatrics Society, 42*, 750–756.

Adams, G. L. (1984). *Comprehensive Test of Adaptive Behavior*. Columbus, OH: Merrill.

Adams, R., Parsons, O., Culbertson, J. & Nixon, S. (Eds.) (1) 1996. *Neuropsychology for clinical practice: Etiology, assessment, and treatment of common neurological disorders*. Washington, DC: American Psychological Association.

Albert, M. S., & Moss, M. B. (1988). *Geriatric neuropsychology*. New York: Guilford Press.

Allison, J., Blatt, S. J., & Zimet, C. N. (1988). *The interpretation of psychological tests*. Washington, DC: Hemisphere.

Altepeter, T., & Handal, P. (1985). A factor analytic investigation of the use of the PPVT-R as a measure of general achievement. *Journal of Clinical Psychology, 41*, 540–543.

Alzheimer's Association (1998). *Is it Alzheimer's? Warning Signs You Should Know*. Chicago: Author.

American Association on Mental Retardation (1992). *Mental retardation: Definition, classification, and systems of supports*. Washington, DC: Author.

American Educational Research Association, American Psychological Association, & National Council on Measurement in Education (1985). *Standards for educational and psychological testing*. Washington, DC: American Psychological Association.

American Educational Research Organization, American Psychological Association, and National Council on Measurement in Education. (1997). *Standards for educational and psychological testing* (2d ed.). Washington, DC: American Psychological Association.

American Psychiatric Association (1994). *Diagnostic and statistical manual of mental disorders* (4th ed.). Washington, DC: Author.

American Psychological Association (1992). Ethical principles of psychologists and code of conduct. *American Psychologist, 47*, 1597–1611.

Anastasi, A. (1958). *Differential psychology* (3d ed.). New York: Macmillan.

Anastasi, A. (1982). *Psychological testing* (5th ed.). New York: Macmillan.

Andreasen, N. C., & Black, D. W. (1995). *Introductory textbook of psychiatry* (2d ed.). Washington, DC: American Psychiatric Press.

Anthony, J. C., LeResche, L., Niaz, U., Van Korff, M. R., & Folstein, M. (1982). Limits of the Mini-Mental State as a screening test for dementia and delirium among hospital patients. *Psychological Medicine, 12*, 397–408.

Axelrod, B. N., Brines, B., & Rapport, L. (1997). Estimating Full Scale IQ while minimizing the effects of practice. *Assessment, 3*, 221–227.

Bayless, J. D., Varney, N., & Roberts, R. (1989). Tinker Toy Test performance and vocational outcome in patients with closed head injuries. *Journal of Clinical and Experimental Neuropsychology, 11*, 913–914.

Bear, D. M. (1986). Behavioural changes in temporal lobe epilepsy. In M. R. Trimble & T. G. Bolwig (Eds.), *Aspects of epilepsy and psychiatry*. New York: Wiley.

Bender, L. (1938). *A visual motor gestalt test and its clinical use*. New York: American Orthopsychiatric Association.

Benedict, H., Schretlen, D., & Bobholz, J. (1992). Concurrent validity of three WAIS-R short forms in psychiatric inpatients. *Psychological Assessment, 4*, 322–328.

233

Benson, D. F. (1994). *The neurology of thinking*. New York: Oxford University Press.

Benton, A., Sivan, A., Hamsher, K., Varney, N., & Spreen, O. (1994). *Contributions to neuropsychological assessment* (2d ed.). New York: Oxford University Press.

Benton, A., Van Allen, M., & Fogel, M. (1964). Temporal orientation in cerebral disease. *Journal of Nervous and Mental Disease, 139*, 110–119.

Berg, R., Franzen, M., & Wedding, D. (1994). *Screening for brain impairment* (2d ed.). New York: Springer.

Bigler, E. D. (Ed.) (1990). *Traumatic brain injury: Mechanisms of damage, assessment, intervention, and outcome*. Austin, TX: PRO-ED.

Brittain, J., La Marche, J., Reeder, K., Roth, D., & Boll, T. (1991). Effects of age and IQ on PASAT performance. *The Clinical Neuropsychologist, 5*, 163–175.

Brody, N. (1985). The validity of tests of intelligence. In B. B. Wolman (Ed.), *Handbook of intelligence*. New York: Wiley.

Brooks, D., & Aughton, M. (1979). Psychological consequences of blunt head injury. *International Rehabilitation Medicine, 1*, 160–165.

Bruininks, R., Woodcock, R., Weatherman, R., & Hill, B. (1996). *Scales of independent behavior—revised*. Allen, TX: DLM/Teaching Resources.

Burke, H. (1985). Raven's Progressive Matrices (1938): More on norms, reliability, and validity. *Journal of Clinical Psychology, 41*, 231–235.

Canter, A. (1996). The Bender-Gestalt Test. In C. S. Newmark (Ed.), *Major psychological assessment instruments* (2d ed.). Boston: Allyn & Bacon.

Caplan, D. (1992). *Language: Structure, processing, and disorders*. Cambridge, MA: MIT Press.

Carroll, J. B. (1997). The three-stratum theory of cognitive abilities. In D. P. Flanagan, J. L. Genshaft, & P. L. Harrison (Eds.), *Contemporary intellectual assessment: Theories, tests, and issues* (pp. 122–130). New York: Guilford Press.

Catron, D. W. (1978). Immediate test-retest changes in WAIS scores among college males. *Psychological Reports, 43*, 279–290.

Catron, D. W., & Thompson, C. (1979). Test-retest gains in WAIS scores after four retest intervals. *Journal of Clinical Psychology, 35*, 352–357.

Cattell, R. B. (1943). The measurement of adult intelligence. *Psychological Bulletin, 40*, 153–193.

Cattell, R. B. (1971). *Abilities: Their structure, growth, and action*. New York: Harcourt, Brace, Jovanovich.

Cattell, R. B., & Horn, J. L. (1978). A check on the theory of fluid and crystallized intelligence with description of new subtest designs. *Journal of Educational Measurement, 15*, 139–164.

Cella, D. (1984). The modified WAIS-R: An extension and revision. *Journal of Clinical Psychology, 40*, 801–804.

Crocker, L., & Algina, J. (1986). *Introduction to classical and modern test theory*. Fort Worth, TX: Harcourt Brace Jovanovich.

Davis, G., & Holland, A. (1981). Age in understanding and treating aphasia. In D. Beasley & G. Davis (Eds.), *Aging: Communication processes and disorders*. New York: Grune & Stratton.

de Leon, J., Ellis, G., Rosen, P., & Simpson, G. (1993). The test-retest reliability of the Mini-Mental State Examination in chronic schizophrenic patients. *Acta Psychiatrica Scandinavica, 88*, 188–192.

D'Elia, L., Boone, K., & Mitrushina, A. (1995). *Handbook of normative data for neuropsychological assessment*. New York: Oxford University Press.

DePaolo, J., & Folstein, M. (1978). Psychiatric disturbances in neurological patients: Detection, recognition, and hospital course. *Annals of Neurology, 4,* 225–228.

Doll, E. A. (1953). *Vineland social maturity scale.* Minneapolis, MN: American Guidance Service.

Drachman, D., & Arbit, J. (1966). Memory and the hippocampal complex. II. Is memory a multiple process? *Archives of Neurology, 15,* 52–61.

Drachman, D., & Hughes, J. (1971). Memory and the hippocampal complex. III. Aging and temporal EEG abnormalities. *Neurology, 21,* 1–4.

Dunn, L. M., & Dunn, L. M. (1981). *Peabody Picture Vocabulary Test—Revised: Manual for Forms L and M.* Circle Pines, MN: American Guidance Services.

Dworkin, J. P., & Hartman, D. E. (1994). *Cases in neurogenic communication disorders: A workbook* (2d ed.). San Diego, CA: Singular.

Eccles, J. (1973). *The understanding of the human brain.* New York: McGraw-Hill.

Ellis, N. R. (1975). Current issues in mental retardation. Position paper of the American Psychological Association. Division on Mental Retardation: *Division 33 Newsletter, 2,* 1–2.

Eyde, L., Robertson, G., Krug, S., et al. (1993). *Responsible test use: Case studies for assessing human behavior.* Washington, DC: American Psychological Association.

Feher, E., Mahurin, R., Doody, R., et al. (1992). Establishing the limits of the Mini-Mental State: Examination of "subtests." *Archives of Neurology, 49,* 87–92.

Folstein, M. F., Folstein, S. E., & McHugh, P. R. (1975). "Mini-Mental State": A practical method for grading the cognitive state of patients for the clinician. *Journal of Psychiatric Research, 12,* 189–198.

Gallo, J., & Anthony, J. (1994). Re: A scoring error in the Mini-Mental State test. *Canadian Journal of Psychiatry, 39,* 382.

Gardner, H. (1975). *The shattered mind: The person after brain damage.* New York: Knopf.

Gardner, H. (1983). *Frames of mind: The theory of multiple intelligence.* New York: Basic Books.

Gardner, H. (1993). *Multiple intelligences: The theory in practice.* New York: Basic Books.

Geffen, G., Moar, K., O'Hanlon, A., et al. (1990). The Auditory Verbal Learning Test: Performance of 16 to 86 year olds of average intelligence. *The Clinical Neuropsychologist, 4,* 45–63.

Geschwind, N. (1972). Language and the brain. *Scientific American, 226,* 76–83.

Geschwind, N., & Galaburda, A. M. (1987). *Cerebral lateralization: Biological mechanisms, associations, and pathology.* Cambridge, MA: MIT Press.

Goldfarb, L., Plante, T., Brentar, J., & DiGregorio, M. (1995). Administering the Digit Span subtest of the WISC-III: Should the examiner make eye contact or not? *Assessment, 2,* 313–318.

Goldstein, K. (1944). The mental changes due to frontal lobe damage. *Journal of Psychology, 17,* 187–208.

Goodglass, H. (1993). *Understanding aphasia.* New York: Academic Press.

Grace, J., Nadler, J., White, D., Guilmette, T., et al. (1996). Folstein vs. Modified Mini-Mental State Examination in geriatric stroke. *Archives of Neurology, 52,* 477–484.

Gregory, R. J. (1987). *Adult intellectual assessment.* Boston: Allyn & Bacon.

Gregory, R. J. (1994a). Classification of intelligence. In R. J. Sternberg (Ed.), *Encyclopedia of human intelligence.* New York: Macmillan.

Gregory, R. J. (1994b). Profile interpretation. In R. J. Sternberg (Ed.), *Encyclopedia of human intelligence.* New York: Macmillan.

Gregory, R. J. (1996). *Psychological testing: History, principles, and applications* (2d ed.). Boston: Allyn & Bacon.

Gregory, R. J. (1998). Clinical assessment and diagnosis. In S. Cullari (Ed.), *Foundations of clinical psychology*. Boston: Allyn & Bacon.

Gregory, R. J., & Gilbert, C. (1993). Retesting effects on the WAIS-R after ten months. Paper presented to the Western Psychological Association, Phoenix, AZ.

Gregory, R. J., Lehman, R. E., & Mohan, P. J. (1976). Intelligence scores for children with and without undue lead absorption. In G. Wegner (Ed.), *Shoshone Lead Health Project*. Boise, ID: Idaho Department of Health and Welfare.

Gronwall, D. M. A. (1977). Paced auditory serial addition task: A measure of recovery from concussion. *Perceptual and Motor Skills, 44*, 367–373.

Gronwall, D. M. A., & Sampson, H. (1974). *The psychological effects of concussion*. Auckland, NZ: Auckland University Press/Oxford University Press.

Gronwall, D. M. A., & Wrightson, P. (1974). Delayed recovery of intellectual function after minor head injury. *Lancet, 2*, 605–609.

Gronwall, D. M. A., & Wrightson, P. (1981). Memory and information processing capacity after closed head injury. *Journal of Neurology, Neurosurgery, and Psychiatry, 44*, 889–895.

Hain, J. (1964). The Bender Gestalt Test: A scoring method for identifying brain damage. *Journal of Consulting and Clinical Psychology, 28*, 34–40.

Halstead, W. (1947). *Brain and intelligence: A quantitative study of the frontal lobes*. Chicago: University of Chicago Press.

Halstead, W., & Wepman, J. (1949). The Halstead-Wepman aphasia screening test. *Journal of Speech and Hearing Disorders, 14*, 9–15.

Hamsher, K., Benton, A., & Digre, K. (1980). Serial digit learning: Normative and clinical aspects. *Journal of Clinical Neuropsychology, 2*, 39–50.

Hart, R. P., Kwentus, J. A., Taylor, J., & Hamer, R. (1988). Productive naming and memory in depression and Alzheimer's type dementia. *Archives of Clinical Neuropsychology, 3*, 313–322.

Heaton, R. K., Baade, L. E., & Johnson, K. L. (1978). Neuropsychological test results associated with psychiatric disorders in adults. *Psychological Bulletin, 85*, 141–162.

Heaton, R. K., Grant, I., & Matthews, C. G. (1991). *Comprehensive norms for an expanded Halstead-Reitan Battery: Demographic corrections, research findings, and clinical applications*. Odessa, FL: Psychological Assessment Resources.

Heber, R. (1961). A manual on terminology and classification in mental retardation. *American Journal on Mental Deficiency, 64* (Monograph Supplement, 2d ed.).

Heinemann, A., Harper, R., Friedman, L., & Whitney, J. (1985). The relative utility of the Shipley-Hartford scale: Prediction of WAIS-R IQ. *Journal of Clinical Psychology, 41*, 547–551.

Heston, L., & White, J. (1991). *The vanishing mind: A practical guide to Alzheimer's disease and other dementias*. New York: Freeman.

Horton, A. M., & Alana, S. (1990). Validation of the Mini-Mental State Examination. *International Journal of Neuroscience, 53*, 209–212.

Hutt, M. L. (1977). *The Hutt adaptation of the Bender-Gestalt Test* (3d ed.). New York: Grune & Stratton.

Hutt, M. L. (1985). *The Hutt adaptation of the Bender-Gestalt Test* (4th ed.). Orlando, FL: Grune & Stratton.

Hutt, M. L., & Briskin, G. J. (1960). *The clinical use of the revised Bender Gestalt Test*. New York: Grune & Stratton.

Ivnik, R., Malec, J., Tangalos, E., et al. (1990). The Auditory-Verbal Learning Test (AVLT): Norms for ages 55 years and older. *Psychological Assessment, 3,* 156–161.

Jennett, B. (1984). The measurement of outcome. In N. Brooks (Ed.), *Closed head injury: Psychological, social, and family consequences.* Oxford: Oxford University Press.

Jennett, B., Teasdale, G. M., & Knill-Jones, R. P. (1975). Predicting outcome after head injury. *Journal of Royal College of Physicians of London, 9,* 231–237.

Jensen, A. R. (1980). *Bias in mental testing.* New York: Free Press.

Joslyn, D., & Hutzell, R. (1979). Temporal disorientation in schizophrenia and brain-damaged patients. *American Journal of Psychiatry, 32,* 1569–1573.

Kaufman, A. S. (1983). Test review: WAIS-R. *Journal of Psychoeducational Assessment, 1,* 309–319.

Kaufman, A. S. (1990). *Assessment of adolescent and adult intelligence.* Boston: Allyn & Bacon.

Kaufman, A. S. (1994). *Intelligent testing with the WISC-III.* Boston: Allyn & Bacon.

Kaufman, A. S., & Kaufman, N. L. (1983). *K-ABC interpretive manual.* Circle Pines, MN: American Guidance Service.

Kaufman, A. S., & Kaufman, N. L. (1990). *Kaufman Brief Intelligence Test. Manual.* Circle Pines, MN: American Guidance Service.

Kaufman, A. S., Ishikuma, T., & Kaufman-Packer, J. (1991). Amazingly short forms of the WAIS-R. *Journal of Psychoeducational Assessment, 9,* 4–15.

Kaufman, A. S., & Wang, J. (1992). Gender, race, and education differences on the K-BIT at ages 4 to 90 years. *Journal of Psychoeducational Assessment, 10,* 219–229.

Keenan, J. (1971). The detection of minimal dysphasia. *Archives of Physical Medicine and Rehabilitation, 52,* 227–232.

Knights, E., & Folstein, M. (1977). Unsuspected emotional and cognitive disturbance in medical patients. *Annals of Internal Medicine, 87,* 723–724.

Kolb, B., & Whishaw, I. Q. (1990). *Fundamentals of human neuropsychology* (3d ed.). New York: Freeman.

Kupfermann, I. (1991). Hypothalamus and limbic system: Peptidergic neurons, homeostasis, and emotional behavior. In E. R. Kandel, J. H. Schwartz, & T. M. Jessel (Eds.), *Principles of neuroscience* (3d ed.). New York: Elsevier.

Lacks, P. (1984). *Bender Gestalt screening for brain dysfunction.* New York: Wiley.

Lacks, P., & Newport, K. (1980). A comparison of scoring systems and level of scorer experience on the Bender Gestalt Test. *Journal of Personality Assessment, 44,* 351–357.

Lambert, N. M., Nihira, K., & Leland, H. (1993). *AAMR adaptive behavior scale—school* (2d ed.). Austin, TX: PRO-ED.

La Rue, A. (1992). *Aging and neuropsychological assessment.* New York: Plenum.

Lesher, E., & Whelihan, W. (1986). Reliability of mental status instruments administered to nursing home residents. *Journal of Consulting and Clinical Psychology, 54,* 726–727.

Levin, H. S. (1983). The Paced Auditory Serial Addition Task—Revised. Unpublished manuscript. Galveston: University of Texas at Galveston.

Levinson, B. M. (1958). Culture pressure and WAIS scatter in a traditional Jewish setting. *Journal of Genetic Psychology, 93,* 277–286.

Lezak, M. (1982). The problem of assessing executive functions. *International Journal of Psychology, 17,* 281–297.

Lezak, M. (1983). *Neuropsychological assessment* (2d ed.). New York: Oxford University Press.

Lezak, M. (1995). *Neuropsychological assessment* (3d ed.). New York: Oxford University Press.

Lishman, L. (1988). Physiogenesis and psychogenesis in the "post-concussional syndrome." *British Journal of Psychiatry, 153,* 460–469.

Luria, A. R. (1973). *The working brain*. New York: Basic Books.

Maas, H. S., & Kuypers, J. A. (1975). *From thirty to seventy*. San Francisco: Jossey-Bass.

Maloney, M. P., & Ward, M. P. (1979). *Mental retardation and modern society*. New York: Oxford University Press.

Matarazzo, J. D. (1972). *Wechsler's measurement and appraisal of adult intelligence*. Baltimore, MD: Williams & Wilkins.

Matarazzo, J. (1986). Computerized clinical psychological test interpretations: Unvalidated plus all mean and no sigma. *American Psychologist, 41,* 14–24.

Matarazzo, J. (1990). Psychological assessment versus psychological testing. *American Psychologist, 45,* 999–1017.

Matarazzo, J., Carmody, T., & Jacobs, L. (1980). Test-retest reliability and stability of the WAIS: A literature review with implications for clinical practice. *Journal of Clinical Neuropsychology, 2,* 89–105.

Matarazzo, J., & Herman, D. (1984a). Base rates for the WAIS-R: Test-retest stability and VIQ-PIQ differences. *Journal of Clinical Neuropsychology, 6,* 351–366.

Matarazzo, J., & Herman, D. (1984b). Relationship of education and IQ in the WAIS-R standardization sample. *Journal of Consulting and Clinical Psychology, 52,* 631–634.

Maxwell, J., & Wise, F. (1984). PPVT IQ validity in adults: A measure of vocabulary, not of intelligence. *Journal of Clinical Psychology, 40,* 1048–1053.

McCaffrey, R., Cousins, J., Westervelt, H., Martynowicz, M., et al. (1995). Practice effects with the NIMH AIDS abbreviated neuropsychological battery. *Archives of Clinical Neuropsychology, 10,* 241–250.

McMordie, W. R. (1988). Twenty-year follow-up of the prevailing opinion on the posttraumatic or postconcussional syndrome. *The Clinical Neuropsychologist, 2,* 198–212.

Melton, G. B., Petrila, J., Poythress, N., & Slobogin, C. (1997). *Psychological evaluation for the courts: A handbook for mental health professionals and lawyers* (2d ed.). New York: Guilford Press.

Mercer, J. (1979). *SOMPA: Technical and conceptual manual*. New York: Psychological Corporation.

Mercer, J. (1994). System of Multicultural Pluralistic Assessment (SOMPA). In R. J. Sternberg (Ed.), *Encyclopedia of human intelligence*. New York: Macmillan.

Miller, W. (1987). The neuropsychology of head injuries. In D. Wedding, A. Horton, Jr., & J. Webster (Eds.), *The neuropsychology handbook: Behavioral and clinical perspectives*. New York: Springer.

Montour, K. (1977). William James Sidis, the broken twig. *American Psychologist, 32,* 265–269.

Moore, M. V. (1969). Pathological writing. *Asha, 11,* 535–538.

Morgan, S., & Wheelock, J. (1992). Digit Symbol and Symbol Digit Modalities Tests: Are they directly interchangeable? *Neuropsychology, 6,* 327–330.

Naugle, R., Chelune, G., & Tucker, G. (1993). Validity of the Kaufman Brief Intelligence Test. *Psychological Assessment, 5,* 182–186.

Nihira, K., Leland, H., & Lambert, N. (1993). *AAMR adaptive behavior scales-residential and community* (2d ed.). Austin, TX: PRO-ED.

Nixon, S. J. (1996). Secondary dementias: Reversible dementias and pseudodementia. In R. L. Adams, O. A. Parsons, J. L. Culbertson, & S. J. Nixon (Eds.), *Neuropsychology for clinical practice: Etiology, assessment, and treatment of common neurological disorders*. Washington, DC: American Psychological Association.

O'Donnell, J., MacGregor, L., Dabrowski, J., Oestreicher, J., & Romero, J. (1994). Construct validity of neuropsychological tests of conceptual and attentional abilities. *Journal of Clinical Psychology, 50,* 596–600.

Papez, J. W. (1937). A proposed mechanism of emotion. *Archives of Neurology and Psychiatry, 38,* 724–744.

Pascal, G. R., & Suttell, B. J. (1951). *The Bender Gestalt Test.* New York: Grune & Stratton.

Pauker, J. D. (1976). A quick-scoring system for the Bender Gestalt: Interrater reliability and scoring validity. *Journal of Clinical Psychology, 32,* 86–89.

Peck, D. (1970). The conversion of Progressive Matrices and Mill Hill Vocabulary raw scores into deviation IQs. *Journal of Clinical Psychology, 26,* 67–70.

Pfeiffer, E. (1975). A short portable mental status questionnaire for the assessment of organic brain deficit in elderly patients. *Journal of the American Geriatrics Society, 23,* 433–441.

Pollens, R., McBratnie, B., & Burton, P. (1988). Beyond cognition: Executive functions. *Cognitive Rehabilitation, 5,* 26–33.

Ponsford, J., & Kinsella, G. (1992). Attentional deficits following closed-head injury. *Journal of Clinical and Experimental Neuropsychology, 14,* 822–838.

Pope, K. S. (1992). Responsibilities in providing psychological test feedback to clients. *Psychological Assessment, 4,* 268–271.

Powell, J., Cripe, L., & Dodrill, C. (1991). Assessment of brain impairment with the Rey Auditory Verbal Learning Test: A comparison with other neuropsychological measures. *Archives of Clinical Neuropsychology, 6,* 241–249.

Prout, H., & Schwartz, J. (1984). Validity of the PPVT-R with mentally retarded adults. *Journal of Clinical Psychology, 40,* 584–587.

Rasmussen, T., & Milner, B. (1977). The role of early left brain injury in determining lateralization of cerebral speech functions. *Annals of the New York Academy of Sciences, 299,* 355–369.

Raven, J. C. (1956). *Raven Progressive Matrices.* New York: Psychological Corporation.

Raven, J. C., & Summers, B. (1986). *Manual for Raven's Progressive Matrices and Vocabulary Scales-research Supplement, no. 3.* London: Lewis.

Reitan, R. M. (1984). *Aphasia and sensory-perceptual deficits in adults.* Tucson, AZ: Neuropsychology Press.

Reitan, R. M., & Davison, L. A. (Eds.) (1974). *Clinical neuropsychology: Current status and applications.* New York: Wiley.

Reitan, R. M., & Wolfson, D. (1993). *The Halstead-Reitan Neuropsychological Test Battery: Theory and clinical interpretation.* Tucson, AZ: Neuropsychology Press.

Reschly, D. J. (1987). *Adaptive behavior.* Tallahassee: Florida Department of Education.

Reschly, D. J. (1990). Adaptive behavior. In A. Thoms & J. Grimes (Eds.), *Best practices in school psychology* (2d ed.). Washington, DC: National Association of School Psychologists.

Restak, R. (1984). *The brain.* New York: Bantam Books.

Rey, A. (1964). L'examen clinique en psychologie. Paris: Presses Universitaires de France.

Reynolds, C. R., Chastain, R., Kaufman, A., & McLean, J. (1987). Demographic characteristics and IQ among adults: Analysis of the WAIS-R standardization sample as a function of the stratification variables. *Journal of School Psychology, 25,* 323–342.

Riley, W., Mabe, P., & Schear, J. (1987). A brief neuropsychological screening battery to detect brain damage in a psychiatric population. *Journal of Psychopathology and Behavioral Assessment, 9,* 67–74.

Robiner, W. (1978). *An analysis of some of the variables influencing clinical use of the Bender Gestalt.* Unpublished manuscript, Washington University in St. Louis, MO.

Roman, D., Edwall, G., Buchanan, R., & Patton, J. (1991). Extended norms for the Paced Auditory Serial Addition Task. *The Clinical Neuropsychologist, 5,* 33–40.

Russell, E. W. (1976). The Bender-Gestalt and the Halstead-Reitan battery: A case study. *Journal of Clinical Psychology, 32*, 355–361.

Russell, E. W., Neuringer, C., & Goldstein, G. (1970). *Assessment of brain damage: A neuropsychological key approach.* New York: Wiley.

Ryan, J. J., Prifitera, A., & Powers, L. (1983). Scoring reliability on the WAIS-R. *Journal of Consulting and Clinical Psychology, 51*, 149–150.

Salvia, J., & Ysseldyke, S. (1988). *Assessment in special and remedial education* (4th ed.). Boston: Houghton Mifflin.

Sattler, J. M. (1988). *Assessment of children* (3d ed.). San Diego, CA: Author.

Satz, P., & Mogel, S. (1962). An abbreviation of the WAIS for clinical use. *Journal of Clinical Psychology, 18*, 77–79.

Scherr, P., Albert, M., Funkenstein, H., et al. (1988). Correlates of cognitive function in an elderly community population. *American Journal of Epidemiology, 128*, 1084–1101.

Schinka, J. (1974). Performances of brain damaged patients on tests of short-term and long-term verbal memory. Ph.D. dissertation, University of Iowa.

Schmitter-Edgecombe, M., Fahy, J., Whelan, J., & Long, C. (1995). Memory remediation after severe closed head injury: Notebook training versus supportive therapy. *Journal of Consulting and Clinical Psychology, 63*, 484–489.

Schoenhuber, R., Gentili, M., & Orlando, A. (1988). Prognostic value of auditory brain-stem responses for late postconcussion symptoms following minor head injury. *Journal of Neurosurgery, 68*, 742–744.

Schretlen, D., Benedict, R., & Bobholz, J. (1994). Composite reliability and standard errors of measurement for a seven-subtest short form of the Wechsler Adult Intelligence Scale—Revised. *Psychological Assessment, 6*, 188–190.

Shipley, W. C. (1940). A self-administered scale for measuring intellectual impairment and deterioration. *Journal of Psychology, 9*, 371–377.

Shipley, W. (1983). *Shipley Institute of Living Scale.* Los Angeles: Western Psychological Services.

Silver, J., Hales, R., & Yudofsky, S. (1992). Neuropsychiatric aspects of traumatic brain injury. In S. Yudofsky & R. Hales (Eds.), *Textbook of psychiatry* (2d ed.) (pp. 363–396). Washington, DC: American Psychiatric Press.

Slate, J. R., & Hunnicutt, L. C., Jr. (1988). Scoring errors on the Wechsler scales. *Journal of Psychoeducational Assessment, 6*, 280–288.

Smith, A. (1967). The serial sevens subtraction test. *Archives of Neurology, 17*, 78–80.

Smith, A. (1968). The Symbol Digit Modalities Test: A neuropsychologic test for economic screening of learning and other cerebral disorders. *Learning Disorders, 3*, 83–91.

Smith, A. (1982). *Symbol Digit Modalities Test manual.* Los Angeles: Western Psychological Services.

Smyer, M., Hofland, B., & Jonas, E. (1979). Validity study of the Short Portable Mental Status Questionnaire for the elderly. *Journal of the American Geriatrics Society, 27*, 263–269.

Sparrow, S. S., Balla, D. A., & Cicchetti, D. V. (1984). *Vineland adaptive behavior scales.* Circle Pines, MN: American Guidance Service.

Spencer, T., Biederman, J., Wilens, T., et al. (1996). Pharmacotherapy of attention-deficit-hyperactivity disorder across the life cycle. *Journal of the American Academy of Child and Adolescent Psychiatry, 35*, 409–432.

Sperry, R. W. (1968). Hemispheric deconnection and unity of conscious experience. *American Psychologist, 29*, 723–733.

Spreen, O., & Benton, A. L. (1977). *Neurosensory Center comprehensive examination for aphasia (NCCEA).* (rev. ed.). Victoria: University of Victoria, Neuropsychology Laboratory.

Spreen, O., and Risser, A. (1981). Assessment of aphasia. In M. Sarno (Ed.), *Acquired aphasia.* New York: Academic Press.

Spreen, O., & Strauss, E. (1991). *A compendium of neuropsychological tests: Administration, norms, and commentary.* (1991). New York: Oxford University Press.

Springer, S. P., & Deutsch, G. (1989). *Left brain, right brain* (3d ed.). San Francisco: Freeman.

Starkstein, S., & Robinson, R. (1992). Neuropsychiatric aspects of cerebral vascular disorders. In S. Yudofsky & R. Hales (Eds.), *Textbook of psychiatry* (2d ed.) (pp. 449–472). Washington, DC: American Psychiatric Press.

Steisel, I. M. (1951). The relation between test and retest scores on the Wechsler-Bellevue Scale (Form I) for selected college students. *Journal of Genetic Psychology, 79,* 155–162.

Sternberg, R. J. (1995). *In search of the human mind.* Fort Worth, TX: Harcourt Brace College.

Storandt, M., & VandenBos, G. (1994). *Neuropsychological assessment of dementia and depression in older adults: A clinician's guide.* Washington, DC: American Psychological Association.

Strange, P. G. (1992). *Brain biochemistry and brain disorders.* New York: Oxford University Press.

Strub, R. L., & Black, F. W. (1985). *The mental status examination in neurology* (2d ed.). Philadelphia: Davis.

Stuss, D. T., Stethem, L. L., Hugenholtz, H., & Richard, M. T. (1989). Traumatic brain injury: A comparison of three clinical tests, and analysis of recovery. *The Clinical Neuropsychologist, 3,* 145–156.

Stuss, D. T., Stethem, L. L., & Pelchat, G. (1988). Three tests of attention and rapid information processing: An extension. *The Clinical Neuropsychologist, 2,* 246–250.

Swiercinsky, D. (1978). *Manual for the adult neuropsychological evaluation.* Springfield, IL: Thomas.

Tallent, N. (1993). *Psychological report writing* (4th ed.). Englewood Cliffs, NJ: Prentice-Hall.

Teasdale, G., & Jennett, B. (1974). Assessment of coma and impaired consciousness. *Lancet, ii,* 81–84.

Teng, E. T., & Chui, H. C. (1987). The Modified Mini-Mental State (3MS) examination. *Journal of Clinical Psychiatry, 48,* 341–318.

Terrell, F., Terrell, S., & Taylor, J. (1981). Effect of race of examiner and cultural mistrust on the WAIS performance of African-American students. *Journal of Consulting and Clinical Psychology, 49,* 750–751.

Thorndike, R., Hagen, E., & Sattler, J. (1986). *Examiner's manual: Stanford-Binet Intelligence Scale (Fourth Edition).* Chicago: Riverside.

Tombaugh, T., McDowell, I., Kristjansson, B., & Hubley, A. (1996). Mini-Mental State Examination (MMSE) and the Modified MMSE (3MS): A psychometric comparison and normative data. *Psychological Assessment, 8,* 48–59.

Tranel, D. (1992). Functional neuroanatomy: Neuropsychological correlates of cortical and subcortical damage. In S. Yudofsky & R. Hales (Eds.), *Textbook of psychiatry* (2d ed.) (pp. 57–88). Washington, DC: American Psychiatric Press.

Trzepacz, P. T., & Baker, R. W. (1993). *The psychiatric mental status examination.* New York: Oxford University Press.

Tulsky, D., Zhu, J., & Ledbetter, M. (1997). *WAIS-III WMS-III technical manual.* San Antonio, TX: Psychological Corporation.

Uhlmann, R., Larson, E., & Buchner, D. (1987). Correlations of Mini-Mental State and Modified Dementia Rating Scale to measures of transitional health status in dementia. *Journal of Gerontology, 42,* 33–36.

Vaillant, G. (1977). *Adaptation to life: How the best and the brightest came of age.* Boston: Little, Brown.

Vance, B., Kitson, D., & Singer, M. (1985). Relationship between the standard scores of PPVT-R and Wide Range Achievement Test. *Journal of Clinical Psychology, 41,* 691–693.

Vincent, K. R. (1979). The modified WAIS-R: An alternative to short forms. *Journal of Clinical Psychology, 35,* 624–625.

Warrington, E. K., James, M., & Kinsbourne, M. (1966). Drawing disability in relation to laterality of cerebral lesion. *Brain, 89,* 53–82.

Wechsler, D. (1932). Analytical use of the Army Alpha examination. *Journal of Applied Psychology, 16,* 254–256.

Wechsler, D. (1939). *The measurement of adult intelligence.* Baltimore, MD: Williams & Wilkins.

Wechsler, D. (1958). *Measurement and appraisal of adult intelligence.* Baltimore, MD: Williams & Wilkins.

Wechsler, D. (1981). *WAIS-R manual.* New York: Psychological Corporation.

Wechsler, D. (1987). *Wechsler Memory Scale—Revised manual.* New York: Psychological Corporation.

Wechsler, D. (1997). *WAIS-III manual.* San Antonio, TX: Psychological Corporation.

Wells, C. E. (1979). Pseudodementia. *American Journal of Psychiatry, 136,* 895–900.

Wertheimer, M. (1923). Studies in the theory of Gestalt psychology. *Psychologische Forschung, 4,* 301–350.

Wetzel, L., & Boll, T. (1987). *Short Category Test, booklet format.* Los Angeles: Western Psychological Services.

Wheeler, L., & Reitan, R. M. (1962). Presence and laterality of brain damage predicted from responses to a short aphasia screening test. *Perceptual and Motor Skills, 15,* 783–799.

White, R. F., Au, R., Durso, R., & Moss, M. (1992). Neuropsychological function in Parkinson's disease. In R. F. White (Ed.), *Clinical syndromes in adult neuropsychology: The practitioner's handbook.* Amsterdam: Elsevier.

Whitehouse, P. J. (1993). Autopsy. *The Gerontologist, 33,* 436–437.

Wiens, A., McMinn, M., & Crossen, J. (1988). Rey Auditory-Verbal Learning Test: Development of norms for healthy young adults. *The Clinical Neuropsychologist, 2,* 67–87.

Williams, M. (1979). *Brain damage, behaviour, and the mind.* New York: Wiley.

Wolber, G., Romaniuk, M., Eastman, E., & Robinson, C. (1984). Validity of the Short Portable Mental Status Questionnaire with elderly psychiatric patients. *Journal of Consulting and Clinical Psychology, 52,* 712–713.

Wolff, K., & Gregory, R. J. (1992). The effect of a temporary dysphoric mood upon selected WAIS-R subtests. *Journal of Psychoeducational Assessment, 9,* 340–344.

Wolfson, D. (1985). Neuropsychology History Questionnaire. Reitan Neuropsychology Laboratory, 2920 South 4th Avenue, Tucson, AZ 85713.

Wooten, G. F. (1990). Parkinsonism. In A. L. Pearlman & R. C. Collins (Eds.), *Neurobiology of disease.* New York: Oxford University Press.

Yesavage, J., Brink, T., & Rose, T. (1983). Development and validation of a geriatric depression scale: A preliminary report. *Journal of Psychiatric Residents, 17,* 37–49.

Yeudall, L. T., Fromm, D., Reddon, J., & Stefanyk, W. (1986). Normative data stratified by age and sex for 12 neuropsychological tests. *Journal of Clinical Psychology, 42,* 918–945.

Yeudall, L. T., Reddon, J., Gill, D., & Stefanyk, W. (1987). Normative data for the Halstead-Reitan Neuropsychological Tests stratified by age and sex. *Journal of Clinical Psychology, 43,* 346–367.

Zachary, R., Crumpton, E., & Spiegel, D. (1985). Estimating WAIS-R IQ from the Shipley Institute of Living Scale. *Journal of Clinical Psychology, 41,* 532–540.

Zangwill, O. (1943). Clinical tests of memory impairment. *Proceedings of the Royal Society of Medicine, 36,* 576–580.

Zimmerman, I. L., & Woo-Sam, J. M. (1973). *Clinical interpretation of the Wechsler Adult Intelligence Scale.* New York: Grune & Stratton.

NAME INDEX

SUBJECT INDEX